D0977225

THE WRECKERS

THE
WRECKERS

A STORY OF KILLING SEAS
AND PLUNDERED SHIPWRECKS, FROM
THE EIGHTEENTH CENTURY TO
THE PRESENT DAY

BELLA BATHURST

HOUGHTON MIFFLIN COMPANY
BOSTON · NEW YORK
2005

To John, with love

Copyright © 2005 by Bella Bathurst
ALL RIGHTS RESERVED

First published in Great Britain by Harper Collins Publishers, 2005

For information about permission to reproduce selections from
this book, write to Permissions, Houghton Mifflin Company,
215 Park Avenue South, New York, New York 10003.

Visit our Web site: www.houghtonmifflinbooks.com.

Library of Congress Cataloging-in-Publication Data
Bathurst, Bella.
The wreckers : a story of killing seas and plundered shipwrecks,
from the eighteenth century to the present day / Bella Bathurst.
p.   cm.
Includes bibliographical references and index.
ISBN 0-618-41677-3
1. Shipwrecks—Great Britain—History. 2. Pillage—Great
Britain—History. 3. Great Britain—History, Local. I. Title.
DA90.B334 2005
909'.096336—dc22   2005045951

Printed in the United States of America

QUM 10 9 8 7 6 5 4 3 2 1

CONTENTS

ILLUSTRATIONS

ACKNOWLEDGEMENTS

Much of this book is based on interviews from around Britain. Most of the interviewees were not wreckers themselves, but people who had a strong connection to the sea and to their local area. One person led to another in a chain of links and associations leading all the way from Shetland to the Scilly Isles. Almost without exception, everyone I spoke to gave up their time and their expertise with a generosity far beyond anything I had a right to expect. Without their help, this book would not exist. I remain unrepayably grateful both to them and to all the other unnamed experts who helped along the way.

Several people provided invaluable background information. Sophia Exelby, custodian of what may well be the UK's finest job title, filled in much of my knowledge on the role of the Receiver of Wreck. Howard Richings, the RNLI's shoreworks manager, gave me both an interview and a list of further contacts, as did John Caldwell in Scotland. Despite my private vow never to step on board a ship with him again, James Taylor, Chief Executive of the Northern Lighthouse Board, is always the best of companions and interviewees. In London, Ben Griffiths provided invaluable legal research, while the staff of the Signet Library, the Scottish Public Records Office, Kirkwall Library, the Maritime and Coastguard Agency, Trinity House and the Morrab Library in Penzance all helped with the unending hunt for material.

In Orkney and Caithness, Willie Mowatt MBE, James Simpson, Jackie Manson, Dr Tony Trickett, Brian Williams, Jeff Temple, John Thornton and George Gunn all offered time and insight. David Stogdon provided a wonderful new perspective on the Stroma men, interrupting his Christmas holidays to do so.

Kirkwall Museum's exhibitions officer Tom Muir filled in vital background history and checked through the manuscript. Further down the west coast, John Macleod, Hector Macleod, Dr Jeremy Hidson, Ken Holland, Roderick and Angus McLean, Lindsay Johnson, Nick Ryan and Sigurd and Rose Scott offered information on everything from smuggling to whirlpools, while Alisdair Sinclair was kind enough to check through the chapter for errors of fact. On the east of Scotland, Chris Marr, Dougie Ferguson and Ron Leask all offered me excellent material, though in the end I was only able to use a small portion of it. On the East Coast, Sid Barnett, Syd Weatherill, Ben Dean and John Porteous provided invaluable expertise on the local salvage industry, while in Norfolk, Richard and Julie Davies made me welcome and put up with endless pestering. In London, Richard Sabin and Bob Jeffries both read through sections of the manuscript and gave me a glimpse of a capital I never knew existed. On the south coast, Andy Roberts, Tess Vandervliet and Bob Peacock expanded my understanding of the Channel and the Goodwin Sands. In Cornwall, Rebecca Pender, Joe Mills, Mike Pearce, Mike Collier, Billy Stevenson and Maurice Hutchens all offered their expertise during a particularly busy time of year. And on the Scilly Isles, Matt and Pat Lethbridge, Peter Kyne, Mark Groves, Frank Gibson and Richard Larn provided me with a clearer view of those exceptional islands than I could have dared hope for.

James and Sarah Dawnay not only provided the loveliest writer's retreat in Scotland but introduced me to Sarah's father, David Stogdon. In Edinburgh, Gus and Elspeth Ferguson offered contacts and companionship with their usual selflessness. My uncle and aunt David and Tessa McCosh had me to stay in Norfolk and pointed me in useful directions, while Rory Day showed me Argyll's own maelstrom. Alex Renton – writer, skipper and friend – not only put up with my lousy crewing, but put aside his own writing in order to perform expert editorial surgery on the manuscript. Richard Ross travelled all the way from California to Stroma, made me smile and kept me going. Euan Ferguson, Ashley

Heath, Alexa de Ferranti, Kamal Ahmed and Angus Wolfe Murray all offered friendship far beyond the call of duty, while my long-suffering family endured three long years of fishy anecdotes and complaint. Down in London, Alan Jones provided beautiful maps while both Michael Fishwick and Helen Ellis made the business of publication more fun than work. In New York, Elaine Pfefferblit, Libby Edelson and Webster Younce's help and insights on publication were invaluable. Most of all, I owe Victoria Hobbs – friend and special agent – a debt I know I can't repay. It is one thing to field seven years' worth of neurotic emails, but to put up with repeated and systematic food poisoning goes far beyond any reasonable job description. This book owes its existence to her unstinting encouragement and patience, as well as to her suggestion that from now on, we eat out.

Any book about the past is in some sense a ghost story. This one started with Robert Louis Stevenson and was written with his history and his family always in mind. One of the many pleasures of researching this has been in revisiting many of the places where the Stevensons worked. Every succeeding year gives me greater admiration for their works both in print and stone. And lastly, there are the ghosts closer to home; those of Johnny Noble and my father. Who, I very much hope, would have enjoyed this book.

INTRODUCTION

While researching another book five years ago, I came across the following passage in Robert Louis Stevenson's *Records of a Family of Engineers*:

> On a September night, the *Regent* lay in the Pentland Firth in a fog and a violent and windless swell. It was still dark, when they were alarmed by the sound of breakers, and an anchor was immediately let go. The peep of dawn discovered them swinging in desperate proximity to the isle of Swona and the surf bursting close under their stern. There was in this place a hamlet of the inhabitants, fisher-folk and wreckers; their huts stood close about the head of the beach. All slept; the doors were closed, and there was no smoke, and the anxious watchers on board ship seemed to contemplate a village of the dead. It was thought possible to launch a boat and tow the *Regent* from her place of danger; and with this view a signal of distress was made and a gun fired with a red hot poker from the galley. Its detonation awoke the sleepers. Door after door was opened, and in the grey light of the morning fisher after fisher was seen to come forth, yawning and stretching himself, nightcap on head. Fisher after fisher, I wrote, and my pen tripped; for it should rather stand wrecker after wrecker. There was no emotion, no animation, it scarce seemed any interest; not a hand was raised; but all callously awaited the harvest of the sea, and their children

stood by their side and waited also. To the end of his life, my father remembered that amphitheatre of placid spectators on the beach, and with a special and natural animosity, the boys of his own age. But presently a light air sprang up, and filled the sails, and fainted, and filled them again, and little by little the *Regent* fetched way against the swell, and clawed off shore into the turbulent firth.

The passage held me. True, it had an unmistakeable air of paraphrase about it – Robert Louis Stevenson having taken the same enterprising approach to his own family's history as he did to Jacobite rebellion or South Seas piracy – but it was also evidently based on fact. The *Regent* was the Northern Lighthouse Board's inspection vessel. Robert Louis Stevenson's father, Thomas, would have been on the yacht with his own father Robert on a tour around all the Scottish lights. In time, seven Stevensons would become engineers to the Northern Lighthouse Board, and Robert Louis Stevenson himself completed an engineering apprenticeship before trading granite for ink. The Pentland Firth lies between the far north-eastern corner of mainland Scotland and the Orkney Islands and is considered to be one of Europe's most hazardous sea areas. These things I knew, but who were these malevolent spectators standing so silent on the beach? Why had they waited there in the dawn for the *Regent*'s destruction? Were these 'wreckers' Stevenson described unique to Swona, or had they also existed elsewhere? I'd heard of pirates, privateers and press men, and I knew eighteenth- and nineteenth-century maritime life provided as many human hazards as natural ones. But I hadn't heard of wreckers or been aware that there were parts of Britain where men – and women, and children – stood with their arms folded waiting for ships to die.

Further reading revealed tantalising details. It seemed that all the Stevensons had at one time or another encountered strong local hostility to the construction of their lighthouses. Concealed within the pages of their Minute Books were hints of protest and resistance, whispers of sabotage, and – once in a while – a yell of outrage when a lightkeeper was caught rigging the wreck return books or 'salvaging' casualties too conscientiously. The Stevensons did their best to keep their keepers on a short leash, but even they were unable to account for the communities around them. In time, each of the family brought back definite evidence – in houses, on farms, below ground – of imports to the islands arriving unscheduled in the night.

Meanwhile at the other end of the country, the Cornish were supposed to be such accomplished wreckers that they regarded it not as a crime but as a profession. In fact, if anyone knew anything at all about the subject, they knew that the Cornish had been wreckers since birth. The only people who did not know this were the Cornish themselves, who swore blind that they had been the victims of a terrible slander and would never have touched a ship in distress. Elsewhere things were just as bad. From all around Britain I started finding stories of people deliberately drowning shipwreck victims, stories of shoreline orgies so dionysian that few participants survived until morning and stories of wreckers burning the boats of Excise men. There were stories of grand pianos sitting unplayed in hovels, of crofts fitted with silver candelabra, and – more recently – of an entire island dressed in suspiciously identical shirts. There were stories of false lights and false foghorns, false harbours, false rescuers, false dawns; even stories of entire coastlines rigged meticulously as stage sets.

Elsewhere in the world things were just as bad. Though few other countries had Britain's unique combination of advantages for a wrecker – island status, a vicious coastline, plenty of expensive traffic – almost every country with a coastline produced their own variants. There were Flemish wreckers, Spanish wreckers, Scandinavian wreckers. The French were such expert wreckers that they had been responsible for drafting the first international law against it back in the thirteenth century. In the Caribbean, wrecks were so frequent that the eighteenth-century colonial government was estimated to derive two-fifths of its income from salvage. America called their wreckers 'moon-cussers' after their habit of swearing at the light of an incriminating moon. The Canadians suffered a sea almost as unpleasant as Britain's, and a similar fund of tall tales. They had whole townships built from wrecked ships' timbers. They had stories of ghostly ladies holding up the stumps of fingers bitten off by wreckers in search of rings. And they had Sable Island, a spit of land which was at one time supposed to have been entirely populated by passing fishermen and shipwreck victims.

But was this all there was? Just stories? No more, no less; all smoke, no fire? If I chose to take the wreckers on would I be walking straight into a twilight of historical whispers and unverifiable anecdotes? Would I spend my time researching things which, like Robert Louis Stevenson's *Records*, were evidently founded in fact but embellished in the telling? And was wrecking something which – if it existed at all – had only existed for a short period, and had now faded out? If it did still exist, would anyone ever talk openly about a criminal activity for which they could still theoretically be prosecuted? Lastly, and most important of all, what exactly was a wrecker?

Like the word itself, wrecking is almost always as opaque as its practitioners. According to the *Oxford English Dictionary* a wrecker is 'one who tries from shore to bring about shipwreck with a view to profiting by wreckage', or one 'who steals such wreckage; a person employed in demolition, or in recovering wrecked ship or its contents'. Salvage, on the other hand, is '1 *vb*: to rescue (a ship or its cargo) from loss at sea. 2 *n*: the cargo saved from a wrecked or sunken ship.' The divisions between rescue, theft, and recovery are often too narrow to be clearly visible, and in different parts of the British Isles it is still difficult to pick out the difference between wrecking, salvage, hovelling, looting, and 'pro-active beachcombing'. Wreckers could be both active and passive: they could actively create shipwrecks, or they could passively make use of wrecks which came their way.

Though most people's awareness of the crime is probably derived from *Jamaica Inn*, Daphne Du Maurier's tale of a group of murderous Cornishmen who lure ships to destruction by putting out false lights along the coastline, there are many parts of Britain (including Cornwall) where there was never any need to deliberately wreck ships. Geography, weather conditions and a hostile sea washed up all the ships they would ever need. Though it is almost impossible to verify, probably rather less than one or two per cent of all British shipping casualties were ever actively wrecked by those onshore. The rest happened for the usual reasons – mechanical failure, human error, navigational miscalculation, storm, gale, lee shore – and were simply exploited by those who found them.

There were also a few instances which fell between active and passive wrecking. As Robert Louis Stevenson pointed out, there were parts of the country where coastliners sinned by omission, having done so little to prevent wrecks that they were, in effect, encouraging them. In some places, beacons and sea-marks vanished and were not replaced. In others, local pilots would threaten to run incoming ships aground unless captains promised them a decent cut of the cargo. And, once in a while, impromptu navigational aids would be sabotaged. In one corner of Scotland a lovelorn bull was apparently put to graze in a field overlooking a particularly hazardous stretch of water. The bull spent his nights broadcasting his desire for a mate, though for a long time the only responses he got were from the horns and sirens of passing ships. When the locals realised that the bull was doing a better job warning skippers of nearby land than a foghorn could ever do, they moved him away and found him a cow.

Whether active, passive or sin of omission, wrecking has existed in some form or another ever since ships first went to sea. In Britain and most of Europe, wrecking's heyday occurred during the eighteenth and nineteenth centuries, when sea traffic was at its heaviest. For much of the nineteenth century and all of the eighteenth, captains setting out from or returning to the coast of Britain faced a formidable set of obstacles. They groped their way across the oceans using the best equipment they had at the time, which did not amount to much. Charts and pilot books were often inaccurate and incomplete; cloud cover made sextant readings impossible; compasses could distort, and barometers only provided sailors with advance warning of their impending fate. In a world in which prizes were still being offered for anyone who could find a way of accurately measuring longitude, it was scarcely surprising that so many ships came to grief.

Nor did things necessarily improve once in sight of land. Until the early nineteenth century, there were almost no navigational aids to help sailors on their way; no lighthouses, no beacons, no VHF or radar. Captains relied as much on a keen-eyed lookout as they did on any more sophisticated technology. Small wonder that there were wrecks, and plenty of them.

For this reason, I have chosen to confine this book to the past 300 years, and to Britain alone. There were wrecks and wreckers before the eighteenth century, and there are wrecks and wreckers in other parts of the world. But Britain's own unique set of circumstances provides an obvious physical borderline. The sheer variety and range of natural hazards around the coastline – riptides on the Pentland Firth, whirlpools on the west coast, sandbanks in Norfolk and Kent, reefs in the Scillies, collisions in the Channel – sometimes makes it seem astounding that anyone made safe landfall in Britain at all. Different conditions called for different techniques – the Pentland Firth pirates were, for instance, as far from the hovellers of Kent in style as they were in miles. And so instead of presenting the book chronologically, I have laid it out by area.

While the twentieth century might have offered many improvements to lifesaving and sea safety, I found that it also provided work for the wreckers. Two world wars, the introduction of new technology and a vast increase in the size and tonnage of shipping often meant more wrecks, not less. Electronics fail, old skills atrophy, and undermanning makes ships vulnerable. And so, from the end of the days of sail to the beginning of the era of GPS (Global Positioning System), there have always been wrecks, and always people who profit by them. As I also discovered, some of those people were still alive, and some of those people would talk.

My last anxiety – that I would be dealing only with a series of unverifiable anecdotes – required a more complex solution. One of the difficulties of researching a book about a crime is that criminals are not generally known for writing about their activities. I found plenty of official and semi-official documents: court proceedings, newspaper reports, travellers' journals, customs correspondence – but much less direct information from the wreckers themselves. For events within living memory, I was lucky. In the years it took to research this book, I have been stunned by the generosity and loquacity of many of the people I have spoken to. The 'wreckers' may be few and far between, and they may have required some convincing that I was not the Receiver of Wreck in disguise or a Customs and Excise officer calling fifty years too late, but when they did talk, they had exceptional tales to tell. My initial fears that wrecking in all its diverse forms was dead, that no-one would be prepared to speak to me, and that there was nothing to find, proved groundless.

But with past incidences of wrecking, the research was more

complicated. Where information from the wreckers themselves did exist, it could not always be cross-checked with other sources or be taken at face value. However long ago it was committed, a crime remains a crime. And so, in stitching together the tale of a particular area or wreck, I have done my best to use material taken from as many sources as possible, and to state clearly which parts of that story have been corroborated by other evidence. Ultimately, however, if I had had to rely solely on material which could be unassailably authenticated, this book would have been a very thin volume indeed. I have therefore chosen to include the stories and incidents which I felt were both relevant and entertaining, and done my best to point out where and when my research has moved from the solid to the speculative.

During the three years it took to research and write this book, I conducted interviews with around 200 people and received help from countless more. Two of those interviewees were women. The sea was and will remain a masculine space. There are plenty of women now working for HM Coastguard, or running maritime museums, or involved in the diving community, but the vast majority of those who still use the sea – either professionally or for pleasure – are men. Parts of this book therefore use 'he' or 'him' when, strictly speaking, I should have included both sexes. But for the purposes of this book I've done the unfeminist thing and taken mankind to represent all humanity. I have done the opposite with ships. The vessels men sailed in are, and always have been, feminine. No one quite knows why – theories range from the anglicisation of classical pronouns or the lovelorn pinings of ancient sailors – but that is how it is and has always been – at least until March 2002, when *Lloyd's List*, the daily gospel of the shipping industry, announced that all ships would henceforth be known as 'it'. The *List*'s editor, Julian Bray, was quoted as saying, 'We see it as a reflection of the modern business of shipping. Ultimately they are commodities, they are commercial assets. They are not things that have character – either male or female.' Leaving aside the understanding that a rusty bulk-carrier full of toxins might not be as generous a reflection on my gender as, say, a slim and elegant tea-clipper, I have still stuck to the old designation. In this book, ships are 'she' – partly for consistency, but mainly just because most people like it better that way.

One last thing. This book is about wreckers and wrecking. It is not about salvage, or about wreck diving, or about the many noble efforts to make the sea safer. So if at times it gives the impression that those who lived around Britain's coasts were, at best, a bunch of alcoholic opportunists and, at worst, a mob of covert murderers, then that is because I have left the more benign sides of human nature to other books and other writers. This book is about what happens where the shore meets the sea, and human need meets human tragedy. Part of that story – a part large enough to fill several further volumes – is connected to lifesaving and the efforts made by all local communities at all periods in history to rescue strangers from danger. Wrecking is one part of the tale of our coasts, but rescue in all its forms, from the RNLI to the efforts of unsung individuals, is another. And though it is not the role of this book to examine the history of all that exceptional sacrifice, it would also be wrong for any reader to remain unaware of it.

The most striking aspects of wreckers and lifesavers are that their twin histories do not necessarily exist in tandem. Broadly speaking, the history of wrecking has remained the same from the beginnings of civilisation to the present day. Shipwrecks bring free loot, and people like free loot. A rare few of those people will provoke a wreck, some will plunder an existing wreck at the expense of the crew or passengers, but the majority will only take things from a ship or a shoreline when they are sure that they are not doing so at the expense of other people's lives. Lifesaving, however, is different. Attitudes to rescuing others at sea are intimately bound up with all sorts of other matters: religion or the lack of it, money or the lack of it, the Enlightenment, state-sponsored humanitarianism, superstition, charity and, above all, the changing values placed on human life down the centuries. In the twenty-first century it is an unquestioned absolute that life is more precious than property. Whether or not Britons believe in God, we undoubtedly believe that sending a boatload of gold ingots to the bottom of the sea is a worthy exchange for the lives of that boat's crew. But we did not always hold such humanitarian views. There have been plenty of times in the past when human life did not carry its current value, and when dispensing with a couple of intransigent passengers seemed a small price to pay for a hogshead of ale or a bolt of raw silk. Life was cheap because life brought no guarantees, and because very few people were prepared to pay the market rate. It was cheap because shipwrecks were simply the price of going to sea, and because every sailor who ever left the land knew the odds were stacked against him.

In 2002 an Oxford University study published in the *Lancet* examined statistics for the most hazardous professions in Britain. The study found that fishing and seafaring were, by a very high margin indeed, the professions with the highest numbers of fatalities. Forget mining, or offshore oil working, farming or crane driving, trawlermen were fifty times more likely to die at work than any other profession. Except, of course, for merchant seafarers, who were twenty-five times more likely to die at work. Between 1976 and 1995, fishermen suffered 103 fatal accidents per 100,000 worker years, whereas construction workers suffered 8 deaths per 100,000 worker years, and those in the service industry only 0.7. As the authors of the study pointed out, mortality rates in both fishing and seafaring are decreasing, but only because the numbers of fishermen and seafarers are themselves decreasing. The numbers of those killed at sea had, in fact, remained almost unchanged since the first Royal Commission was appointed in the 1830s to enquire into the causes of shipwreck. From the first moment at which the first sailor set a course for the unexplored horizon, mariners have always known that those who managed to survive the hazards of shipboard life – disease, accidents, overcrowding, malnutrition, the cruelties of on-board discipline – were just as likely to perish through shipwreck, storm or collision. And all seafarers knew that the laws of a stable world do not apply in a place where nothing, not even the floor beneath their feet, remains at rest for long.

And so sailors went to sea, and the sea (or disease, or corruption, or wreckers) killed them, and for centuries that was just how things were; they took the money, but they paid the price. It was not until well into the eighteenth century that seafarers began to fight back. Even when they did, it was not the men who actually had to face the danger who began agitating for change, but shipowners depressed at having to write off 10 or 20 per cent of their revenue to shipwreck every year. Saving lives at sea therefore began not through some sudden impulse of compassion, but because someone worked out that it would be cheaper to keep sailors alive. Within the space of a century, Britain gained lighthouses, lifeboats, load lines, watertight bulkheads, effective anti-scorbutics, cork lifejackets, and several parliamentary committees. In the process, they also lost the notorious coffin ships on which emigrants vanished into the New World, plus many of the crueller excesses of shipboard life. The English lighthouse authority – which up until the early eighteenth century had been much more interested in making money on patents than in spending it on lights – began to follow the example of the Scottish authority, which occasionally got around to building things. By stringing a chain of lights around the British coastline, the Stevensons in Scotland and the Douglasses in England were indirectly responsible for saving an uncountable number of lives. In 1823, William Hillary published his pithily-titled pamphlet 'An Appeal to the British Nation on the Humanity and Policy of Forming a National Institution for the Preservation of Lives and Property from Shipwreck', and the following year the RNLI was founded. After prolonged agitation, Samuel Plimsoll introduced compulsory load lines, indicating the point to which a ship could safely be weighted.

In 1824, *Lloyd's Register of Shipping* began keeping annual figures for United Kingdom and worldwide shipping losses. Those naked statistics and the shocking facts they betrayed did as much to alter public opinion as a thousand brave men ploughing through gales. The changes continued into the twentieth century with proper medical and lifeboat provision for passengers, VHF, satellite-based navigational systems such as Decca, Loran and GPS; radar, sonar, shipping forecasts, coastguard patrols, Search and Rescue (SAR) helicopters, and so on. Though it was impossible to quantify how many lives each new piece of technology was responsible for saving, the RNLI celebrated its centenary in 1924 with the announcement that in the hundred years since Hillary's pamphlet almost 60,000 lives had been saved.

There is no question that the past two centuries have seen an exceptional reversal in attitudes to lifesaving, and that all of Britain has benefited as a result. There are still tragedies, disasters and abuses, and the sea still remains a lethal place, but the sheer fact that so much time and courage is devoted to lifesaving at sea is, and should remain, a source of national pride. The Stevensons and the lifeboats represent the lighter side of humanity; now here is the dark.

Great Britain

ONE

False Lights

The human body is better at life than it is at death. We are blunt objects made for subtle intents; we can turn our bodies to almost any task and find that we already have the necessary equipment inbuilt. We can survive injury, starvation, pain, breakage, disease, time and despair. We are designed to last and built to survive. We have almost everything we need to repair and defend ourselves, and what we lack, we find elsewhere. Every one of us inhabits our own biological masterpiece. But, like every grand design, we have our flaws. Many of them are surprising; while we remain resistant and adaptive to injury or disease, we are peculiarly vulnerable to changes in temperature. Raise or lower our core body heat by just a few degrees, and we start to lose function. Make the difference more extreme, and our organs cannot work. Maintain the heat or the cold for too long, and we die.

Originally designed for the tropics, we remain elementally temperamental. Whether living in the Arctic or at the Equator, all of us have to maintain our core heat to within roughly half a degree of 37° Celsius. Half a degree is a change so slight that in the air around us it would feel imperceptible. Our external world is subject to huge surges and lapses in temperature; Britain, with its irresolute weathers, still varies between −20° in winter and +35° in summer. But in order to keep ourselves alive and functional, we need to keep our core body temperature stable at all times, whether in winter, summer, ice or fire. It is an extraordinary feat, and it takes an extraordinary amount of energy.

Most of the time, clothes (or the lack of them) help to do the job for us. Over the centuries, we have evolved the capacity to moderate the effect of the environment on our bodies with the addition or subtraction of a layer of fur or wool or denim or Gore-tex. Apply the right layers of clothing and the internal temperature of someone in −40° Greenland will stay at the same level as someone in t-shirt and shorts in +40° sub-Saharan Africa. The trouble arises when we get wet. Water is our greatest vulnerability; we cannot live without it, but we cannot live within it. Like the earth itself, we are seven-tenths water. It is the great equaliser; the source of our subsistence. Everything we are or were or aim to be begins and ends at sea level. It dictates our capacity to survive and thrive as a nation, our view of ourselves, our defence, our past, our future. It gives us life, and it kills us. Most of the world's oceans are filled with water lower than the temperature which we can safely tolerate for any length of time (20°C). Water conducts heat twenty-four times more efficiently than air; a body in water will cool four times more rapidly than on land.

Those who fall into the sea – whether through accident or design – find themselves in a foreign element. Water aims to equalise as rapidly as possible; it wants you to become part of it, fast. It has no difficulty at all absorbing something as vulnerable as a human body. First it steals heat, then it steals energy, then – if it is rough, which the seas around the British Isles tend to be – it replaces the air in the lungs with water. And finally, it takes you down.

Unfortunately a man overboard is notoriously difficult to spot. Once in the water, there is very little to be seen – just a head and a bit of splashing. The speed of the current will carry the victim soundlessly away while a ship takes time to turn and return. A small sailing yacht will probably only have a crew of two or three, and using one to keep a permanent lookout while using another to reef and steer is not easy. Add to that the hazards of poor visibility or bad weather, plus the strong possibility that the victim is not wearing safety gear, and an unscheduled swim does not seem such a shrewd idea.

According to recent scientific advice, in order to have the best chance of surviving sudden immersion you should make sure you are in a calm and temperate sea – preferably the Mediterranean in mid-summer. You should also be male, and fit, but probably have a reasonable amount of fat as well. If female, then you may have a worse chance of surviving the initial shock of shipwreck but a better long-term prospect of survival, since women's bodies store a higher percentage of fat than those of men. If you have the misfortune to fall into a cooler sea, then you should have spent time acclimatising yourself to the impact by taking regular cold baths. If you insist on drowning yourself in the waters around the British Isles, then try to do so on the west. The North Sea, lacking the benefit of the warming Gulf Stream, is generally at least two degrees colder than the Atlantic. If possible, you should be wearing a well-designed lifejacket, correctly sized and tied, and fitted with a splashguard. You should also be wearing clothing which provides a good 'boundary layer' around the skin (a wet suit, for instance). You should enter the water slowly and with caution, and remain as still as possible for the first couple of minutes while your body acclimatises. You should remain aware of the effects of cold on the nervous and circulatory system, and perform any tasks requiring manual dexterity as soon as possible after entering the water, since the cold will rapidly begin to numb your hands. As the amount of oxygen finding its way to the muscles decreases, even the strongest swimmers will eventually find themselves treading water. If you find a lifeboat or life-raft, but have the misfortune not to be rescued within a few hours, it may or may not be a consolation to know that you will survive for about a week with no fresh water, and between forty and sixty days with water but no food. Cannibalism is not recommended – like other meats, human flesh is comprised mainly of protein, and digesting protein depletes more of the body's water stores than carbohydrates do. On no account should you drink sea water. As any gardener who has ever sprinkled salt on a slug could tell you, salt shrivels things. When salt water touches the lungs, it tightens the alveoli, fatally reducing oxygen capacity. If you wish to survive drowning, try to do so in fresh water.

Though the notion that anyone who falls overboard is going to do so calmly and slowly in a freshwater sea while wearing the right clothes and having taken years of preparatory cold baths may seem ridiculous, there is at least a chance that a modern boat will be equipped with safety equipment and that the local coastguard could be alerted. A shipwreck victim in the eighteenth or nineteenth centuries had no such hope. Safety equipment as such did not exist. There was no coastguard, no SAR helicopter, no lifeboat. In a gale, the crew's best chance of survival was to bind themselves to the mast and wait it out. They knew there could be no emergency flare, no Mayday alert, no warning call from sea to land, no Emergency Position Indicating Radio Beacons, no fluorescent lifejackets equipped with whistles and splashguards.

The only advantage that an eighteenth-century victim might have had over a twenty-first-century one was the availability of buoyant material. Modern yachts are built of fibreglass and modern ships of steel. Unless there is sufficient air left in the hull, both types go straight to the bottom of the sea if they capsize. Eighteenth-century vessels built of wood at least offered the mariner the consolation of watching his erstwhile safe haven float past him as he drowned. Presuming, of course, that he had actually managed to come up for air, since he probably could not even swim. Until well into the 1960s swimming classes were not compulsory in British schools. In many parts of the country people still remember being hurled off the local pier by their parents or elder siblings in the hope that they would float. If they floated, then they could survive, and that was all the tuition they needed. Besides, it wasn't as if even that rudimentary lesson helped. There are still areas of Britain where until very recently, fishermen would even ignore the impulse to remain buoyant. If they fell overboard, they folded their arms, filled their boots, and met their fate. Once the sea has claimed someone, so the thinking went, no man – on land or on deck – could challenge that claim.

It is therefore unsurprising that most maritime safety organisations concentrate more on keeping people out of the water than on dealing with them when they fall in. Fortunately for most people in Britain there are now few moments when we need the sea. In the past, anyone who wanted to earn a livelihood, travel, emigrate, exchange knowledge, conquer the colonies, take their goods to market, work, teach, fight, learn, or survive, had to take a boat. They could not fly or take a train under the Channel. They were stuck, moated by the surrounding oceans. They had no choice but to trust to fate and an adequate captain. Either way you look at it, we are sodden from both above and below, surrounded by ocean and fogged by grey weather. No part of England is more than seventy-five miles away from the sea, and – no matter how far we appear to grow away from it – the sea still shapes our identity, our history and much of our wealth. Dampness is our defining characteristic, and every foreigner that ever read about England knows it as a place of unceasing rain. This is a liquid land, and even those who never go near the sea will ever completely avoid its clammy grip. In recent years, water has begun to creep deeper into our homes and our supposedly storm-proof lives. Whether or not global warming or over-development of the flood plains is the culprit, the waters go on rising, month after month.

Our relationship with water marks much of our history. We may not be far from our continental neighbours, but we persist in behaving as if we are worlds apart. Even now, the British regard the rest of Europe as a club we would rather not join. Depending on our mood, we can either welcome its invasions (tourists, workers, decent food), or turn our backs to it; more usually, we manage a combination of the two. The distance between Dover and Calais is seventeen miles, but it marks a fathomless distance of difference to us. Our encircling waters have protected us, fed us, enriched us and occasionally trapped us. Anyone with plans to invade France, or Italy, or Spain, had merely to muster an army and march across the mountains, but anyone deluded enough to think of invading Britain pitted themselves against an exquisite set of natural defences: dirty seas, high cliffs, vile weather and a combative population. Thus the only possible attractions for attacking us were either to rob us, or to tame us, or both.

From our side, we regarded the water as both a challenge and a hazard. Since we were surrounded by it, we had to learn to cross it. Over the centuries we became knowledgeable about our particular patch of ocean, and the understanding made us bold. We sailed further, bought, sold, colonised, stole and appropriated, and then brought our spoils back in triumph across the water. We were rich – disproportionately so, and we came to regard the ocean as both our God-given element and our lake of liquid gold.

All that imperial loot came at a price, however. According to the *Shipwreck Index of the British Isles*, published by Lloyd's Register, and currently the most comprehensive estimate of UK losses, there are between 30,000 and 33,000 known wrecks around the British coastline. Though the figures include both domestic and foreign shipping, the final total is undoubtedly an underestimate. Though the *Index* has recorded all known ships from the point at which reliable records began to exist, there will be many thousands more vessels which, because they were small, or unregistered, or working illegally, vanished without ever making it safely into the books. Lloyds Register, which began producing annual figures for British and world-wide shipping casualties in the 1880s, only dealt with vessels above 1,000 tons, a statistical benchmark which exempted many smaller fishing vessels and almost all small inshore craft.

Still, even the figures which do exist make for interesting reading. The areas of England with the greatest numbers of wrecks per mile of coastline, are, perhaps predictably, Norfolk, west Cornwall and the Goodwin Sands (off Kent) with 25.6, 26 and 32 wrecks per mile respectively. Less predictably, the county with by far the worst shipwreck record in the whole of the British Isles is Durham, a small county with only twenty-six miles of coastline. The reasons for its appalling total of 43.8 wrecks per mile lie both in the geography of that coastline, and in its erstwhile economic identity as the home of shipbuilding, coal, and iron. The rivers Tees, Wear and Tyne are all local to Durham and collectively launched more ships than either the Clyde or the Mersey, or indeed any other river in Europe. Beyond the mouths of those rivers, small colliers steamed up and down the east coast with coal for all quarters of the British Isles. In part, the huge numbers of local shipping casualties were due to the volume of seaborne traffic in the area. But they were also due to the curse of the North Sea and the east coast: steep seas and lack of adequate safe harbours. In addition, as the 1836 Shipwreck Committee heard, the shipbuilding standards in the area were often outrageously low, and attempts to improve standards or safety derisory.

Other parts of Britain were similarly troublesome. Though the *Shipwreck Index* does not provide county-by-county statistics for Scotland, there is strong evidence that certain coastal areas equalled or even exceeded the worst of England's totals. In particular, the Pentland Firth and the north-east coast were areas that even skilled navigators avoided if possible. Scotland is effectively governed by three seas: the Atlantic on the west, the North Sea on the east and a combination of the two in the north with a character all of its own. On the west coast, the majority of ships would be coming to or from the Clyde, heading from Glasgow down to western English ports or over to America and Canada. As with County Durham, much of the shipping around the east was local and small scale: fishing vessels, freighters going to and from the Continent, and – later – boats servicing the offshore oil industry around Aberdeen. Shipping round the north included a bit of everything: whaling vessels, East Indiamen dodging blockades further south, American ships heading towards Norway or Sweden, submarines and warships entering or leaving Scapa Flow, fishing trawlers, tankers on their way to Flotta or Sullom Voe.

But all the figures for Britain combine to emphasise one thing. Though a steady 20 per cent of all shipwrecks were and still are caused by what could be classified as human error – inaccurate charts, insufficient fuel, incompetent crews, drunken captains, absent lookouts, corrupt pilots – the majority of them are caused by what insurance companies still classify as 'Acts of God'. Passengers could sail on the best-equipped ships with the most experienced captains using the most up-to-date charts; they could choose the safest and best-lit routes; they could personally refuse to put to sea until every last block and tackle had been checked and rechecked; they could vet the captain and dismiss the crew, but if the wind turned or the sea rose, they could still find themselves backing inexorably onto a lee shore or yanked by the currents onto a sandbank or staring upwards into a lump of blue-black sea with their name written on it. And nothing at all, not technology, not skill, not experience and definitely not prayer would ever have saved them from their fate.

There were and are parts of the British Isles where the sea is inclined to give sailors the benefit of the doubt. But there are also many places where there are no second chances and where the sturdiest ships in the world still sail with trepidation. The distribution of wrecks around our coastline – bone piled upon bone for two millennia or more – tells a tale more eloquent than mere statistics. Some of those ships lie on the sea bed because of mendacious shipowners or sleeping captains; some of them are there because of malfunctioning engines or missed stays. But most of them are there because the sea put them there, and because that sea never did care whether they lived or died.

For as long as there have been wrecks, there have been people fighting over them. Wading through the centuries of judgements, precedents, clauses, disputes, definitions and counter-claims in Britain's courts of law gives the reader the strong impression that the human passion for argument is almost as strong as the human desire to stay afloat. The legislation started with the Greeks, and it is not finished now. In part the arguments have persisted because the sea gives the law some unusual problems. Due to its inconvenient habit of rising and falling twice a day there are considerable difficulties in deciding exactly where it starts and stops, whether objects in shallow water should be considered submerged or land-bound, and where high- and low-water marks should fairly be drawn. It even took several centuries before the law could make up its mind about exactly what constituted wreck. The legal historian Lord Coke, writing in 1817, defined it thus:

> Flotsam is when a ship is sunk or otherwise perished, and the goods float on the sea. Jetsam is when the ship is in danger of being sunk and, to lighten the ship, the

goods are cast into the sea, and afterwards notwithstanding the ship perish. Lagan or ligan is when the
goods are so cast into the sea, and afterwards the ship
perishes, and the goods are so heavy that they sink to
the bottom; and the mariners to the intent to have
them again, tie to them a buoy, or cork, or such other
thing that will not sink, so that they may find them
again.

'Derelict' is a ship or cargo which has been abandoned by her
owners with no hope of recovery or repossession. To clarify
things further, the law states that though a salvaged wreck can
sometimes revert to being a ship, a condemned wreck is not a
ship but another species of thing entirely.

But in this abundance of wordage there are some conspicuous
absences. While there are plenty of prosecutions for piracy,
for plunder and riot, for smuggling or even for stealing wreck
from local customs houses, there are very few prosecutions
for wrecking itself. The lack of cases provides the most effective
argument of those who suggest that the wreckers, like sirens or
sea monsters, were no more than a myth dreamed up by outsiders. If, through twenty centuries of law, so few people were
accused and so few convicted, then surely it follows that there
was no wrecking. Besides, even if it were true that wrecking
was often prosecuted under different names, then why, in all
those miles and miles of words and deeds and articles, are there
no convictions for the crime of showing false lights, and only
one known case which even mentions it?

Oddly enough, the best counter-argument to the sceptics also
exists within the law. It is the legislation itself which gives the
best indication of the extent of wrecking and the different forms
it took. Though there are very few individual cases of wrecking
or of showing false lights, there is unquestionably a vast amount

of legislation forbidding it. Since monarchs and governments do not usually spend their time inventing non-existent crimes, or lawyers prosecuting non-existent offences, the volume of wordage is startling. So either wrecking existed and was usually prosecuted under different titles, or 2,000 years' worth of legal scribes have somehow got it wrong.

In earliest times the sea was regarded as another of the monarch's chattels, along with countries, money and people. In mediaeval rulings, all salt water was regarded as a subject of the English Crown in the same way that a soldier or a serf would be, and the sea was considered 'the packhorse of the King'. In 1236, following protests by shipowners, a charter granted by Henry III finally allowed the owner of wrecked goods to reclaim his property, so long as he did so within three months. Crucially, the same charter included a clause stating that if any man or beast escaped alive from a ship, then that ship could not truly be considered a wreck.

Forty-four years later, Edward I reiterated the same ruling. His version, the First Statute of Westminster, would become notorious. Though the 'man or beast' rule was initially inserted to ensure that wreckers did not seize and destroy ships which could have been refloated, in practice it became a permit to murder. As far as any wreckers were concerned, if all that stood between them and £100,000 worth of brandy or silk were a couple of half-drowned midshipmen then they would do everything they could to help those midshipmen to a speedy death. As far as the wreckers were concerned, property came before life, and the law endorsed their view.

The 'man or beast' ruling persisted for many centuries in different forms, and it was not until 1771 that it was finally and explicitly repealed. Even then, its effects lingered on in the common lore of the land. In more remote parts of the country, nineteenth- and even early-twentieth-century wreckers were supposedly drowning their victims according to the old rule.

In 1266 the Rules of Oleron, drafted by the French but adopted in some form throughout Europe, became Britain's earliest identifiable form of sea code. Its articles give a faithful account of maritime practices at the time, and a fetishistic account of mediaeval punishments. Article XXV states that corrupt pilots,

> do like faithless and treacherous villains, sometimes even willingly, and out of design to ruin ship and goods, guide and bring her upon the rocks, and then feigning to aid, help and assist the now distressed mariners, are the first in dismembering and pulling the ship to pieces . . . all false and treacherous pilots shall be condemned to suffer a most rigorous and unmerciful death, and high gibbets shall be erected for them in the same place . . . where they so guided and brought any ship or vessel to ruin as aforesaid, and thereon these accursed pilots are with ignominy and much shame to end their days; which said gibbets are to abide and remain to succeeding ages on that place, as a visible caution to other ships that shall afterwards sail thereby.

Any landowner in league with corrupt pilots was to suffer an equally inventive and time-consuming death:

> If the lord of any place be so barbarous, as not only to permit such inhuman people, but also to maintain and assist them in such villainies, that he may have a share in such wrecks, the said lord shall be apprehended, and all his goods confiscated and sold ; . . . and himself to be fastened to a post or stake in the midst of his own mansion house, which being fired at the four corners, all shall be burnt together, the walls thereof shall be demolished, the stones pulled down, and the

place converted into a market place for the sale only of hogs and swine to all posterity.

Likewise, Article XXXI states:

> If a ship or other vessels happens to be lost by striking on some shore, and the mariners thinking to save their lives, reach the shore, in hope of help, and instead thereof it happens, as it often does, that in many places they meet with people more barbarous, cruel and in-human than mad dogs, who to gain their monies, apparel, and other goods, do sometime murder and destroy these poor distressed seamen; in this case, the lord of that country ought to execute justice on such wretches, to punish them as well corporally as pecuni-arily, to plunge them in the sea till they be half dead, and then to have them drawn forth out of the sea, and stoned to death.

The next few centuries saw the gradual shaping and reshaping of the laws governing both salvage and the disposal of wreck. Significantly, the 1410 charter incorporating Trinity House (the lighthouse authority for England and Wales) not only made specific mention of false lights, but cited the wreckers' activities as one of the reasons for its establishment:

> [All] godly-disposed men, who for the actual sup-pression of evil-disposed persons bringing ships to destruction by the showing of false beacons, do bind themselves together in the Love of our Lord Christ, in the name of the Master and Fellows of the Trinity Guild to succour from the dangers of the sea all who are beset upon the coasts of England, to feed them when ahungered and athirst, to bind up their wounds and to build and light proper beacons for the guidance of mariners.

Though the sentiments were noble, Trinity House failed to live up to its own poetry until well into the nineteenth century, preferring to leave the construction of lighthouses to individuals and the collection of light dues to violent legal argument.

Under an act early in Henry VIII's reign, the Lord Admiral of England was to appoint vice admirals for each county, who – along with designated lords of the manor – were given rights to all wreck in their areas in return for the submission of annual accounts. The system ultimately proved as open to corruption as the Statute of Westminster, since the vice admirals proved as venal as any wrecker. The preamble to another act in 1713 revealed how lively wrecking remained:

> Whereas great complaints have been made by several merchants, as well Her Majestie's subjects as foreigners trading to and from this kingdom, that many ships of trade, after all their dangers at sea, escaped, have, unfortunately, near home run on shore, or been stranded on the coasts thereof; and that such ships have been barbarously plundered by Her Majesty's subjects, and their cargoes embezzled, and when any part thereof has been saved it has been swallowed up by exorbitant claims for salvage.

The same act gave customs officers and JPs the power to order the rescue of vessels in distress. For the first time, it also offered official salvage awards as encouragement. Not that legislative bribery seemed to make much difference. Forty years later, the preamble to Act 26, Geo II of 1753 conceded that 'Notwithstanding the good and salutary laws now in being against plundering and destroying Vessels in Distress, and against taking away shipwrecked, lost or stranded Goods, many wicked enormities had been committed to the disgrace of the nation.' Crucially, the same act also contained the first explicit legal reference to false lights, explaining that:

If any person or persons shall plunder, steal, take away, or destroy any goods or merchandise, or other effects, from or belonging to any ship or vessel ... which shall be in distress or which shall be wrecked, lost, stranded, or cast on shore on any part of his Majestie's dominions (whether any living creature shall be on board such vessel or not) ... or shall beat or wound with intent to kill or destroy, or shall otherwise wilfully obstruct the escape of any person endeavouring to save his or her life from such ship or vessel, or the wreck thereof; or if any person or persons shall put out any false light or lights with intent to bring any such ship or vessel into danger, then such person or persons so offending shall be deemed guilty of felony; and on being lawfully convicted thereof shall suffer death as in cases of felony, without benefit of clergy.

Subsequent clauses outlawed the taking and concealing of wreck, and the offering of wreck for sale, on pain of seven years' transportation to the American colonies. A further act of 1826 reiterated the ruling against 'false lights', but also widened it to include the display of 'misleading signals'.

The legislation made little difference however. In 1861, the Malicious Damage Act found itself travelling over much the same ground as before:

Whosoever shall unlawfully mask, alter, or remove any light or signal, or unlawfully exhibit any false light or signal, with intent to bring any ship, vessel or boat into danger, or shall unlawfully and maliciously do anything tending to the immediate loss or destruction of any ship, vessel or boat ... shall be guilty of felony, and being convicted thereof shall be liable ... to be kept in penal servitude ... or to be imprisoned for any term exceeding two years, with or without hard labour, and ... if a male under the age of sixteen, with or without whipping.

By 1894, the shipping, salvage and anti-wrecking laws had been sufficiently codified to allow for a single Merchant Shipping Act to deal with all three. The 1894 Act abolished the vice-admiral system, and replaced it instead with individual 'Receivers of Wreck' and local customs officials, responsible for both suppressing looting and for reuniting lost cargos with their owners. The Receivers were permitted to use force – up to and including enlisting the help of the army – to quell rioting, and were legally exempted from responsibility for any deaths which might occur during their attempts to keep order.

The scaffolding of the 1894 Act remains standing to this day, though the eighty or so individual Receivers have now been amalgamated into one post held by an individual working as part of the Maritime and Coastguard Agency. In theory, the Receiver is also responsible for prosecuting cases where wreck has been taken but not reported, and for ensuring the protection of the most sacred wreck sites, including the *Stirling Castle* (sunk during the Great Storm of 1703) and the *Association* (the British naval flagship that sank off the Scilly Isles four years later).

In the twenty-first century, most of the Receiver's time is not spent blunderbussing gin-crazed Cornishmen in craggy coves, but in an office in Southampton issuing directives. Preventive work is now done by leaflet and website rather than with the help of dragoons. And the majority of that work is not directed at local coastal communities, but at the diving fraternity, some of whom have taken over where the old wreckers left off. With the twentieth century's improvements in underwater technology, it has become possible for divers to go further and deeper than ever before, and thus to reach the remains of wrecks which would once have lain undisturbed. Since many areas of the sea bed along the British coastline are more ship than sand, and since many of those ships are alluring both as exploration sites and as sources of booty, serious diving has fast become a significant sport. Stealing from submerged wrecks has two significant advantages over stealing from wrecks aground: you are far less likely to be observed, and you are guaranteed never to leave fingerprints. In theory, anything found on a wreck in British waters should be reported immediately to the Receiver, but, as one professional diver put it: 'Maybe 5 per cent of all the wreck that's found ever gets officially declared. And that's an over-estimate.'

Sophia Exelby is now the UK's only Receiver of Wreck. She is a brisk, competent woman in her early thirties who came to the job with a background in marine archaeology and a civil servant's sense of protocol. She spends much of her time trying to encourage the diving community and general public into reporting wrecks they discover. But since there is currently no legal time limit on reporting wreck, she has to rely more on incentives than on sanctions. If, for instance, you take twenty boxes of training shoes or three seventeenth-century fish knives from a wreck either on land or underwater, the law states that you must report your findings to the Receiver. If you do not you could be fined £2,500 for each offence, as well as having to pay the person entitled to the wreck (or the Crown if it is an unclaimed wreck) twice the value of the recovered artefacts, plus loss of any salvage rights. If no rightful owner is found or comes forward within a year and a day, those items will, most likely, remain yours. However if you do not declare your findings the Receiver cannot prosecute – or would find it very difficult to prosecute – since there is no deadline. And if, five years on and ten boxes of trainers down, the Receiver or her staff were to appear at your front door asking exactly what those things were on your feet, you could declare that you were definitely just about to fill the form in, but that it had just slipped your mind. In other words, the law as it currently exists has neither teeth nor clothes.

Exelby looks uncomfortable at this suggestion: 'Well, yes, but prosecution is only one aspect of law enforcement. There is monitoring, and there are cautions, there are rulings, and there is education, and all those together make a package. And although prosecution is the highest level or the strongest measure, there are many other measures which are at our disposal which we can use, which also have a deterrent effect.'

Had there been any recent prosecutions for theft of wreck? 'Not at the moment, no.' And had there been in the past? 'I don't actually know that. I don't think so. I don't believe so. To my knowledge there hasn't been one taken forward.' So as far as the Maritime and Coastguard Agency is aware, there has not been a single prosecution for wrecking in the twelve years since the post of Receiver was created? 'There are other offences under the Act. There are three or four offences for various aspects of misappropriating wreck, such as hiding it or keeping it hidden or taking things and selling them overseas to foreign ports. I can't remember them all off the top of my head. But none of those offences is dependent on a time.'

Doesn't she find such legislative toothlessness frustrating? 'It would be unfortunate to take forward a prosecution which wasn't strong enough in terms of evidence, so that the courts turned it away and said, "this is a load of rubbish". We can't go trying to enforce the law when it might just be a local gripe, or local rivalries,' she replies. Can she search? 'We can search premises, but we need good enough evidence to do it. You can't just go and knock people's doors down, you need to be fairly certain of your case before you do so.'

Though frustrated by the lack of time limits within the

current legislation, Exelby believes it is possible to encourage more people to come forward. 'Our opinion is that people should understand that there's no reason not to report, because in I think 90 per cent of cases the finder gets title to the artefact that they have recovered or they get a salvage award based on the value of that find. So it's really in people's interest to report – it's an incentive to honesty, if you like: carrot-driven rather than stick-driven.' But, as she concedes, it is a policy which leans heavily on a belief in the finer side of human nature. Besides, when tougher powers are needed, Exelby remains trapped by the burdens of proof. 'Offences under the Protection of Wrecks Act would be things such as diving within a protected area. But to prove that an offence had been committed, it would have to be something which you could actually see, and that's also difficult. You can say that the wreck has been tampered with on the sea bed, but you can't necessarily say who has done it. There are so many parameters which are a bit woolly on that one as well.'

It is tempting to conclude that the law today is no stronger than it was 200 years ago when a wreck was defended by no more than the efforts of an exhausted crew and a single outraged customs officer with a stick.

Even if all those centuries of laws and sanctions had been more effective, they could never have fully compensated for older, more feral forms of rule. Westminster could pass anti-wrecking statutes on a weekly basis, but none of them would make any difference to a hungry people on a distant island. And so, over the centuries, the law went one way and the wreckers went another. In different parts of the country fragments of legislation broke away from their original sources, floated into local lore and remained there, rusting but still roughly functional. In many cases, those parts of the law which were most likely to benefit the wreckers were also the most likely to have lingered in the collective memory. The 'man or beast' rule was never meant to benefit anyone but shipowners and wreck victims, but it remained the wreckers' licence to kill long after the original legislation had been repealed. Similarly, the 1808 ruling that those who presented a shipwreck victim's corpse to the authorities for burial would be paid a bounty of 5 shillings remained a part of unofficial coastal law long after the law had been abandoned and 5 shillings had become 25 pence. As Robert Louis Stevenson pointed out in his *Records of a Family of Engineers*, what made sense in Westminster was nonsense by the time it reached Shetland.

> The danger is to those from without, who have not grown up from childhood in the islands, but appear suddenly in that narrow horizon, life-sized apparitions. For these no bond of humanity exists, no feeling of kinship is awakened by their peril; they will assist at a shipwreck . . . as spectators, and when the fatal scene is over, and the beach strewn with dead bodies, they will fence their fields with mahogany, and, after a decent grace, sup claret to their porridge. It is not wickedness: it is scarce evil, it is only in its highest power, the sense of isolation and the wise disinterestedness of feeble and poor races. Think how many Viking ships had sailed by these islands in the past, how many Vikings had landed, and raised turmoil, and broken up the barrows of the dead, and carried off the wines of the living; and blame them, if you are able, for that belief (which may be called one of the parables of the devil's gospel) that a man rescued from the sea will prove the bane of his deliverer.

There were other kinds of law as well: the unwritten rules of the sea set down by time and habit. In certain parts of the country there remains a belief that anyone who finds something on a beach, drags it above the high-water line and marks it with a stone has asserted his claim to that object forever. During the 1839 Commission of Inquiry into the establishment of a national constabulary, the Commissioner of the Liverpool Police explained the habits of the wreckers along the nearby coastline. 'Such was the feeling of the wreckers,' he said, 'that if a man saw a bale of goods or a barrel floating in the water, he would run almost any risk of his life to touch that article as a sort of warranty for calling it his own. It is considered such fair game, that if he could touch it, he called out to those about him, "That is mine." That is marked as his, and the others would consider that he had a claim to it, and would render him assistance.'

There is not a single line in all the laws of England or Scotland which supports the notion of 'finders keepers', but the unofficial rule still persists in people's minds. A refinement of the same idea was to be found in the old belief that 'from immemorial usage' the proceeds from any wreck should be divided three ways: a third to the landlord, a third to the finder, and the remainder to the vice admiral. A case brought by Lord Dundas as the Vice Admiral of Shetland against two shipowners was heard before the Edinburgh Court of Session in May 1800. As the prosecution explained:

> The liberal share which is thus allotted to the salvors and to the heritors, has taken its rise from the peculiar circumstances of the country ... From the remoteness of their situation, and the impossibility which thence arises of the officers of the law taking wrecked and stranded goods under their protection, they are peculiarly exposed to the hazard of depredation; and it

is necessary to reward in a liberal manner the fishermen and others ... in order to encourage them to make those exertions which are necessary in such situations for the safety and protection of wrecked and stranded goods.

It is that gap between law and lore which is part of what makes the concept of wreckers and wrecking so beguiling. Anyone who burgles or robs or loots goods from a derelict house knows they are breaking the law. Anyone who came across a wrecked car and helps themselves to a couple of tyres and a fan belt knows they are stealing. Even those who, in the midst of a riot, step through a smashed shop window and make off with three incompatible hard-drives and an obsolete TV do so in the knowledge that they are taking advantage of the breakdown of civil society. Anyone who takes another man's property on land knows they are castigated by all the lawmakers from Moses onwards. They might not agree with those laws, but they know they exist. They might believe, along with Proudhon, that property is theft, but they also know that the law considers theft to be theft. So what exactly makes ships and the sea so different? Why should it be that anything touched by salt water is also considered to have been washed clean of ownership? Why should it be that what comes from the sea has no history?

There are plenty of good social, historical and economic explanations for wrecking, but nothing will ever really explain its metaphysical causes. The wreckers have always occupied a no-man's-land somewhere between water and earth, and through all the 2,000 years' worth of legislation, they have persisted in the belief that they have an absolute right to anything off an abandoned vessel. It never seemed to matter whether that wreck had taken two years of international travel through the seas to arrive on their beach, or whether it arrived yesterday stamped with an identifiable mark from an identifiable owner on an identifiable ship. The wreckers would probably argue that they just made the best of what came their way, but they were also taking advantage of a subtler transformation. The sea does not sort objects according to weight or value, but by whether they float or not. Once stripped of context and immersed, those objects have also cast off their former identities and become something else. Add poverty and remoteness to the equation, and it is not really surprising that the wreckers thought as they did. They wrecked for the same reasons that Mallory climbed Everest; because it was there. They wrecked because they were poor, because they lived on the coasts, and because a ship on the rocks was irresistible during a Shetlandic winter or a Hebridean famine. In the more remote parts of Britain they wrecked because they had to. Treeless islands such as Tiree or Barra saw wrecks and jettisoned deck cargo as a kind of divine hardware store, providing them (albeit erratically, and at high rates of interest) with fence posts, joists, rafters, floorboards, and boat hulls. Families who lived along the main coastal trading routes would find their only luxuries – silk for a dress, china for the kitchen, tools for the farm – laid out for them on the rocks and reefs of an inhospitable coast. Whatever washed up on a beach was considered 'the sea's bounty', God's gift to the borderliners – even if God at times appeared to be a present-giver who insisted on disinfecting all his gifts with salt water first.

There were other, more subtle temptations to wrecking other than mere necessity. Anyone who breaks into someone's house or flat with intent to steal from it will be confronted by a thousand tokens of possession and identity. But anyone who breaks into a container vessel is confronted by a mass of anonymous objects. Their endless replication makes them seem impersonal, and their homelessness makes them seem unwanted. The ship and its contents are en route from one country to another; from manufacturer to retailer, from retailer to customer, from customer to landfill site. Unless the wrecker steals up to the captain's cabin and pilfers a watch or a wallet, he is probably not going to be confronted by any discomfiting signs of ownership or with the victim of his crime. If something evidently belongs not to an individual but to an organisation or a group, then – so the thinking goes – it does not really belong to anyone at all. Finding a container-load of cotton shirts, stamped with their brand and still sealed in plastic packets, is somehow not the same as finding a suitcase filled with someone's old clothes. In the first instance, so the thinking goes, the company probably produces thousands of shirts a day, is insured, and will regard the loss of a few short-sleeves as – quite literally – a drop in the ocean. It's business, not personal. But in the second instance, those clothes belong to someone. Someone who does mind, and who probably doesn't have insurance, and who would very definitely take exception to seeing their best coat on the back of a beachcombing thief. In law, there is no difference between the collective and the individual. But in the mind of the wrecker, there most definitely is.

Besides, who exactly is a wrecker? Just for a minute sit back and consider yourself. Let's just say that you live in a place where unbidden gifts arrive on your doorstep at night, and from time to time deliveries of firewood or timber appear unpostmarked near your home. Once in a while, you and the dog go out for a walk to find precisely the thing you need laid by the side of the path – a fence post of just the right size, a crate of untouched oranges. Whoever – or whatever – put them there has vanished, and you can be sure they're not coming back. Sometimes this silent deliverer of gifts, who expects no remuneration and asks for no thanks, does wonderful things: provides exactly the right roofing material for your house, a bolt of undamaged canvas, even an unsolicited crate of vintage port. You know that such items are unclaimed, and that unless you take them, they will remain so. No-one will see you find it, no-one will know you have it, and no-one will ever challenge your right to it. By taking it, you will not be stealing it, you will be salvaging it. And you know salvage is as legal as breathing.

And then you find out that more of the same is going to arrive. You realise that there will be whole containers full of such items – not luxuries, but things you really need: children's clothing, household equipment, tins of fruit. You know that in this next delivery, there will be more than enough of everything for everyone, and that you will be able to take as many bottles of gin and as many spare car tyres as you want. You know that this time people will see you, but no-one will mind, because they'll all be out there on the headlands with tractors, carts and jemmies, joyfully helping themselves in a great free-for-all. You know that they, like you, are savouring this, and that your whole hard-worn community is rejoicing in its bonanza.

Then you discover that, with a little extra effort, you will be able to reach right in to the source of these gifts, to go further and deeper than everyone else, to pluck out items which would otherwise be lost. With the aid of a boat, you can get right down into the half-sodden hold to rescue items otherwise destined to rot with time. You know that the source of these gifts will itself provide all sorts of extras: raw materials, tools, vital supplies. With the help of some wire cutters and an axe, you can liberate any amount of fabulous riches. You need feel no guilt, because if you do not act, then you are storing up problems for everyone, contributing to ecological disaster, degrading your pristine piece of sea for years to come. The local authorities know this too, and would actively encourage you to get out there and start picking things off. You imagine that the ultimate owners of all this free booty live in a far-off country, and that they do not care about this. If you don't do something about it now, then they will just spend three years arguing over how to avoid dealing with any of it, by which time every last piece will have gone to waste. If you step back and think about it for a minute, you know that all of this represents a kind of divine justice, the sea playing Robin Hood.

And then time passes, and another winter comes. You sit huddled at home through months of gales, punished by the cold northern darkness or incessant Cornish rain. There was a bad harvest last year and some of your livestock died. It rains so hard that water pours in through the roof, spoiling what is left of your stores and rendering every possession spongy to the touch. There's a death in the family and rumours of redundancies at the area's main employer. Just when you think you can take it no more, when there's nothing in the larder and you're down to rationing soap, you hear on the grapevine that something is coming your way. A ship approaching local waters, laden with everything you need and might wish for: tractors, timber, alcohol, seeds, tobacco. If you do nothing, then that ship will pass by on its way to an undeserving destination, and you and your equally hard-pressed neighbours will just have to watch it vanish. All it would take is something very minor – a small incentive to the local pilot, the unexpected failure of the nearby foghorn or radar beacon. Nothing one could really call sabotage; just anticipated winter damage. And one bright morning after a particularly severe storm, there on the beach is everything you prayed for laid up on the sand. The ship itself has vanished and there's no sign of the crew, but you feel sure – or as sure as one can be – that someone else will probably have rescued them. And as you cart off the wood and make free with the drink, you only thank God and the fates for hearing your prayers.

It is possible. It happened, and will doubtless happen again. But would you also choose to remember, as you piled your house high, that wrecking is not a victimless crime, and that every gold coin lying unclaimed at the bottom of the ocean was paid for with the bones of ten men dead?

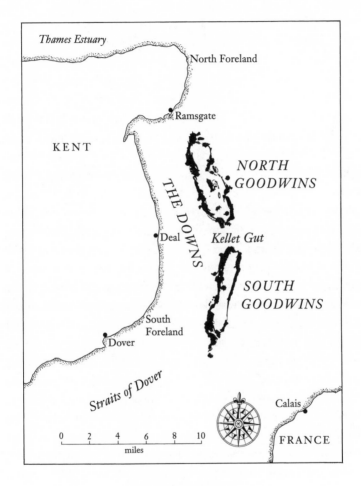

Goodwin Sands

TWO

Goodwin Sands

At 8 a.m. on a day that breaks no records, Ramsgate seafront is deserted. A middle-aged man swings a metal detector in long slow circles round the breakwater while someone from the council drives a machine up and down the beach, laying out the sand smooth and flat in the places where the water does not reach. On one corner of the esplanade, a figure wrapped in wintry rags goes on sleeping through the sound of the machine and the mewling gulls. Even now, the pavement is warm and the sun uncomfortable. According to the radio, this might well be the hottest day of the year, perhaps the hottest day for a decade. A boy on a bike is out early, riding up and down. When people pass by, he stands up on the pedals and guns the bike faster and faster until the handlebars waggle from side to side and his shoulders shake with the effort. After two or three circuits of the pavement, he comes racing down the walkway to the beach, launching himself in the direction of the miniature fairground. The bike's front wheel hits the soft sand and the boy hurtles over the handlebars, landing with an audible thud. He picks himself up and looks around, grinning sheepishly.

Down on the pier by the marina, Bob Peacock's car has purple pimp-glass windows and several items of diving equipment in the back. A solid, stocky man in his mid-forties with an air of good-natured authority, Bob greets me, collects a few extra items from the boathouse and drives further down the

28

harbour. We leave the car and load the oxygen tanks onto his boat. Two other divers, Pete and Dave, are waiting behind the breakwater for Bob's approach. They leap on board and we motor out of Ramsgate towards France. The tide has just turned, and as the sun strengthens, the water begins to glitter. Behind us, Kent's white cliffs – the unscrubbed colour of a nation left out in the rain – recede in the heat haze. In the boat's wheelhouse, the dashboard is covered with electronics: radar, GPS, a computerised chart showing the boat's course across the water, and a depth finder tracing out the surface of the sea bed in pretty multi-coloured spikes. A magnetometer shaped like a giant light bulb lies on the floor of the boat's saloon. The stern is undecked, with a ladder and tailgate; lockers running down both sides contain cylinders, masks and meters.

Half an hour out of Ramsgate, Peacock shuts off the engine. The rumble of machinery is replaced by the slipslop of the sea against the hull and the splutterings of the VHF. The boat rocks in the water, rotating slowly towards the sun. Ramsgate and England have been reduced to a mirage, a pale strip of haze balancing just over the horizon. As I watch from the wheel-house, Bob and Dave strip off, douse themselves with talcum powder, and wriggle into black rubber dry suits. On top of the suits they attach a series of pipes, cylinders, metering equipment, masks, snorkels and bags. Finally, they reverse into the straps and belts attaching their oxygen cylinders which, when full, are so heavy that the men cannot comfortably stand upright. Their flippers make it almost impossible to walk, and the mask makes it difficult for them to see where they are going. They stagger blindly over to the tailgate and drop backwards into the water.

Pete and I sit in the middle of the English Channel and wait. Pete is waiting for his own turn underwater, and I am waiting for land to appear. Not to reach land – though unmoored, the boat isn't going anywhere – but for solid ground to rise up from the water. Sitting here, the notion seems ridiculous. We're stuck on a boat surrounded by sea; the nearest land from here is several miles away in either direction. There's just ocean and sky and a couple of divers paddling around somewhere below us. The electronic depth finder registers around 30 or 40 feet of water beneath the boat, and there isn't a single lighthouse or beacon in sight. But the charts on the screen tell a different story. In lines of stratified yellow and blue, they say that some-where close by, there is something as solid as fact. At present that something is probably about 7 or 8 feet underwater, but in an hour or so it will be concrete enough to walk on. Even now I'm not sure I believe it. But I also know that this place is littered with the remains of those who did not believe in the Goodwin Sands.

The Goodwins are a series of sand banks lying north-north-east towards the Netherlands, and they are stuck directly in the centre of the world's busiest shipping lane. All told, the Sands stretch for more than ten miles north-south, and more than four miles east-west, with their seaward side reaching six miles into the narrowest point of the English Channel. Roughly speaking, they are split into three separate parts: the North Goodwins, the South Goodwins and the South Calliper. Between the South Goodwins and the South Calliper runs the Kellett Gut, a deeper channel of water considered a safe passage for boats of shallow draft. But – and it is often a fatal but – not a single one of these measurements is actually true.

The Goodwins are notorious not merely because they stick out, as Bob Peacock puts it, 'like a pothole on the M25', but because that pothole has a habit of wandering. These sands are quicksands. What appears as deep water one week may be solid ground the next, and what was sand at Easter could just as well be chalk before Christmas. Even the Kellet Gut, which on current Admiralty charts looks as reliable as a river bed, has a habit of vanishing. In 1926 it was considered to be navigable by ships of deep draught, but the surveys of 1865 and 1896 found no evidence of a channel at all. It was open to shipping in 1850, but fifteen years later had disappeared completely. Every single tide that rises or falls over the Goodwins will move the top foot of sand slightly; a couple of winter gales may make the difference between safe passage and shipwreck.

Broadly speaking, the movements of the Goodwins follow a seven-year pendulum swing from east to west and back again, but winter gales and the Channel's individual micro-climate mean that the only thing which remains absolutely consistent about the Goodwins is their treachery. Ships are unable to give them too wide a berth because the Channel itself is less than twenty miles wide at this point, and boats which do not run aground on the Sands might just as easily run straight into England or France. Matters are further complicated by tidal variation in the area. Spring tides can rise or fall by 16 feet; during a low spring tide, around twelve miles of the northern and ten miles of the southern sands appear above the surface, but at low neap tides nothing at all can be seen of them.

It is thought that the Goodwins were once an island named Lomea, low lying but static and fertile. In 1014, according to legend, the sea wall collapsed, the waves rushed in and the islands were overwhelmed. Now, twice a day, the Goodwins become islands again, intermittent Atlantises appearing and disappearing with the tides. Hence the diving and the divers – the sea's resurrection men. This comparatively small area of the Channel has been responsible for more wrecks, and the consequent loss of more lives, than any other sea area around Britain. As Richard Larn, author of the *Shipwreck Index of Great Britain* puts it: 'Of the countless thousands of natural obstacles which represent a hazard to shipping in the western world, there is no single headland, island, rock, sandbank or bar which has earned such infamy or been more feared by seamen than the Goodwin Sands.' The Sands' mutable habits, the volume of

31

traffic through and across the Channel, and the fact that the Sands provide a breakwater for ships sheltering in the Downs (the stretch of water between the Goodwins and the Kent shore) has ensured that over the years, this apparently placid stretch of coastline has acquired a reputation as violent as Cornwall or the Pentland Firth. Present-day Admiralty charts of the semi-circle of Channel guarded by the Goodwins between Folkestone and Broadstairs show a sea black with wrecks, foul ground and obstructions. Over the centuries the Goodwins became known as the 'ship swallower', for their anthropomorphic greed in seizing vessels: all 1,000 tons of one nineteenth-century ship, the *Ogle Castle*, disappeared within an hour. When the visibility and weather conditions are good, this place is a diver's paradise.

Bob Peacock is the skipper of the only local boat with an official licence to dive on the Goodwins, and in summer he makes the trip as often as he can. So far, he and his shifting group of assistants have found 1,800 wrecks on the Sands. The finds range from small pieces of flotsam to complete and un-touched hulls. It is not merely that there are the remains of so many ships here, or that those ships are of such archaeological value, but that the Goodwins protect what they also destroy. Far below, the sea bed is chalk. Most vessels will vanish through the sand and then settle, embalmed until the seas change shape again.

During the Great Storm of November 1703 – still considered the worst storm ever to hit the British Isles – part of the English naval fleet under the command of Sir Cloudisley Shovell had taken shelter in the Downs (Shovell would ultimately meet his fate after being shipwrecked and washed up on a beach in the Scilly Isles four years later). Overnight the wind increased to the point where unbroken seas were sweeping over the main-masts. Though many of the vessels were new and had struck all sails, by 1 a.m. on 27 November they had begun to drag their anchors. Most were driven onto the Goodwins, watched by their helpless compatriots on shore. In all, four major battleships and almost 1,200 lives were lost that night. Casualties from other parts of the country pushed the total number of deaths up to 2,000 – the greatest single loss the Royal Navy has ever suffered, either in war or in peace.

As with several other vessels, the seventy-gun man-of-war *Stirling Castle* came to rest on the Goodwins. Shortly after the storm the Sands took one of their regular trips westwards, burying the ship as they went. For almost three centuries she remained undisturbed, until 1979, when a small group of divers found her. Cordage, pewter mugs and old wine bottles were strewn on her decks. Below, the divers found shaving kits, porcelain, wooden plates; everything from old grapes to shoemakers' lasts. Scattered around the surrounding sea bed were the remains of what at first appeared to be cow bones, but were later identified as human tibia. As the divers noted, the bones were clustered most thickly around the areas in which there were also most wine bottles. Knowing the likely fate of the ship, it seems that many of the crew drank themselves to stupefaction before they drowned. When the licence became available for diving the protected sites around the *Stirling Castle*, the *Northumberland* and the *Restoration* (all three of which sank during the Great Storm), Bob Peacock applied. The licence, granted on a 'look but don't touch' basis, allowed Bob to clear the site of detritus before his surveying commenced, thus revealing how much of each ship remained intact.

Bob himself knows the Goodwin Sands well enough not to take liberties. Did he, I ask, ever find them sinister? 'They're unforgiving. You make a mistake, they catch you out. If you get above a Force 6 here, what you end up with is all white water – the shore just boils. It's not a nice place to be. The other side of the Sands is not so bad, but here, there's no protection.' Pete, his diving companion, had been working the Goodwins for the past twenty years: 'It's horrible when it's misty. Before I saw the sense of my ways, I used to do quite a bit of fishing over here. We were always out fishing for bass and all sorts. Few times, the same place I've gone along, I've actually hit the bottom of the boat and then carried on, turned round and come back out. The day before, you'd come through clear. You know it's low because it goes on the sounder. You think, well, there's only two, three hours after so we should have a clear run. But it moves all the time. If you put your hand down sometimes, it's like something's grabbed your hand – it sucks your arm down. Probably pull it off, if it could. It's like it's alive, like little marbles.'

Everyone who has fished or dived in the area has been caught out by the Goodwins at some point – by the rapidity with which fogs descend, by the way in which the Sands pick themselves up and walk, by the pathways and channels silently opening or closing. When the tide is fully out, the surface of the Goodwins is solid and almost rock-like. But when the tide returns, that solidity wavers. George Carter, once a keeper on the North Goodwin lightship, wrote of a trip he took on foot out to the North Sand Head:

> Beneath my feet, the sand quivered slightly. The flood-tide was returning and the Goodwins were coming to life. Before my eyes the whole face of the sand began to change. The gullies, 'fox-holes' and swillies were linking up, and the water in them started to flow. The pleasant tinkle was gone, replaced by a more sinister sound – the soft roar of the returning flood. The Sands were losing their stability; they quaked and shook beneath my hurrying feet, while the low hummocks melted and ran like hot wax.

The returning tides can move shockingly fast; during spring tides, it races at over 5 knots on some parts of the Goodwins. No-one seems to know if the Calliper Sands (a corruption of 'galloper') got their name because the tide returned faster than a horse could gallop. But what is certain is that the tides in this area are unusually pronounced. In summer it is possible to hold cricket matches in areas which, two hours later, will be covered by 16 foot of water.

Perhaps the only way to negotiate them with any degree of safety is to keep some form of 'live' chart, which marks the changes they make as fast as the sea itself: a fixed paper chart would be out of date by the time it is printed. Though there may be an element of predictability in the way that the Sands move, regular rumblings in the Channel's own internal equilibrium means that any skipper who comes too close may find himself watching uselessly as the depth finder registers 40 metres, then 20, 15, 10 . . . 5 . . . 2 . . . To exacerbate matters further, the Goodwins have proved difficult to light and mark. Over the centuries various attempts have been made to alert sailors with fixed lights driven into the chalk bottom. None have proved successful. Nor did an 1841 proposal to build a harbour and breakwater in Trinity Bay between the South Goodwins and the South Calliper. The alternative option – the four light vessels presently moored at the northern, southern, western and eastern extremities of the Sands – have proved as vulnerable as any other ship. In 1954, the South Goodwins light vessel broke her moorings in a gale and was driven ashore on the very spot she was supposed to be marking. All seven of her crew were drowned when she capsized; the only survivor was a birdwatcher visiting from the Ministry of Agriculture.

While the other two dive, Pete remains on board, half-man, half-rubber. The computerised chart shows us twisting ourselves into an electronic scribble. Inside the wheelhouse the depth finder pans round the ocean floor, reducing water and sand to a tiger-striped carpet of colour. Stones and hummocks of sand appear as black, but every so often the screen scans past a spike of red metal – a cannon, a binnacle, possibly a submarine conning tower. The graph gives all of this information quite calmly. It does not include reality's grainy visibility, its shifting temperatures or its difficulties with subaqueous breathing. According to the computer, everything from top to bottom exists in air-bright water, but in reality the first 10 metres of sea filter out 90 per cent of all light. People describe diving in poor visibility in the same way others have described glaucoma: the descent into dusk, the blurriness, the confusion, the gun-barrel vision, the objects looming huge out of the grey.

Partly because of that darkness, diving is only possible in relatively shallow water, though the whole kit – rubber masks and silly feet – only serve to emphasise how alien all divers are to this element. As they slide slowly through the metres, do they become curiosities themselves? What do the fish make of these subterranean fetishists, miming and poking through the blizzards of sand? Without all this comic technology, there would be no wreck exploration and no penetration of these depths. As it is, Bob and Dave cannot stay down for more than forty minutes, and will not know until they dive whether or not they will be able to see anything except their own dials and meters. They are also limited by the tides: diving is only possible at slack water and best during neaps when the tides are weaker.

After a while, Peacock and Dave heave themselves out of the water, strip off their gimp kit and adjust the boat's position by a few feet. Pete splashes himself with talcum powder and falls backwards into the sea. The sun burns, and around us the sea behaves as it does when there's 400 fathoms below the keel instead of a mere few metres. Bob sits in the wheelhouse unravelling a warm cheese and ham pasty and dabbing at the electronics. He looks at his watch. 'We'll be back in Ramsgate by noon,' he says. The useful thing about diving on the Goodwins is that you can combine it with a more sensible life. Peacock and his co-divers come here as a hobby. Occasionally that hobby can prove lucrative, but generally they do it just for the pleasure of indulging an available obsession. Since they cannot stay down for long, and since the trip from Ramsgate is only worthwhile on the balmiest of summer days, it is the sort of part-time occupation which lends itself well to a double life. 'I got up this morning at 5 a.m., we've got twenty-five staff, and it's wages day today,' Bob tells me, 'I'm manager of a residential home, but I have managers who can do some of the work for me, so I can walk away, you know? Pete, he works round this area, and so does Dave. It means you can have a dive, but not disrupt your whole day.' Bob used to work in a power station, but took up diving after they started shutting the stations down. 'I was born in Ramsgate – I've always been interested in the sea. I got my first boat, and then I sold that and got *Tusker 2* ' – named, I subsequently discover, after his favourite beer. 'After the initial excitement of learning to dive, you try and give yourself other interests. I've always been interested in history, and when I started diving the wrecks, I decided I'd like to learn more about it. So I did some research on that, and that led into archaeology, and understanding the principles of working underwater. It can get boring if you keep diving the same sites, but that's where the archaeology comes in. Then you're looking at smaller things, you're trying to extract information from finer details. That one today, it's probably going to take thirty or forty dives to establish what we actually have.'

A few moments later, Pete surfaces. 'Crap vis',' he grumbles as he removes his mask and stands dripping on the deck, 'couldn't see more than a foot in front of me.' Bob waits resignedly until Pete has removed his tanks and then turns the boat back towards England. It's hot and getting hotter; the water flings little glimmers of light onto the walls of the wheelhouse. Around us there is just the same scene as there was two hours ago: the sea, the sky, the little white strip of England. The water hasn't changed, the weather hasn't changed and England hasn't moved. Perhaps the Goodwins won't appear. I lean back against the gunwhales. The boat motors northwards.

Five minutes away from the wreck site, Bob shouts something over the sound of the motor. 'There you go!' he yells. 'There's the Goodwins for you!' I look up. To begin with, I can't see anything more than a slight tremor in the water on the port side. The sea is still the same colour, the water still stretches as far as I can see. But as I watch, the ripples become smaller and more agitated, as if the sea is encountering some form of sub-terranean resistance which had not been there five minutes before. Over to the west, it is just about possible to make out what looks like a faint rind of white surf. A little further on, the slight whiteness becomes more distinct. The computerised chart shows us moving slowly over a curve of pale blue, with the Kellet Gut just to starboard.

And then, suddenly, there are islands rising up from the sea. In place of unimpeded water, there is a huge golden dune stretching out to the west. Round its edges, the water whitens and surges, reshaping itself around the sand's resistance. Already its seaward sides have been colonised by a party of seagulls and a few grey seals, lying heavy as wrecks on the edge of their new shore. Over on the other side of the boat, there is surf and tropical orange as far as the eye can see. I almost expect to see someone trundle past with a hot-dog stall and a sun lounger, looking for the optimum sunbathing spot. And these beaches aren't small, they are great big swathes stretching towards the Kent coast. The speed with which they have been appropriated by the birds and seals only emphasise the sense that these beaches have always been here, that it could only have been absent-mindedness or myopia that stopped me seeing them before.

There is nothing which prepares one for the strangeness of this elemental conjuring trick. In some parts of Britain, the variation between the tides is so great (upwards of plus or minus

20 feet) that England or Scotland or Wales gain an additional mile of foreshore every twelve hours. There are offshore reefs which appear and disappear with the rhythm of the water level, rocks and sandbanks which only ever show themselves at the spring and autumn solstices. If you potter around on a beach for long enough, you get used to the landscape's twice-daily exits and arrivals. Literature is littered with legends of lost and found lands; Atlantis was supposed to have been located somewhere in southern Cyprus, and Robert Louis Stevenson invented a treasure island which later turned out to be a perfect (and perfectly unconscious) copy of an island where his Uncle David once built a lighthouse. Even Britain itself rises and falls with the millennia. But to watch a fully-populated 9-mile island surface from a clear blue sea is different.

'I've had picnics on the Goodwins,' says Bob, following my thoughts, 'and there have been people who have gone bowling on the Sands. You can do that. You can get a boat to take you out here, mess around for a couple of hours and go back to Ramsgate when the tide turns. They used to land a hover-craft on them – it just depended where the wind was.' He revs the engine and we motor off again. I turn to say something to Pete. By the time I turn back, the Sands have slid away. Not just receded behind us, but gone, completely vanished. There was land, and now there is no land, no birds, no seals, no un-arguable expanse of sand and surf. Nothing. Just the sea again, and the approaching cliffs of Ramsgate. It is that disappearance – the reverse of their earlier metamorphosis – which makes the Goodwins so eerie. One minute, they are there, as sure as land can ever be. The next, there is nothing. Just the bright deceiving waters of the English Channel.

Andy Roberts is a Deal man who also has first-hand knowledge of the Goodwin Sands. Before joining the Maritime and Coastguard Agency he piloted the hovercraft which used to pass the Sands every day on its way from Ramsgate to Calais. He's a warm, energetic character, with a sharp stare and a tidy beard. His conversational style, with its combination of officialese and casual mannerisms, gives an impression of someone comfortable with his responsibilities. Like Bob Peacock, he has been at sea since childhood, and now stares out towards France from the first floor of the coastguard station along the Deal seafront. Looking through the high-powered binoculars at the white water which marks the edge of the Goodwins, he recalls seeing them close-up. 'When I worked on the hovercraft, when there were big storms, we used to go up onto the Sands and run along them. Sometimes you'd see ships or bits of ships regurgitated, and then three months later they would have vanished again. It must be a maelstrom underneath there. You think of the people who were shipwrecked there, and they got off the boat and they're standing around on the Sands waiting for the tide to come in . . .' He pauses. 'Their death is arriving, and there's nothing they can do. All they can do is wait for the tide to come in. If they could only talk, those Sands, they'd tell a tale or two.'

But the Goodwins do talk. They murmur, they rage, and occasionally they even confess. 'There's 3,000-odd wrecks out there on the Sands. You know that expression, "worse things happen at sea"? It came from the Great Storm of 1703, because Deal was devastated by that storm, and whenever anyone in Deal spoke about it afterwards, the answer was, "worse things happen at sea", because 2,000 people had been drowned just a few miles away.'

As Roberts points out, it was hardly surprising that the Goodwin Sands became a perfect Mecca for wreckers. Over the centuries, the inhabitants of the coastal towns overlooking

the Downs – Deal, Ramsgate, Walmer, Sandwich, Dover – concluded that the best way to live with the Sands was to go into
business with them. Like politicians dealing with intransigent
donors, the local fishermen understood that dealing with the
Goodwins required a combination of guile, respect, venality
and boldness. Those who approached without caution risked
being swallowed themselves, but those who studied the tempers
of the tides could return with a year's salary stashed in the
hold. Besides, even without the Goodwins on their doorstep,
the sheer quantity of shipping passing through the Channel
would have provided plenty of employment mending, resupplying and piloting ships. The Downs had been used for centuries
as safe anchorage by ships waiting for a fair wind to carry them
down towards the Bay of Biscay, since the Goodwins acted as
a natural breakwater against bad weather coming from the
Continent. Entire naval or merchant fleets would often linger
in the Downs for weeks or even months, embayed by gales or
undertaking repairs. In part, the immensity of the naval losses
during the 1703 storm was due to that reliance on a single
small stretch of water. A sizeable portion of the English naval
fleet had taken shelter en route to overwintering in the River
Medway; when the storm arose they had nowhere to hide.

But the Great Storm was an exception by any standards,
and in general the combination of a safe anchorage, a 9-mile
sandbank and a major shipping channel provided the local boatmen with plenty of legitimate employment. The 1867 'Report
on the Subject of Wreck and Salvage' for Lloyd's Salvage
Association detailed the working methods of the Deal men:
'Each port has its peculiar kind of boat. Ramsgate boats,
Broadstairs boats, and Deal boats, all differ from one another,
and are immediately distinguished by a person who knows them
as he does. No-one whose attention has once been directed
to it can mistake a Deal boat.' As with the Scilly gigs and
the Pentland yawls, the Deal boatmen adapted their boats to

suit their environment. A Deal lugger was a long, lean, speedy clinker-built boat, open-decked except for a 10-foot stretch at the stern to provide lockers and berths, and propelled by a single square-headed lugsail. Crucially, they were boats with a very shallow draught, making it possible for them to sail over sandbanks in just a few feet of water and allowing the boatmen to get to parts of the Goodwins which other boats could never hope to reach. Sometimes, explained the Lloyd's author, the Deal boatmen would 'provision a lugger and set off on a ten or twelve days' cruise, seeking jobs'.

All of which sounded perfectly innocuous. The trouble arose when the boatmen gave their jobs a more entrepreneurial twist than strictly necessary. Over the centuries, the Kent men had perfected their nautical skills to the point where they had evolved several separate sub-species of wrecker. In place of the ordinary Cornish version, the Kent men had hovellers, smugglers, pilots and salvors all working the Sands and all devoting themselves to different aspects of both healthy ships and wrecks. In general, each boatman had one main source of employment – such as fishing, salving or piloting – but would also supplement his income by taking other, smaller jobs as and when they arose.

This blending and intersecting of roles made it difficult to say with authority who did what, or who could be considered either angel or devil. The confusion between differing job descriptions arose both out of necessity and because such distraction could prove useful as a method of misleading officialdom. Pilots would perform a perfectly legal service in guiding an East Indiaman past the Goodwins one day but be first on the deck of a disabled frigate the next. Hovellers could be resupplying a ship or finding medical care for its crew at the same time as stripping that vessel of every last rivet when it then ran aground. All four breeds of boatmen would race to sea at the first cry of a ship on the Goodwin Sands. Sometimes, it was claimed, there would be over a hundred boats casting off from Ramsgate or Deal. Competition occasionally became so ferocious that boatmen would remain at sea for several days during a gale in the hope of making it to a shipwreck faster than their neighbours. At times, the rivalry became so great that there was not only bad blood between the separate coastal towns, but rivalry between the two different parts of Deal itself. To outsiders, the fine geographical or professional distinctions between the boatmen were irrelevant; they were villains to a man, and that was that. In his account of the 1703 Great Storm, Daniel Defoe earned permanent opprobrium for his views on the Deal men:

> *Those sons of plunder are beneath my pen,*
> *Because they are below the names of men . . .*
> *The barbarous shores with men and boats abound –*
> *The men more barbarous than the shores are found:*
> *Oft to the shattered ships they go,*
> *And for the floating purchase row.*
> *They spare no hazard, or no pain,*
> *But 'tis to save the goods, and not the men*
> *Within the sinking suppliant's reach appear*
> *As if they mocked their dying fear*
> *If I had any Satire left to write,*
> *Could I with suited spleen indite,*
> *My verse should blast that fatal town . . .*
> *That barbarous hated name of Deal should die,*
> *Or be a term of infamy –*
> *And till that is done, the Town will stand*
> *A just reproach to all the land.*

More than a century later, the Deal men's reputation had not improved. The Reverend Robert Eden, Rector of Leigh in Essex, a little further round the coastline from Deal, described the impact of their reputation in his 1840 *Address to the*

Depredators and Wreckers on the Sea Coast. 'I well remember,' he wrote,

> from very early days, hearing and reading of a class of men called 'wreckers' who dwelt upon the sea coast, and whose fiendish habit was to rejoice in every wreck which occurred, to gloat in savage pleasure over the groans and agonies of the perishing sufferers and to live by the plunder which they then heaped to themselves – a plunder which was too often stained with blood – a plunder which was always stamped with the curse of God. And I well remember thinking that it could not be possible, that Englishmen could so act.

As the Lloyd's salvage report pointed out, the villages nearest the Goodwins were well prepared:

> Deal might have been built for smuggling; which is the same thing as saying it is exactly constructed for wrecking. The streets run parallel to the beach, and close to it and are connected by numerous narrow alleys out of which open doors, leading into yards and sheds. The beach extends some miles and at various parts of it, on the shingle itself, stand roomy wooden sheds, belonging to the boatmen. There cargoes of a whole fleet of ships, once landed on the beach, might be so effectually disposed of in these yards and sheds in a few hours, that not a trace of them would remain.

Nor was this mere paranoia on Lloyd's part. The report listed several known incidences of wrecks being disguised, including ropes being cut or spliced, sails cut up, and metal melted down within hours of salvage.

As often as not, the hovellers were smugglers with extra time on their hands. They supplemented their income by assisting the vessels anchored in the Downs and by waiting for storms.

The captain of a ship at anchor could use the hovellers as couriers, shopkeepers or pilots, paying them to ferry letters to and from the shore, to resupply the ship's provisions or guide them past the Goodwins out to sea. During the sea's peacetimes, the hovellers relied on the traditional rules of supply and demand. When a ship arrived in the Downs, the waiting boatmen would launch their luggers and sail towards it, knowing that whoever reached the ship first or negotiated the best terms got the job. A captain who needed a couple of extra lengths of rope, a spare sail or an able seaman would pay the hovellers for their skill and speed as suppliers. The arrangement worked much like a concierge service: in return for an agreed fee, the hovellers would provide the goods and experience that ships could not supply for themselves.

During the summer months the hovellers would remain on shore, smoking, gossiping and repairing their boats. But when the weather turned and the barometer fell, they would train their telescopes on the stretch of visible sand seven miles beyond the shore. Once a gale was at its height, they would race their boats into the surf and sail out towards the Goodwins. They were looking for ships in distress, either in order to find work as pilots, or as salvors or – if they thought they could get away with it – as straightforward wreckers. In cases where ships proved unsalvable, the hovellers would occasionally work in conjunction with the lifeboats to take off the crew and to render assistance.

That was the theory, anyway. In practice, it was alleged, captains supplied and hovellers demanded. Those who refused their services found themselves the victims of seaborne extortion rackets, their cables cut, their anchors stolen and their crews overpowered. The 1867 Lloyd's report claimed that:

> Foreigners who have had any experience of this coast
> dread, above all things, the costly assistance of its

hovellers. The following particulars are supplied to me by a consul of the country to which the vessel belonged: the captain was steering, in a heavy sea, straight for the Brake Sand. A lugger offered to put one or two men on board, but the captain was more afraid of the lugger than of the dangerous bank, and would not let the men come on board. 'I have been here before. I know you. If you once get on board you will have half my ship and cargo. I shall take my chance.' He steered on to the sand before the eyes of the boatmen and every soul on board perished.

A very different view of the service the hovellers provided was given by George Byng Gattie, civil servant, author, and patriotic citizen of Kent. In his *Memorials of the Goodwin Sands*, published in 1890, Gattie devoted a chapter to the particularities of hovelling and in it mounted a passionate defence of the trade. As he saw it, the hovellers were heroic practitioners of a noble trade, and had been slandered both by their fellow countrymen and the French. 'Taking the whole body all round,' he wrote, 'the hovellers are as honest, well-conducted and respectable a set of men as are to be found anywhere round our coasts.' According to Gattie, Daniel Defoe's account of the Great Storm of 1703 was highly partisan and 'libels the Dealmen in the grossest and foulest manner possible, charging them with visiting wrecks for the express purpose of saving whatever valuables they could for their own use, but leaving the crews to drown or perish! A more abominable and cruel falsehood it is impossible to conceive, for anybody who knows anything of the peculiar feelings of a Deal hoveller is well aware that his first thought, in all his daring and desperate expeditions to the Sands, is to save life and NOT property.' The hovellers would race each other to a wreck, Gattie claimed, not with the intention of removing the ship's best pickings, but with the hope of being first to reach a soul in distress, adding: 'An incidence of a hoveller hesitating for a moment when there is a chance of saving life has, we believe, never been known.'

It was true, Gattie conceded, that the hovellers were occasionally accused of terrible crimes. Over the years, they had been forced to defend themselves against charges that they deliberately slipped anchor chains, that they were habitual drunkards or incurably addicted to smuggling. Most of the charges were, he considered, no more than the foul-minded libels of landsmen. Admittedly, hovellers had sometimes been hauled up before the local courts on charges of wrecking or extortion, and once in a while someone had been convicted of cutting cables. But though it was also true that many of the Deal men freely admitted to smuggling, Gattie believed that 'he was not one whit worse than his neighbours in the adjoining counties ... This class of simple, half-educated man, who have not gone very deeply into the theories of Adam Smith or John Stuart Mill, or made fiscal questions their special study, can never be brought to understand how or why, having fairly and honestly bought and paid for goods in a foreign country, they are breaking any law in landing and selling their lawfully purchased property.' Worst of all, in Gattie's view, was the allegation that the hovellers were overly fond of a drink. 'This is a most unjust and unfounded accusation ... a vile calumny entirely devoid of truth.' On the contrary, Gattie claimed, 'It is scarcely a matter of wonder that these men, who are accustomed to lead a hard laborious life, often exposed to winds and waves, snow and rain, in an open boat, without deck or shelter, for hours together, when they come ashore with, perhaps, every stitch upon them wet through, and half-frozen besides, should straightway indulge in that genuine sailor's comfort, a little grog; and who would blame them?' Taken all in all, he (unreassuringly) considered the hovellers to be 'honest, hard-working, well-conducted, and respectable a set of men as are to be found anywhere round our coasts'.

Then there were the official salvors. If a ship was seen in distress, a group of the boldest sailors would race out to her from one of the nearby towns. If her hull was found to be damaged beyond repair, or – as in the case of many older ships – she was not deemed worthy of refloating, the salvors would negotiate terms with the captain to make the ship secure and to save the cargo. Those terms often caused friction. Shipowners and insurers on both sides of the Channel complained that the Kent salvors were little better than pirates. The French in particular alleged that the salvors condemned ships which were still seaworthy, that they forced captains to accept extortionate terms, that they boarded ships without consent, that they were more interested in saving cargo than they were in saving either passengers or crew, and that in some cases, they might deliberately wreck or scupper a salveable ship.

In 1857, the AB *Kimbal*, an American vessel, ran aground on the Goodwins. She was boarded by Deal boatmen who negotiated terms with the captain for saving both cargo and passengers. The captain then ordered his own effects to be placed in one of the luggers, and sent his steward with the boat back to shore. 'When the lugger approached the shore after dark,' reported Lloyd's,

> the boatmen told the steward they could not run their lugger ashore through all that surf. He must land in a small boat. At daylight, he could return and they would land the things. At daylight the lugger had disappeared and the captain's effects and merchandise were never seen again. The next afternoon, when the captain reached the beach, and learned that he had been robbed of all he possessed in the world, he is reported to have been wholly overcome with grief: and to have exclaimed that he should return to his own country and

report, that he had lost his ship in a country where the inhabitants were more savage than those of Patagonia ... the next day, after the loss of the ship, her provisions, stolen by the boatmen, were hawked about the streets of Maidstone for sale.

By 1867, the French had become so indignant at perceived malpractices that a group of salvage experts issued a report on English wrecking. In it they complained that: 'by the side of the lifeboats and their gallant crews, there exists a perfect fleet of boats, manned by grasping sailors, who prowl constantly in the neighbourhood of sand banks on the lookout for vessels which they may save, *volens volens*, from dangers, often imaginary, with a view to extorting indemnification from the owners, whom the law places completely at their mercy.' They cited instances where pilots had claimed salvage for bringing a ship safely into port, of coastguards speculating on wrecks, of professional salvors exaggerating claims, 'Or, lastly, these same salvors, suddenly transforming themselves into a company of pirates, board vessels which do not ask for any assistance, and engage in a struggle with the crew, who they overpower ... It is a notorious fact that vessels in danger sometimes prefer running the risk of being lost to putting themselves into the hands of salvors; in no case do they willingly accept the assistance of the latter, except in the last extremity.'

If this seemed far-fetched, then it was backed up by the 1866 'Letter from the Committee of Maritime Underwriters in Paris': 'We certify,' they wrote,

that it is of public notoriety in France, among those who are acquainted with matters of navigation, that on the English coasts the trade of salvage or ... of simple assistance rendered to ships in peril by boatmen, fishermen, pilots and steam-vessels, is exercised under very oppressive conditions, which appear to us little worth of a civilised nation and for which we can scarcely find a parallel, unless among the wreckers of the Bahamas ... we complain of these abuses, less in our own interest as underwriters ... than in the interests of navigation itself, of morality, and of civilisation. It is certain that salvage, such as we see it practised on the English coasts, is a remnant of barbarism.

Lastly, there were the pilots. As in other parts of the country, the Kent pilots would race out to a ship's signal, and the first man on board would pick up the commission to guide the ship out to sea or into safe anchorage. As the Lloyd's report put it, 'the pilot acts as a sort of advisor to the captain; ready at hand for all matters connected to the navigation of the ship which require local knowledge; and he is a watchman by night'. Unlike the hovellers, the pilots operated under a licencing system, licences being granted to freemen of Dover and Sandwich usually through a system of patronage. The system worked much like black taxis and minicabs do; both licenced and unlicenced pilots would compete for fares, and it was up to the captain to choose between the accredited pilots or those who, for a lesser fee, might guide them to safety or leave them sinking on a sandbank.

William Stanton was rare among boatmen for his willing-ness to put pen to paper. Born in 1803, he was raised in Deal, educated in Walmer and had put to sea by the age of eight as both pilot and salvor. In 1834, Stanton charmed the Duke of Wellington both into giving him dinner ('a most splendid set-out it was,' he recalled, 'of every luxury you could think of') and into approving his full pilot's licence. Stanton made his living in the same way as the rest of the Deal men: through a combination of guile, courage, sharp practice and – if necessary – violence. Stanton's account of the night of 31 December 1830 offers a pungent impression of his working methods. Though his version of the story should probably be taken with caution and a sea's worth of salt, it does also give a sense of just how hard even for those born within sight of the Sands found negotiating the Goodwins.

During a high south-west gale, a German-registered brig, the *Alexander*, was spotted in trouble on the banks. Several Deal men put to sea, sailing rapidly towards the grounded ship. The tide was falling and by the time they reached her side, there was only five foot of water below their keels. Stanton and a friend of his, John Wilkins, leapt aboard. The brig's mainmast and rudder had gone, but – as far as Stanton could make out – the *Alexander* did not seem badly holed. The captain told them that the vessel was new, 'only five days since she was built, being iron-knee'd and copper-fastened, and very flat-bottomed, and that she would stand beating over a cliff'. She was carrying a cargo of linens valued at £25,000, and when the captain took Stanton aside and offered him £500 for saving her, Stanton rejected the offer, hoping that saving such a valuable ship would mean he could make a better settlement later. Ordering the remains of the mainmast to be cut away, Stanton set about trying to refloat the ship. 'While doing this,' he noted, 'a young gentleman came and insisted on my calling a boat to take him on shore directly as he was the super-cargo, and did not mind what the expense was. I told him to pack up his valuables and he should go when the boat came.' At first, the brig did well, rolling off the sea bed and sailing rudderless over the Sands towards safer open water. But after an hour or so, her bow dipped seawards. Stanton sent the carpenter below to see what the problem was. 'He came up: his countenance told me enough. He said there was more than four feet of water in her forward.' Stanton set all hands to pumping the bilges, but it was already too late. 'I saw quickly she was done and beat and a wreck.'

The wind had risen again, and Stanton signalled for the remaining Deal luggers to come alongside to take off the crew and passengers, and to salve as much of the cargo as they could. As Stanton was battling to get a line to one of the boats, 'the young man came to me with a bundle under his arm, and says, "why have you not got a boat for me, according to my orders? I insist on you calling a boat for me immediately, for I am the owner's son, and a gentleman, and I will stop here no longer for anyone!" At last he became quite troublous.' Stanton lost his temper, and shouted at the boy that if he did not sit in the cuddy and wait, the next boat ashore would not take him aboard. 'He went in quite astonished,' Stanton wrote, 'and there I saw the poor fellow drown among the tables and chairs.'

Turning back to his task, Stanton realised that the luggers could not reach them and that the brig was on the verge of breaking up. As he began to shout orders for all those remaining on board to climb the foretop, the deck began to splinter beneath his feet. As the two halves of the Alexander bowed seawards Stanton found himself stranded aft alongside the captain and the remaining crew. Struggling to haul himself up the almost vertical decks, Stanton finally reached the foretop (the platform at the top of the foremast). As he did so,

> the captain laid hold of me, begging and crying of me to save him, as if he thought I knew of some supernatural means to do so. On my looking down upon them aft, there was a heart-rending scene as ever eyes beheld: the men were drowning one at a time, the most awful deaths imaginable. One fine-built man actually died hanging by his wrist over the port side . . . his shrieks and cries are more than my pen can describe, and their looking up to us in the foretop, in a most pitiful manner, for help which was impossible for us to render, and we appearing in a safe place to them.

But their haven proved to be a false one. Stanton knew the foretop was eventually going to fall and – since the only parts of the brig remaining above water were the bowsprit, the fore-chains and a small section of bow – he did his best to cajole the others into moving. By now, most were either mute with terror, or had resigned themselves to a quick death. Stanton's companion John Wilkins had lashed himself to the forelift, and when Stanton tried to urge him towards the bowsprit, he refused to move. Yelling through the gale, Stanton told Wilkins he planned to 'die like men and strive to the last'. Wilkins remained, silent and unresponsive, neither moving further to save himself nor letting go. 'I never got another word from his lips after this time. He was a fine strong-built young man, stood six feet, and in the height of his prime.'

By now, the storm had reached hurricane force, with a vicious cross-tide and mountainous surf. As the remaining men groped their way to the only parts of the ship which remained above water, a wall of grey-green sea rose up, washing the captain and three men off the bowsprit. The next wave left no-one alive except Stanton and one other sailor, who lashed themselves to the chains with the only binding they had to hand – their cravats. The fabric was insufficient; the next big sea that broke over them washed the two away from the remains of the ship and out over the Sands. As he drifted half-conscious across the Goodwins, he saw the two local boats still standing off. Somehow, he alerted their attention:

My legs refused their office, and my lips they told me were as black as ink . . . just at the time they got me in the boat we drifted into such a quantity of bale goods all around us; they asked me if I could stand it if they picked up some bales. I answered, "if you do not intend taking me on shore directly, throw me overboard again and let someone pick me up that will!" Not another word was spoken, but they clapped all the muslin on for Ramsgate. Poor fellows, the bales were very tempting

53

to needy men, but I felt very ill, and I might expect to get worse.

Fed, bled, and rested, Stanton made his way to Deal, where he assumed his family would be anxiously awaiting his return. But, when he got home, he found his wife unimpressed by his heroic survival. She, 'knew nothing of my day's encounter, for she began telling me she was invited to a party, as it being the Old Year Out and the New Year In. She little thought the narrow escape I had from taking my exit altogether.'

Some time later, Stanton went to court in Dover to claim a salvage award. Though an award was made to the men who eventually managed to retrieve £6,000 of cargo from the brig, Stanton was told by the court that 'there was no precedent to award for saving life'. Stanton's experiences perfectly illustrate the peculiarities of salvage law, and the disincentive to save life which existed right up to the founding of the Royal National Lifeboat Institution in 1834. He, meanwhile, retired in 1867, and spent the remainder of his days writing up his *Journal of a Deal Pilot*, which offers an account of his working life at once both blunt and coy. 'In later and more prosperous times,' remarked Ashton Long in the journal's foreword, 'I fear the (Deal pilots) got an evil reputation . . . the evil was beginning in Stanton's time, as he found when the Dover dock men refused to run off a rope without excessive payment. As is usual in such cases, the inevitable occurred: they abused their privileged position, were given plenty of rope, and hanged themselves.'

A milder generation of Englishmen are still dealing with the Goodwins, though these days the hazards are of a different kind. Since the recent reorganisation of the Coastguard service,

Andy Roberts has been responsible for a section of coastline running from Herne Bay to Rye. The Channel itself is bisected by an invisible 12-mile borderline, the southern part controlled by the French and the northern by the UK's Maritime and Coastguard Agency. Anything which might affect both sides of the line – a mid-channel collision, a powerless vessel – is subject to negotiation between the French and British authorities. But even with the assistance of the French, Roberts and his colleagues in Dover are responsible for an area which includes not only the Goodwins, but the narrowest part of the Channel and Beachy Head, Britain's coastal destination of choice for the suicidal.

Merely policing the Channel itself would, Roberts says, keep him busy enough. At present, this narrow stretch of water takes over 600 shipping movements a day. Some of those – like the ferries – are regular and scheduled, but the rest – the supertankers, the freighters, the holiday yachts – vary from place to place and time to time. What are the weather conditions like in this part of the country, I ask. Is this, like the east coast, a bad area for fogs? 'It's no more or less foggy than other parts of the UK, but you know yourself how quickly it comes down when you're driving. And out there, no-one slows down for fog. When I used to drive the hovercraft, we would still keep going at 60 mph through the fog, back and forth.'

According to Lloyd's, Roberts tells me, 'only 14 per cent of the world's collisions happen in poor visibility. With poor visibility, people reckon the crew are on the bridge, on edge, concentrating totally. When it's perfect visibility, people tend to concentrate less.' When something does go wrong, the coastguard will not necessarily be the first to know since many skippers remain reluctant to issue Mayday calls even in extremis. This is partly due to the obscurities of salvage law, but it is also driven by a misplaced sense of self-sufficiency. According to Roberts, 'the reluctance is there because of the embarrassment. The fishermen are the worst – when you get a fishing vessel saying "Dover Coastguard, this is a fishing vessel, I've got a bit of a problem"', Roberts smiles, '. . . then you know you're just picking splinters out of the water. Maybe it's a macho thing or maybe it's just the sense that they can look after themselves, but they won't issue a Mayday call until it's almost too late. Yachts will do it. Imagine they've got a westerly Force 6, they've been sailing for twenty-four hours, three people on board, one of them is seasick, and that person is dehydrated, freezing cold – would spend thousands to get off that boat, would charter a helicopter if he could. He's here in the Channel and he calls Dover and says, "I've got a crew member who's very sick and I'm not sure my engine's working." You could be really hard, you could say, "Well, that's your problem," but you know what he's really saying is, "I'm in the cack, I need help." They're not actually sinking, they're still seaworthy, but they're in trouble and if you left them alone the trouble could get worse.'

Just as alarming – though in a different way – are the increasing numbers of asylum seekers found in these waters. Most are coming over from the Continent, looking for a new life in Britain. 'We picked up maybe a dozen last year, trying to get over in those little inflatables that you buy from a garage forecourt. We've had others that have been picked up over here by a ferry going back to Calais. We've had one jump off the SeaCat ferry last year when he was arrested. By the time the lifeboat picked him up twenty minutes later, he was dead, drowned. It's just awful. I don't know what drives them. I don't know – they're there, and there are hundreds a day coming.'

Most incongruous of all are the Channel swimmers. 'We have 70-odd of them a year,' says Roberts, 'and they're swimming the busiest thoroughfare for shipping in the world.' He then goes over to a table and points to a chart: 'That's the deep-water route for ships with a draught of more than 23 metres. Navigating the Channel is not an easy feat if you take all the variables into account – fog, sandbanks, density of traffic, poor visibility, speed and the kinetic energy of a ship. I sailed on a 400,000-ton tanker once, with another 100,000 tonnes of cargo. The width of a ship like that is the length of a football pitch – they're huge, huge beasts, and they're coming up the deep water route all the time. Something that size is probably doing around 17 mph and if they had to stop in an emergency, it would take about seven miles to come to a complete halt. It can't stop, and it can't alter course – it can't come out of this deep-water channel because of its draught. And then you have a Channel swimmer in front of it. The swimmers start off from here [on the English coast] and because of the currents and the tides, they'll follow a curve. It's no good that swimmer waving his passport and saying, "Stop! I'm British!" The tanker is coming up here, and it's going to keep going.' He laughs. 'Makes you realise how sane you are, doesn't it?'

Reeling off a list of hazards stretching the length of the Channel from Kent to Cornwall, Roberts sounds much like someone reciting mythical trials set for legendary sailors. If, as he says, you can pass the ship-swallowing Sands, then you must dodge Dungeness's creeping coastline. If shoals and shifting beaches don't bring you down, then you'll need to watch out for the white cliffs from which people fling themselves. If you can get past them, you might make it to the mid-Channel maelstrom. Out in the deep water you then have to pick your way through the Lilliputian figures on lilos floating below your bows. If you miss the swimmers, then you must take care to avoid the vast steel leviathans bearing down at 25 knots, seeing nothing and stopping for no-one. If the giants don't crush you, then you must try to make it past Dorset's Charybdis at Portland Bill. Finally, if you can make it safely through all of these, you must face a final challenge, Cornwall's three great slaughterers: the Bishop, the Wolf and the Western Rocks.

Even then, you must always keep in mind that those are just the visible hazards, and that both above and far below, packs of silent submarine predators might be hunting: 'Warships don't have to follow any rules – they don't have to call into the Coastguard. The SAS exercise off here to prepare for terrorist attacks, and no warship has to notify us. The supply ships are also considered military vessels, so they don't have to notify us either – they do, but if they're on manoeuvres, they don't want anyone to know. Subs are a case in point – it could be part of the test; can they get through the Dover Strait without being detected? Basically, we don't know what the military are doing, we just get phonecalls telling us that there are Apache helicopters buzzing around all over the place.'

To illustrate the number of potential Coastguard headaches, Roberts plays me a video: 'We use this for training,' he says, 'just to give people a flavour of what it's like out there.' The tape snows for a while and then goes dark. A faint pixellated outline appears at the top and bottom of the screen, identifiable as the coastlines of Britain and France. Between the coastline are other lights moving apparently at random between the two solid lines. The tape is a fast-forwarded recording of radar signals from all shipping moving through the narrowest point of the English Channel during six hours on an average autumn mid-afternoon in 2001. Each light represents a single vessel, but at this level of magnification the radar cannot discriminate between the light of a 100,000-ton oil tanker on its way to a refinery in Mexico from a 38-foot yacht on its way to a beach in Spain. Speeded up, the lights move like fireflies across the screen, each on its own indistinct mission. At first the movement of the lights seems to follow no coherent pattern, but gradually order begins to appear. The lights moving east-west are closest to the English side of the Channel and the lights moving west-east take the French side. Directly crossing the two horizontal streams are another set of lights, this time moving vertically up and down the screen north-south from England to France and from France to England. Though the separate coastlines appear distinct, the Goodwin Sands do not. They register only as an absence, a space between Ramsgate and the main shipping channels. An inexpert or inattentive captain could miss their existence without even thinking. To complicate matters further, each individual light is moving at different speed, some streaking across the screen, some dawdling at walking pace. To continue Bob Peacock's analogy of the Channel as the ocean's motorway, it is as if someone had pasted the M6 over the top of the M4, removed all divisions between lanes, and left each driver to fight things out between themselves. Except for a few basic maritime courtesies, there is nothing at all to stop any of these ships – from the largest to the smallest – colliding.

Looking at the little pinpoints floating silently across the screen, I think of the old wreckers' tale of false lights. The radar's orderly anarchy has become their twenty-first-century equivalent, high-tech lanterns suggesting a cohesion which does not exist. Roberts switches off the video. 'My God,' I say, 'that's frightening.' Roberts nods. 'Cruise ships now can take 4,000 to 5,000 people on board. You've got tankers carrying 400,000 tons of Mexican crude. And it's all coming through this Channel, perhaps in thick fog, or bad weather, or with a Channel swimmer in the middle ... If you think of all the variables, there's a recipe for disaster. Lloyd's reckons that once every five years, a roll-on, roll-off ferry operating out of a UK port will be involved in an incident that will involve a mass evacuation of that vessel. There's 40,000 ferry sailings a year out of UK ports and 50 million people carried per year. And if we had a major collision, with that amount of people sailing, it would make Lockerbie look minor.' And now, as he points out, there's the potential threat of a seaborne terrorist attack to add to the equation.

Looking out of the window at the distant froth around the Goodwins, it occurs to me that it is no wonder Britain remained uninvaded for so many centuries. What with the wreckers, the salvors and the suicides, who would ever want to cross this wretched stretch of water? And who, frankly, would want to associate with a bunch of natives who consider swimming with supertankers a valid way of having fun? I say goodbye to Roberts and walk back down the Deal seafront, thinking again of that radar screen with its little criss-crossing dots. But it was not the presence of those tiny electronic insects which seemed most alarming. It was the absence inside them, that tiny oval patch of blackness on the right-hand side of the screen. No lights, no warning sign, no borderline; just a void. Something you would not even notice until you heard the soft scrape of sand against the hull and the sound of the tide going out. Something moving against the side of your final safe haven, something gurgling like the sound of a throat. Just a rush of water and a trickle of sand. And then . . . Nothing.

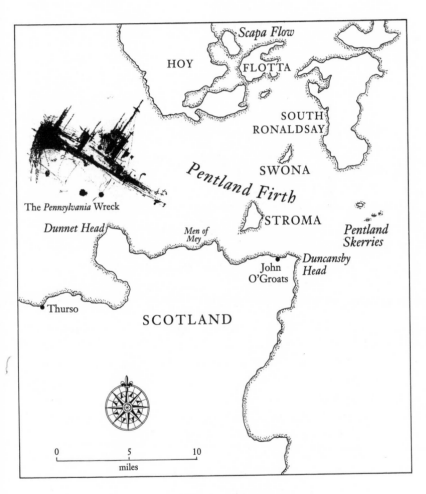

Scapa Flow

HOY

FLOTTA

SOUTH
RONALDSAY

SWONA

Pentland Firth

The *Pennsylvania* Wreck

STROMA

Pentland
Skerries

Dunnet Head

Men of
Mey

Duncansby
Head

John
O'Groats

Thurso

SCOTLAND

0   5   10
        miles

Pentland Firth

THREE

Pentland Firth

F rom where I am standing, it all looks perfectly clear. There's the mainland behind us with the cluttered harbour at Gills Bay vanishing back into the land, there's Dunnet Head on one side and John o'Groats on the other. Away over on the cliffs to the far right is the lighthouse at Duncansby Head, fenced about by railings to stop the long-departed keepers from being lifted bodily off the cliffs by the winds which hurtle round this corner of the north. Off on the starboard side is an iron beacon shaped like an old-fashioned birdcage, standing guard over the white water to the west. From sea level, it is just about possible to see from here to the folded slopes of Hoy and the entrance to Scapa Flow. Smoke is visible from a couple of the houses on Orkney, and though the clouds above our heads race along way over the speed limit, there is a warm and springy glow to the whole scene. True, there seems to be a certain amount of disturbance in the water out in the Firth, but nothing particularly troubling. Maybe a few odd little flashes of white by the Pentland Skerries – white where white definitely should not be – and a few unexpectedly large waves flinging themselves against the mainland. And there do seem to be several large rocks, visible even from this level, stuck smack in the middle of a shipping lane. Plus a couple of prominent marker buoys standing sentry over some unspecified hazard. But nothing exactly savage; nothing to really justify this stretch of water's accursed reputation. Looking out over the Pentland

Firth, it occurs to me that there is something seductive about the ways in which the sea deceives. There is not enough here on a bright day in June to show the truth about this place; that this stretch of water, in darkness, in fog or in winter, is murderous.

On the boat, the wind picks at the supermarket bags. Today's travellers include two engineers from the Northern Lighthouse Board, on their way over to a fortnight's work at the island lighthouse, Margaret Gibson, a sparky woman in her seventies who was born here, myself, and James Simpson, skipper and Laird of Stroma. Not that 'laird', with its ripe and tweedy implications, seems the right word for Simpson. He's a tall man, slightly stooped, with his spine curving protectively over his belly. Today – and, you suspect, every day – he is dressed in a flea-bitten pullover the colour of mould, a checked shirt and olive coveralls. He is old, but it is not his age you notice so much as the way he stands in the wheelhouse with one hand on the tiller, one eye out for the land and one ear tuned to the conversation. He has the solidity and assurance of someone who is a part of this place. He looks like the kind of person who would not need to shout to command.

Above us, clouds rip across the sky, accelerating towards the mainland. Ahead of us, the island creeps closer. Once the bags of goods are unloaded, Simpson, Margaret and I take a stately ride on an ATV to the lighthouse. The island of Stroma is not large – two miles long by one mile wide – but it is singular. Like many of the outposts in Scotland's archipelago, it is treeless, and, to an eye accustomed to benign lowland curves, comparatively bleak. There could be no secrecy here, no hiding place. From the top of the island it is possible to pick out every tuft of grass from Thurso to Kirkwall and every passing boat from the North Sea to the Atlantic. No-one could do the weekly wash here without half the Highlands knowing the colour of their smalls. In this landscape, with its ripping winds and flinging rain, you would expect the houses to be hunkered down into the ground, buried deep in whatever clefts and dells could be found. But they're not; they parade down the main road in a line of strict horizontals and verticals, upstanding against the sea and the land. As on the Caithness mainland, the walls of each croft are all built of thin slivers of oatmeal granite bricked up into a form of stone Morse code – dot dot dash, dash dash dot. Many of the doors gape open, showing black against the stone. The window of one croft has a small, perfectly round bullet-hole through one remaining pane. The skeletal hull of a boat leans against the grass, a few old bits of farm machinery rust away in the middle of an abandoned vegetable patch, and the bones of a long-dead whale stand propped against the side of a garden wall.

As we ride by, Simpson points out the different crofts – some large and relatively opulent, some no more than miniature butt-and-bens. 'There would be about fifty houses or crofts,' he explains, 'small crofts, but they were reckoned to be better off than the fisherman in, say, Wick or Keiss. They set the croft down before they went off on the herring fishing – the herring was a big industry in that days. When the men went to the herring fishing, they had the croft ploughed; the women fed the sheep and the cattle and milked the cow, and when they came home from the fishing they had tatties for the winter feed and then they cut their harvest. When the herring fishing was finished, it was harvest time – it was a seasonal fishing, and it suited the Stroma men perfectly because their wives attended to the crofts. You could say the women in Stroma were liberated well before women's lib. They'd got men's work to do – milk cows, make butter; they were very industrious women. And then when the husband comes home they'd have a fat pig to kill – that was your winter meat, all salted.'

Occasionally, the island would be cut off by bad weather for a few weeks during winter. People got by on the stores they'd gathered in the summer, though occasionally there were more

64

serious absences. Throughout its history, Scotland has been victim to as many famines as Ireland, but since the country was not so single-mindedly dependent on the potato, and was 'helped' in times of need by both the Kirk and the lairds, those famines were rarely as destructive as elsewhere. Was it a hard life? Simpson considers. 'The only thing I would think would be a difficulty is if you were a smoker and you ran short of fags. That was terrible. I was a smoker and on Stroma I was short of tobacco. I tried smoking tea – you get the smell when you came in the house – and then I had sugar beet that we used to feed the animals with, and I steeped the sugar beet in water, and dried it on the stove. And, you know, it was not a bad smoke.'

On the way past Stroma Mains, the largest farm on the island, Simpson starts quoting: 'Woe unto them that join house to house, that lay field to field, till there be no place, that they be placed alone in the midst of the earth! . . . Woe unto them that rise up early in the morning that they follow strong drink; that continue until night, till wine inflame them!' What does he mean? 'Isaiah,' he says. 'That's what happened. They took the land on either side, and look at the luck it brought them.' The majority of crofts on the island would have worked between two and six acres of land. The Mains was amalgamated from several smaller crofts and the old cemetery, extending first to 130 acres and then to 230, a Highland Clearance in miniature. But it, like every other house on this island, is now abandoned. No-one, not even Simpson himself, lives here.

Stroma was inhabited until 1962. In 1914 there were 300 people on the island; by 1957 the population had sunk back to forty-five. First the shop went, then the nurse, then the school. Even the belated construction of a harbour in 1956 did not stop the slow seepage of people. There is still some argument about the reasons for the depopulation. Some say it was the introduction of the eleven-plus exam, a move which forced the island's children to cross from Stroma's school to the mainland ones, and thus to gain a taste for life on a bigger island. Some say it was local council's failure to take account of local conditions and its refusal to provide regular transport for the islanders and their livestock. Some say it was the lack of a decent harbour. Behind all these reasons lies the blinding geographical one: proximity to the mainland proved Stroma's blessing, but also its downfall.

In 1947 the whole island was bought by a Yorkshire umbrella manufacturer named John Hoyland, who fell victim to the old Scottish curse on absentee landlords. Every single one of his tenants left, and as they went, they demanded compensation for the various improvements each had made to their crofts. Unsurprisingly, Hoyland then tried to sell the island. Equally unsurprisingly, no-one wanted it. Rumours bloomed and faded; for one wildly implausible moment, Stroma was going to be home to a nudist colony. Then, when there were no more than sixteen people still living on the island, Hoyland offered the island as a prize on an American quiz show. Finally, in 1960, it was bought by James Simpson: born on Stroma, brought up there; the first islander to pass his driving test, and the last ever to use its roads.

Later, back in the warm kitchen of his farmhouse on the mainland, Simpson considers the wisdom of his offer. 'I had no intention of buying Stroma, but I had time on my hands, and I was in seeing the accountant. He sent me up to this lawyer – never met him before, and I said, "I see Stroma was sold last week, and it's not sold this week. Is it on the market?" "Yes," he said, "Stroma's for sale." I said, "What kind of money?" So he told me what kind of money, and there and then, the lawyer wrote that I, James Simpson, offered to buy the island of Stroma at a certain figure, and I signed my name at the end of it. I went off on holiday, and when I got back there was a letter saying my offer was accepted. Lena [Simpson's wife] nearly flew at me for being so stupid. She says, "Stroma? What on earth are you going to do with an island?" Next day a letter came in saying would I withdraw the offer because a better one had come in. So that made me all the more determined. I was hard put to pay the money, though.'

So there he is now, holding sole dominion over a number of beautiful but derelict crofts, a small amount of grazing land, and a community of viciously territorial terns. In the absence of people, Stroma has become a breeding ground for the birds. Flocks which used to nest on the mainland have moved over here, and the colony is now protected under law. As I walk back up the track from the lighthouse at the far end of the island, the terns, incensed at the human intrusion, started mobbing me. Looking up, I found myself staring at several large white missiles coming at me with malice aforethought. Realising that being strafed by high-velocity guano is not doing anything for either my dignity or my coat, I dive for respite into one of the derelict crofts.

Inside, I find the shocking white pelvic bone of a cow submerged beneath a sea of sheep droppings. The windows, cut deep into the feet-thick walls, have been blocked up with a couple of planks nailed together in the shape of a St Andrew's cross. The daylight which shines through provides the only illumination in the house. In another, the sea-green structure of an old box bed still stands in the divide between two rooms. The floor below has gone – either deliberately removed, or accidentally destroyed by the trampling livestock – but the bed and the limed matchboard ceiling above it are intact, untouched even by the damp. The kitchen table still stands in the parlour and a framed and fading photograph gazes out from the top of the mantelpiece. In the grate there are five plastic fishing buoys and by the sink is an old bottle of sheep drench. In the croft near the Baptist kirk, the upstairs rooms have been emptied of everything except fading yellow wallpaper and the mummified body of a rabbit. As I walk from room to room below the coombed ceiling, there is a sudden scritter of feet directly above my head and then the answering echo of rafter-dust falling. The rooms are tiny, each doorway barely measuring more than five and a half foot high. A man the height of James Simpson would have to bow himself in or out every time.

Back outside, the terns attack with renewed enthusiasm. Bolting from croft to croft, I hear a strange sound coming from the shoreline – a low, plaintive mumble rising and falling. A seal colony. The seals watch me walking towards them. When I get too close, the colony rises as one, flumping over the rocks and into the sea. I sit on the rocks and watch them. Fifty dark faces stare back at me, huge-eyed and curious. With their bodies underwater and their silent interested gaze, it is not hard to see why so many people considered the seals too close to humankind for comfort. Bobbing there by the shore, waiting for me to do something, they look disconcertingly like shipwreck survivors.

I turn away and walk back up the hill, through what remains of Stroma's old township. The houses along the main road down the spine of the island seem to have rotted at different rates. Those crofts, which have somehow managed to keep their glazing and their roof-slates, are in much better condition than the others. In some, the furniture is still laid out as if only recently abandoned: iron bedsteads with mattresses, tables, armchairs, cupboards full of boots and bottles, everything arranged with the same care and compaction as it would be on a boat. But most crofts have already lost the war with the weather. As soon as the tiles go, the damp begins to sidle into the mortaring; within a couple of years all that is left are a few bony ribs and the stark gable ends. Even so, these places have done well to last as long as they have. They were built for resistance, to resist the intrusion of the sea, the air, the sun, and the wind. And, perhaps more pointedly, to resist outsiders.

The number of seals and terns is evidence that the fishing

round here must still be plentiful, and the nettles in front of most crofts is proof of the land's potential fertility. Given the possibility of a good living and the evidence of so much activity in the past, it is tempting to see Stroma's abandonment as the result of some appalling trauma. Abandonment is always taken as a sign of failure, a collective death. There's plenty of abandonment to be found in Scotland – the Highland Clearances saw to that. But Stroma does not feel sad. True, there is sorrow in seeing the once meticulous vegetable patches turned over to weeds, or wondering how many more winters the box beds will stand before they start to rot. But that isn't the whole story. What is interesting about Stroma is not the fact of its abandonment, but the tale of its past.

An official book published in 1992 to commemorate the islanders' lives includes photos, reminiscences, essays on the school, the kirk, the food, the crops, the fishing; all the social and anti-social aspects of their past. What it does not include is anything about wrecking. Which is a curious (and, as it turns out, a deliberate) omission. Because, apart from being almost universally remembered as a happy place, Stroma was overwhelmingly a wreckers' island.

Standing in the lantern room of Stroma lighthouse, it is easy to see why. It is early afternoon now, and there is near-perfect visibility for a distance of ten miles or more at all points of the compass. Down below, the sea is midway through the ebb tide. Throughout the Firth, the water is arguing with itself, jostling and barging, rising and returning, endlessly restless. Directly below, spray mobs the submerged reefs. The current pushes through alleyways of rock, bangs round the edges of headlands, punishes the base of the beacon out by the Skerries. Whitewater seethes around the base of the cliffs, crashing up, receding, crashing again without rhythm or coherent motion. Broad plumes of spray appear where clear sea should be, and the grass on the cliff tops grows in tight, salt-licked quiffs. The battle between one current is fought in foaming haste against the opposing roost, and the sea often passes through in three dimensions. When the wind gets up, or when there is a particularly strong spring tide flowing, the water thrashes at itself, finding its own violent passage from one place to the next. It looks ill-tempered, impatient, a furious place. If there could be such a thing as a liquid riot, then it would be found here in the Pentland Firth. Step back a few yards inland, and there's not much noise apart from the birds and the wind. But stand over the sea, and the noise is almost constant: a thick rush of sound as the water finds its way in or out of the Firth. The terns hover above, watching but never landing.

A few weeks earlier, on an equally windy, equally sunny day, I had stood over on the other side of the water, at the furthest edge of South Ronaldsay. In Scapa Flow to the north, the sea was calm enough to see the islands reflected, and it was high summer in the sky above. But in the Firth, it looked like war.

The distance between the mainland and the most southerly of the Orkney Islands is seven miles. Through that thin passage, the North Sea and the Atlantic race each other twice each day. All the tides and eddies of the great wide west and north meet the currents of the east and south, and funnel themselves through a passage which, in oceanic terms, is barely wider than a drainpipe. Twice a day through this reversible river, two seas hurtle together. Towards the narrowest point in the Firth, the current (either east or west) picks up speed, joins the confused currents around the land, and begins to leap and tumble. When it enters the Firth, water travelling in one direction with the flowing tide would be travelling at a speed of around two or three knots. White with fury, it races past the land, leaving a wake of whirlpools, roosts and overfalls in its path. When it bolts out the eastern end near Duncansby Head, it will be running at 10 knots or more, over three times its usual tidal speed.

Where it meets the land, it breaks far more violently than you would expect, even on the calmest days.

Mix bad weather or a spring tide into this equation, and things become even more difficult. Due west of Orkney, the nearest land is Canada, 3,000 miles away. Due east, it is Norway. Given the time, the winds and the distance, it is perfectly possible for a light breeze in mid-Atlantic to hit the Pentland Firth as a full-blown gale. Any rough weather blowing westwards will often meet a tide coming in the opposite direction right in the middle of the Firth. It has been estimated that for fifteen days out of every month, the winds in the Firth rise to Force 7, and to Force 8 (with waves 30 foot high or more) seven days out of every thirty-one. As the Admiralty chart for the area cautions: 'Spring rates of 12 knots occur, and extreme rates of 16 knots have been reported' – a speed almost unheard of in the seas around the rest of Europe. In most parts of the country, wind speeds of 70 or 80 mph are considered extreme, but during the Great Gale of 1953, the local anemometer registered a speed of 120 mph before it too blew away. Bruce Brown, the last keeper of Duncansby Head lighthouse, recalled seeing his wife, Hazel, almost taking an unscheduled flight to Orkney. 'Hazel was on the way back from the doctor once. I was sitting here [in the keepers' lounge] and Hazel suddenly went flying past the windows. If she hadn't got a grip on the dyke, she'd have been away out to sea.'

To complicate matters further, neither the mainland nor Orkney are solid landmasses. The shores of both are a confusion of creeks, reefs and islands which, like Stroma, Swona, Copinsay and the Pentland Skerries, stand directly in the path of the current. Each of these in their turn set up their own individual maelstroms, many of which are sufficiently notorious to have earned their own names: the Swilkie, the Men of Mey, and the Bores of Duncansby. The tides too have their stings. Because of their power, they can recoil at the edges or rebound off the land, they can dawdle along and then spring suddenly forwards with the merest swing in the wind. And, despite the scouring tides, the sea bed of the Firth is not smooth. Below the water lie not only the usual snags of reefs and shoals, but the bones of every ship that ever came to grief here. Because the currents are so powerful, a ship that goes down north of Stroma can easily end its days cluttering a corner of Duncansby. One dive expert recalled leading a trip out to the Firth which nearly ended in disaster. Two experienced divers found themselves towed along so fast by the current that, within a few minutes, they ended up a mile away from the dive boat with a dwindling supply of oxygen and not much chance of hailing the skipper. In the end, they were saved only by luck and the captain's best guesswork.

In most cases, guesswork is not enough. As almost anyone on the islands will tell you, in-depth knowledge of the Firth is not to be bought, and nothing but years of practice can really show sailors how to navigate this place. As one fisherman who has lived in a house overlooking these waters all of his life noted: 'In bad weather, I was always at my best. On a fine day, that was the time that a treacherous thing could happen, not a coarse day. I've seen me get tricked on a fine day at sea. Not with a gale of wind, but with the sea.'

Those who do use the Firth to best advantage do so with caution. George Gunn, who fished the area for several decades and who now lives in John o'Groats, is clear about the best way to treat it. 'We took chances, but we knew when to take them – we didn't just take them willy-nilly.' What did he think made a good Pentland navigator? 'Remember that the sea is always the master. Realise that. You're not the master, by no means. You might be the skipper, but the sea is always the master. People forget that before they ever start the sea – they think they know everything afore ever they start. That's why some of them get lost. We didn't have all the navigational gadgets, but we knew exactly where we were.'

No survey or Admiralty chart can ever hope to correctly identify each of the Pentlands' hazards, since what appears in soundings one day might be a mile or more to west or east by the next. Add to this the prevailing weather conditions around the Firth – smothering fogs, scorching winds, gales which arrive with no apparent preamble – and the abrupt cornering of the coastline at Duncansby Head, and it is a wonder that anyone ever makes the passage at all.

But they do. Like the English Channel, the Pentland Firth sees an exceptionally high number of shipping movements every year – around 6,000 in the mid-1990s, and far more in the past. These are not the aimless putterings of private yachts as they might be on the west coast or in southern England. Until the 1970s and the precipitate decline of the Scottish fishing industry, shipping movements in the area tended to be split three ways: passenger ferries plying to and from Orkney, fishing trawlers, and commercial cargo vessels. In theory, their captains do have alternatives. In the days of sail, many found the prospect of the Firth so daunting that they went the long way round to the Continent, either via the northern passage between Orkney and Shetland, or through the English Channel. The route through the Firth is faster (literally, if you get the tides right), but it is also infinitely more hazardous. It also guards the entrance to Scapa Flow, once Europe's finest natural anchorage, and now, as a consequence, Europe's finest wreck dive site.

Aside from smaller traffic entering the Firth on the way to mainland Orkney or one of the smaller islands, there is also the Flotta oil terminal, responsible for a threefold increase in shipping tonnage between 1990 and 2000 alone. Most tankers are large and powerful enough to enter and leave Scapa Flow at all times of day, but even they seem to pause suspended in the water, making such slow headway against the currents that they remain stationary for minutes at a time. One ex-submariner recalls travelling through the Firth on the way to Norway in 1969: 'We would do 12 knots on the surface flat out in those old diesel submarines. But we went north of Stroma and Pentland Skerries doing over 25 knots. There was a huge wind behind us ripping the sea up, and we were right on the peak of the tidal stream. We just whanged through it like a cork fired from a bottle. It was amazing fun!'

Until the late eighteenth century, neither side of the Firth was well lit. Mariners coming from Canada or America and navigating by dead reckoning could find themselves many miles off course by the time they reached British waters. Captains could find themselves wrapped in fog from Newfoundland to Bergen, making it impossible to take an accurate sextant reading and leaving them fatally dependent on compass readings and guesswork. Charts would often be either incomplete or inaccurate, and any pilot guide to the Firth would be more likely to induce panic than complacency. Captains could, and frequently did, sail blinded by cloud across the Atlantic and then guess their way through an unlit Firth, relying on nothing more than prayer and a farsighted lookout. Today, most of the ships passing through here would be equipped with more navigational aids than they know what to do with: sonar, radar, GPS, VHF, fish-finders, magnetometers, computerised charts, hourly weather checks. And if all those electronics should fail, there are five major lighthouses overlooking the Firth; Dunnet Head, Duncansby Head, Stroma, Swona and the Pentland Skerries. Plus, of course, the supplementary aids of foghorns, long-range forecasts, and the promise of assistance from local pilots. Even then, ships still go astray, tripped by a strong spring tide or a current unmarked in any guidebook.

The combination of wind, weather, tides, and the configuration of the land make the Pentland Firth both one of the most compelling parts of the British Isles and a wrecker's heaven. Those who once lived on the Caithness mainland, the south of Orkney and the two inhabited islands – Stroma and its smaller northerly neighbour, Swona – never had to create a shipwreck; they happened without prompting. Precise figures on the numbers of wrecks in and around the Firth over the past 300 years are difficult to obtain, but the most detailed recent estimate calculates that, between 1830 and 1990, over 560 vessels were either refloated after getting into difficulties, or – more likely – were entirely ruined. Since the Shipwreck Index of Great Britain places the total number of recorded wrecks around Scotland at around 7,500, the Pentland Firth's toll seems alarmingly high.

The sea alone might have made the Pentland a hopeful searching ground for pirates, but the area also provided other reasons to go wrecking. Orkney is geographically closer to Norway than to England. All the islands still retain the fishy stink of their Viking past. Floating around in the background are all the generations of sea raiders and maritime opportunists who used the nearby seas as skilfully and aggressively as did the British Navy in the time of Nelson. Though Orkney is comparatively low-lying and fertile, the islanders were never rich, and could rarely afford to turn away the opportunity for extra gain. Since Orkney is also almost entirely treeless, all timber had to be imported from elsewhere. And, most importantly of all, the ocean is inescapable. Caithness men might have been able to turn their backs on the sea; Orcadians never could. It was said of them that they were 'farmers with boats', as accustomed to harvesting water as landsmen are to harvesting earth. What was true of the north side of the Firth was doubly so for the islands in the middle of it. Apart from subsistence farming on the crofts in Stroma, almost all the islanders' money came from fishing, boat building, piloting, smuggling, illegal whisky distilling, and wrecking.

In 1814, Walter Scott accepted the engineer Robert Stevenson's invitation to join him on the lighthouse yacht's annual tour of the Scottish lights. They sailed slowly up from Leith, stopping off to inspect the various east coast keepers and their charges, before arriving in Orkney. As Scott later noted, his first visit to the Pentland Firth did at least impress upon him the urgent need for lights:

> The wrecks on this coast were numerous before the erection of the lighthouse on Sanday. It was not uncommon to see five or six vessels on shore at once. The goods and chattels of the inhabitants are all said to savour of flotsome and jetsome, as the floating wreck and that which is driven ashore are severally called. Mr Stevenson happened to observe that the boat of a Sunday farmer had bad sails – 'If it had been His [i.e. God's] will that you hadna built so many light-houses hearabouts,' answered the Orcadian with great composure, 'I would have had new sails last winter.' Thus do they talk and think upon these subjects; and so talking and thinking, I fear the poor mariner has little chance of any very anxious attempt to assist him.

As Stevenson himself noted, the islanders of Orkney:

> certainly had their share of wrecked goods, for the eye is presented with these melancholy remains in almost every form. For example, although quarries are to be met with generally in these islands and the stones are very suitable for building dykes, yet instances occur of the land being enclosed ... with ship timbers. The author has actually seen a park paled round chiefly with cedar-wood and mahogany from the wreck of a Honduras-built ship; and in one island, after the wreck of a ship laden with wine, the inhabitants have been known to take claret with their barley-meal porridge ... It may further be mentioned that when some of

Lord Dundas's farms are to be let in these islands a competition takes place for the lease, and it is bona fide understood that a much higher rent is paid than the lands would otherwise give were it not for the chance of making considerably by the agency and advantages attending shipwrecks on the shores of the respective farms.

On South Ronaldsay, Willie Mowatt MBE has held several jobs during his seventy-seven years, though only some of them were legal, and most remained entirely unrecognised by the honours system. He is a strong, thick-set man, as solid as a shire horse. Though age has made him deafer and his eyes are rheumy with age, he shows few other physical signs of decrepitude. At home, the cat sits in the best chair, and Willie pores over his collection of cuttings taken from what he calls the 'barrel organ' (the microfiche) in the local library. 'I've worked for everything,' he says; 'I've been a Pentland Firth sea dog all my time, as well as a blacksmith and all trades, except preaching. And piracy too.' Officially, Willie Mowatt has been a blacksmith, farrier, crofting assessor, fisherman, lifeboatman, Excise man, and amateur historian. In 2001 Willie was given the MBE; the citation noting his 'services to the local heritage of South Ronaldsay'. On the wall at home he keeps a photograph of himself and his wife standing stiff-collared in front of Buckingham Palace.

Unofficially, he was also a wrecker. 'Oh, I know all about it,' he says. 'I've been the chief pirate of the Pentland Firth. In my day, in my day. I was at them when I was ten-year-old.' The knowledge that he was given an award under the honours system for, among other things, plunder, theft and concealment of stolen goods, causes him enough pleasure to silence him (except for a few watery wheezings) for several minutes. 'We helped with the ships, and we'd get them afloat and everything –

we was very helpful in every respect, but when she became a wreck, that was ours.'

Among those who are old enough to remember, there are several wrecks now sewn tight into local legend. Chief among them is the *Pennsylvania*. On 27 July 1931, the 6,000-ton Danish freighter struck the west side of Swona. She was a general cargo vessel, loaded to the gunwhales with merchandise for export. Mowatt remembers the *Pennsylvania* as 'the best. I think so. She was coming from America – load of cars, general cargo. There was three weeks of thick fog – at that time a hell of a thick fog. And they think that his [the captain's] course from America was dead reckoning – none of the modern stuff, none of the radar, nothing, just the old-fashioned navigation. And that island of Swona was in its way, that was the trouble, or he'd of been through the Firth no bother. But with the dead reckoning and the fog – I know that the fog signal at the Pentland Skerries blew solid for three weeks non-stop, and that ship was caught in it.'

When the ship struck, in a calm sea and virtually zero visibility, both the Danish captain and the thirty-one crew refused the assistance of the Longhope lifeboat and remained on board to await the arrival of a tug from Copenhagen. No-one knows exactly why the captain was suspicious of local help, or why he chose to put both his and his crew's lives in danger by remaining on board, but the delay proved fatal to his ship. The *Pennsylvania* was in a dangerous position, badly holed, with 23 foot of water in the forehold and trapped in the path of a nine-knot current. By the time the tug had made its way across the North Sea, the current had swung the ship around and broken her back. Eventually, however, both crew and captain were rescued and taken to Wick before making their way back to Copenhagen.

But what they and the shipowners considered an expensive misfortune, the pirates of Caithness and Orkney considered the best thing to happen to them in years. Within a very short space of time, evidence of unusual activity was observed around the ship's split spine. The men came silently at first, unnoticed by the official salvors or – for a time – local coastguard. It is a matter of some dispute whether the Stroma men arrived before or after the lifeboats, but there is no question that they got the cream. It is said that they had managed to get two brand new American Cadillacs off the ship, into their own boats and back to the island without the aid of lights and before anyone noticed anything had gone missing. As the *Pennsylvania* settled back onto the rocks, the disappearances increased. Goods began to slip away, apparently lost underwater. The raiders were also helped by the weather, since the sea remained uncharacteristically smooth for several days after the wreck, making it much easier to offload cargo.

And the loot . . . The loot had to be seen to be believed. There were items in the hold of the *Pennsylvania* to silence even the most avid materialist. There was a piano, typewriters, toys, prams, several slot-machines fitted for Baltic currency, gramophones, 500 boxes of spark plugs, basins, swivel chairs, card tables, sewing machines, apples, watches, flour, women's clothing (including suspenders), hogsheads of American tobacco, car parts and, of course, the two Cadillacs. Much of the cargo presented no difficulty to the unloaders, but other parts proved more troublesome. At one stage a boat was seen rounding the island, heavily laden and covered with a tarpaulin. According to the local paper, the *Orcadian*, the boat was accosted by two coastguards. Seeing them, the skipper kept the boat a little way offshore but within hailing distance. 'Good load of peats,' he shouted, gesturing to the lump under the tarpaulin. Unpersuaded, the coastguards demanded a clearer look. The skipper refused. Realising that insistence would either lead to a fight or to the Stroma men bolting, the coastguards let the boat go, returned to Kirkwall and reported the incident to the local Receiver of Wreck. According to another source entirely: 'They hove-to for such time as the coastguard got the hell out of it. And they landed anyhow and they had two wardrobes aboard. One of the fellows [in the boat] took a bit of a fright and he made to hurry out right over the boat, and he went right through the mirrors – terrible bad luck. He cleared out for the rest of the evening anyhow – I think he ended up in jail. He turned up later on, I understand, just the same.'

That same source, Willie Mowatt, remembers that, 'There was another Stroma man, he had a whole case of rubber boots, and he thought he was dead right with his rubber boots for all his days. Until he found out they were all just for the one feet.' There were also more unexpected items. 'Another Stroma man thought he had a great case – well, he thought it was silk, and when he got it ashore and took this stuff home, he found it was a case of shrouds! But no pockets for loot!'

James Simpson has another story of the *Pennsylvania*, though it is a tale which Mowatt considers a gross slander against Orcadians. 'The story I heard was this Orkney man, after the sale, when they'd made a lot of money, this Orkney man had a box under his arm, and they were in the pub on the mainland. Some of the Stroma men says: "What's that in the box?" "Well, boy," he says, "there's enough in that box to last me and the wife for the rest of our life." So then they got tittle-tattle here – he must have found treasure on that ship, he must have found money. So the man got drunker and drunker, and still this box stayed under his arm, a shoe box. And they says again, "What's in your box?" And he says, "Well," he says, "there's enough in that box to last me and the wife and our two sons for the rest of our lives." Oh my goodness me, they were thinking, this must be a treasure. They was trying to find a way of tackling him, take the box from him. Anyway, the Orkney man got drunker and drunker, till the box fell with a clash on the floor, and burst open. And you know what was in the box?'. He looks at me. 'Condoms.' Willie Mowatt is unamused. 'It didn't reduce the population in Orkney just the same. As far as I knew the kids had them for balloons.'

When the local authorities found out what was happening in the *Pennsylvania*'s wrecked hold, they did their best to put a stop to the looting and to protect what remained of the vessel. Their efforts, however, proved too little, too late. In a subsequent report, the local Receiver of Wreck recorded his visits to over forty people on Stroma and South Ronaldsay and his attempts to recover some of the cargo before it was sold off. His account sounded a note of high indignation: 'The goods,' he wrote,

> have been concealed. I visited the men yesterday and while [one man] admitted that he had been at the wreck, the others refused to make a statement. They would not even admit that they had been to the wreck ... In every case, the parties who brought the goods ashore from the wreck had no intention of either reporting or handing them over to me. They all plead ignorance, however, and state that they were under the impression that the steamer being a wreck, they could take as much goods as they wished.

Informed that they would be prosecuted under the Merchant Shipping Act for concealing stolen property, most either paid the nominal sums required, or produced a few token goods. 'Plunder was produced from the hearts of haystacks, from amid growing oats, from the beds of lochs and the dark recesses of the seashore,' reported the *Orcadian*: 'Several days were occupied in visiting the raiders' homes and in selling to them the goods they had already stolen.' The paper struggled for a while to maintain a tone of high-minded censoriousness, and then gave up. 'True Orcadians,' it concluded, 'will have a sort of sneaking regard for any who risk their lives in acquiring loot, worthless though it may really be.' In a later edition, subheaded 'Humours of an Orkney comedy,' the paper considered that,

'The wreck has revealed the extraordinary outlook which the average Northerner has on such plundering. Whether they live in town or country, in the isles or on the mainland, the majority consider a wreck legitimate prey.'

In the end, it was considered that the Stroma men had already taken so much from the wreck that it would be easier for all concerned if they were to buy it. The Danish underwriters gave up all hope of salving the ship or what little remained of her cargo, and sold her for £100 to a syndicate of Stroma men, belatedly making official what had for weeks been going on unofficially. As Simpson remembers: 'There was Orkney men, and there was Stroma men, and there was men from John o'Groats, and they broke up the framework of the ship – the doors and the parts – and they took it across to the mainland. They had two or three sales, and they made a lot of money with it in that way. The *Pennsylvania* had everything from needles to anchors – typewriters, adding machines. I remember my father's adding machine, it was a big clumsy thing, but you'd get the answer same as a modern one. There was ladies' under-clothes, there was corsets – you name it, it was on that ship. Oh, there was strange things on the island after that. They had all these things that they'd never heard of before in this part of the land.' A wreck sale was held on Huna, attracting a large attendance, and by mid-October the ship had vanished into the Firth, broken up by heavy seas.

It is a reasonable bet that neither the local Receiver of Wreck nor the rivalrous islanders ever found all the loot. Although Stroma may appear a bald place, as naked now as it must have been when first created, it is in fact the kind of openness which offers plenty of concealment. And the Stroma men were expert at finding places to hide things. Down the cliffs, in caves – small items could be hidden in fields, or dug into the turf, or pushed into corn stooks. In fact, the only place where things would never be hidden was in the crofts themselves. Willie Mowatt recalls many items being hidden from the cargo of the *Pennsylvania*. 'They [the Stroma men] had an enormous load of tins of sardines just ready for household use, and great big frying pans too. They was hidden in the loch – in the long grass, clear of the house, of course, not far from the landing spot at the south end of the island. There happened to be a day about that time of year when there was shooters that came from down in England for shooting wildfowl, and they had their man with a dog for picking up the game. So these dogs got on this scent of this fine frying pan – they wouldn't leave the damn spot, and the shooters didn't know what on earth was the matter. So they investigated, and there was this pile of loot, with the sardines and the fat in the frying pans that had attracted the dogs.'

Once the loot was off their property, concealed in a cave or a peat stack or by a loch, no-one could prove who it belonged to. David Stogdon, the RNLI's Inspector of Lifeboats for Scotland from 1952 to 1960, remembers making several visits to Stroma. The islanders maintained a strict control over who entered and left the island. Those who were not wanted were told that if they tried to land on Stroma without permission, they might find themselves trapped. Police boats could go missing, develop an unexpected leak or spontaneously combust. If that didn't work, they would be told that attempting to land put them under risk of direct attack. 'The Stroma men were,' says Stogdon, 'a law unto themselves.'

Customs officers, policemen, coastguards and Receivers of Wreck might all have been repelled, but the lifeboatmen were liked and trusted partly out of respect for their work and partly because they were a voluntary, non-governmental organisation. Stogdon was also accepted by the Stroma men because he had sailed every inch of Scotland and the Firth since childhood, and knew exactly what he was talking about. He remembers being greeted on his arrival by William Bremner, then the appointed head of the Stroma gathering, and given a tour. What he saw would have made a conscientious Excise man weep. After a tour of the makeshift island graveyard, he was shown into the islanders' crofts. 'Every house,' he says, 'was stuffed with wreck.' What sort of wreck? 'Well ... clocks, telescopes, binnacles ... I seem to remember enormous dining-room tables in small cottages. And then of course from time to time they'd have cargo parts of lorries or something like that which could be put together to make a lorry and taken ashore on two or three fishing boats in calm weather. They'd land it quietly somewhere, drive it along and sell it.'

Stogdon was also shown how, and where, the wreck was hidden. 'Bremner said, "Of course, the trouble is, people come from the mainland to find out what we've got, so we have to have a way of hiding it." And he showed me where stuff had been put below the water. It was put there so if a search took place, they would find nothing. The booty was underwater, down rocky narrow crannies, probably quite deep, on chains, and then coming up on a thread to a little cork. You'd pull up the cork, and then the thread, and you'd get a bigger rope, and then you'd get a bigger rope than that, and then you'd get the end of a chain, and then you'd have to get a hoist rigged to bring up whatever was down there.' He laughs. 'But for the coastguard coming to look, they could look all day and never see the tiny corner with the cork. Because they were so remote, these corners which were deep enough and the right size to take booty, that anyone who didn't know it very very well wouldn't know where to look.'

The islanders also had a tried-and-tested method of confusing any officials sent to search the island. One of the wives would take up a bundle of something – a bag of oatmeal, a sack of potatoes, a baby – wrap it well, and run from one end of the island to the other with it. Another wife, in another corner of the island, would do the same. And another, and another, each with their own suspect bundle, and each running in different directions. One of the wives might well have a piece of genuine wreck under her shawl or her cloak, but most of them would be running around with perfectly innocuous items. The coastguard would, of course, have to set a man to hurry after each one of the wives, thereby not only using up all their manpower, but exhausting them in the process. As Bremner added, 'We're used to coping with interference in our profession.' Perhaps unsurprisingly, the customs officer and coastguard never did find much.

But how on earth had they managed to conceal a full-size dining-room table, I wondered? 'They aren't concealed,' says Stogdon, 'they're in their houses. They've come off a casualty so long ago that they're safe using them now. And the clocks and all that kind of thing were only on view when a long period had passed. Is what I imagine.' James Simpson remembers a number of different hiding places, including a hatch underneath the font in the local Baptist kirk. There were also alternative tricks when the customs made an unexpected raid. 'I remember one story when the customs came to this house. They were smuggling – it was a Dutchman, a Dutch ship that had just come in, lying off by a couple of miles, and they were selling off the booze and the tobacco cheap, duty-free. And the customs had heard about this and they made a search, and they had a whole lot of loot in the house. The old wife went to bed with all this tobacco and bottles round her, and when the customs came the family says, "Oh my God, it's an awful sad house. Old granny's about to pass away, please don't harass us." And here she was lying in bed, nothing wrong with her, hiding all the loot, the booze and the fags under the sheets.' In the days when there were frequent outbreaks of cholera, typhoid or smallpox, it was easy to assure the curious customs officers that a house was under quarantine and one or other member of the family was inside, burning with fever. Likewise, a pious party of well-dressed men could also convince officials that it was an act of profanity to search the kirkyard for wreck.

James Simpson considers the islanders' particular character. 'The Stroma pirates, they call them, but they were no pirates in any way. My father never locked the door, nobody ever locked their doors, there was nothing ever under lock and key. But if a ship went ashore, and they thought there was a boat at the bottom of the sea, by jings they would work hard to salvage what they could from the wreck – and quite rightly so. I suppose it was a great provocation for an island to see all these things. These wrecks lasted a couple of days, and then it all went to the bottom of the sea, and nobody got any benefit.'

But the story of the *Pennsylvania*, and of the other great general cargo wrecks, conceals an equally compelling truth. In order to get to wrecks and then to lift off cars or dining tables, the Stroma men – and those who came after – had to be extraordinarily skilful sailors. To work the Firth as pilots, fishermen or pirates required not only the kind of blood-born navigational skills which have almost completely vanished in the modern age, but a knowledge of the way each eddy, roost and stream would work at different times of the month and in different sea conditions. That depth of knowledge could only be taught by years of experience in fair weather and in foul.

David Stogdon points out that the first people to arrive at the scene of any shipwreck would not be the lifeboat or the coastguard, but the Stroma pirates. As he notes, the islanders had an advantage that the Orcadians and the mainlanders did not. 'Either it was the lifeboat from Longhope or from Stromness [in Orkney], or it was from Thurso, and they would take time. The one which was furthest away might be launched because it had the tide with it, and the one that was nearest would only be launched if the tide was with it – if the tide was against it, it would hardly move. The lifeboats did about eight knots, and the tide would be nearly that – about six knots, perhaps. But the Stroma men knew every inch of the Pentland

Firth. Living on Stroma, you were in it – in the turn of the tide, in the size of the sea. Wrecks were given them, virtually, because it was a dangerous place and they were dead on the right spot for it. And they took what came into their hands.'

Does he believe that the Stroma men would save life before saving loot? Stogdon is ambivalent. 'There's a lot I don't know about it,' he concedes, 'because I only went to see them to find out if they were being helpful to the lifeboat. The lifeboat might find every time that they'd got there first, but it didn't matter – the lifeboat would assist in taking people off, or might take over the people from the Stroma men.' And would the Stroma men help the lifeboat crew? Stogdon thinks for a while. 'Um – I don't think so. No, no, I'm sure they wouldn't. The Stroma men were there to steal. They didn't have much time to strip the boat before she went down completely, I imagine. They [the crew and passengers] were probably quite safe, but the Stroma men just got on with their work of stripping. I assume lives were not lost. I can't help feeling . . . they were such nice people, Bremner and the wifies. I've never considered that the wreckers on Stroma would ever cause a loss of life. They would save people, I'm sure.'

So did the lifeboats consider the Stroma men a help, or a liability? 'Do you know, I don't know. I never asked that. But I would think that they didn't – they just knew that the Stroma men just would be there first, because they were so on top of where the casualties were, whereas the lifeboats had some way to go. So I think the lifeboats would feel that it was saving life from the Stroma men as well as everyone else – I mean, the lifeboats are responsible for saving lives, not property, and so that's all they're concerned with. They don't tow something with no life on board, because it's property, and because that's not their job.'

To illustrate his point, Stogdon recalls the way in which events unfolded when a vessel went ashore during his visit.

Stogdon was taken by Bremner (who was not himself a wrecker, but who was responsible for the apportionment of any wreck) down to the headland overlooking the Men of Mey. 'I saw them doing it. The fishermen from Stroma went so quickly – I mean, as I turned round on the island to talk to Bremner, they'd already started to go. There weren't many boats, and they were quite small, but they were very effective. It was fascinating seeing them arrive and jumping straight up. Crooked Jack with his one leg, he was the first on board to strip the boat. The poor people on board – I think there were about thirteen or fourteen – were desperate to get off. They thought the end of the world had come, because the Men of Mey were roaring, the tide was roaring in. They were all trying to get into the fishing boats to be rescued, and of course, there wasn't any fishermen in them – they'd all gone stripping.' Stogdon smiles, half-rueful, half-admiring. 'It was the most amazing sight. The lifeboat was approaching from Stromness – I think it was Stromness – but that's some way off, and it would take her some time to get there. It's a long way.' What did the Stroma men want first? 'Well – binnacles, telescopes, sextants, and then any money they could find, I presume. There wouldn't be much of value in that kind of small fishing boat, but every boat had something of value.'

All three men – Simpson, Mowatt and Stogdon – recall the man named Crooked Jack, 'the greatest pirate in my time,' according to Willie Mowatt. Crooked Jack's real name was John Sinclair, and at some point earlier in his life his leg had been amputated just above the knee. He got around with the aid of a pair of customised crutches, and once aboard a boat was known as the best and boldest of all the Pentland Firth navigators. Like a true pirate, it is also said that he also occasionally wore a parrot on one shoulder, though one suspects the parrot at least was apocryphal. In any case, neither the subtraction of a limb nor the addition of a bird impeded his skill as a wrecker. When news of a ship aground arrived, he would be first down to the shore and first on board the casualty.

Like all the other Stroma men, Crooked Jack had spent many years refining his ship-stripping skills. On fishing vessels and smaller craft, he and the Stroma men would go first for the brasswork, then for any cigarettes or alcohol, and finally for anything else of value, including the fabric of the boat itself – engine parts, fenders, good-quality navigational equipment, non-ferrous metals. They used axes to hasten the work. Mowatt recalls: 'You had to watch yourself. Oh, they didn't like competition.' All the wreckers were accustomed to working at speed, listening both for the thud of the lifeboat's arrival or for the rending of steel plates as the ship began to break up.

Watching the Stroma men at work gave Stogdon a new respect for those who navigated the Firth so skilfully. He points out that a ship like the *Pennsylvania* was unrepresentative of the wrecks the Stroma men usually dealt with, since despite heavy fog on the day she grounded, the sea remained calm. More usually, the Stroma men would be sailing out to a troubled ship in the thick of a winter gale, hauling themselves through the shrieking winds and looming seas.

Over on South Ronaldsay, Willie Mowatt is torn between his respect for the Stroma sailors and indignation that anyone should get the better of an Orcadian. He does, however, take pleasure in the Stroma pirates' audacity: 'Oh yes, they was good sailors, definitely – the very best. It was impossible to beat the pirates of Stroma. Generations of pirates, them. They knew what they were doing – that was their trade. It was traditional. It was just bred in them; they didn't do it by any tuition, it was just a case of "look for the best".' As he concedes, there were some sea raids which only Stroma men would have the impunity to attempt. 'In the '14-'18 war, when they sank the blockships [the wrecks sunk around the eastern approaches to Scapa Flow to block the entry of enemy submarines] Stroma men came across and looted them too for copper and brass. And they was caught by the Admiralty boys. They looted them for copper and brass and anything else besides. They went to [the scuttled German Fleet in Scapa Flow] as well, they took the coal from them and any scrap they could get.'

Whether or not this is true – and whether or not it really was Stroma men instead of South Ronaldsay sailors, who would have been much closer to the wrecks – remains unverified, and probably unverifiable, though there are also rumours that men from Burray, Graemsay and Holm were all interested in the ships for reasons that had nothing at all to do with defence of the realm. Besides, five minutes later, Mowatt reconsiders: 'There was as good pirates on this island as ever there was on Stroma,' he says hotly – 'Every bit. Everywhere there was an island, it was the same, there's no difference among any of them.'

Aside from perfect seamanship, both the Stroma and the Orcadian pirates had unshakeable confidence in their own boats. The Stroma yoles (or yawls) were solid, clinker-built, open-decked boats, up to 30 feet in length and 10 foot across, rigged with two masts and an extra jib. Most were broad beamed but shallow, with short keels designed to sit snugly on the sea and to be capable of sailing at speed. The stem was curved to allow the boats to run up a beach easily, and all of them provided plenty of space for cargo. James Simpson remembers them with great fondness. 'The Stroma men were good seamen and they built lovely boats. There's no-one so good the length and breadth of Britain. They were boats that were meant for cargo for the island – they needed a boat to carry a few tons, whereas a Shetland boat was a narrow boat, more for speed, for racing, it was no use for cargo. The Stroma carpenters built a very good yole, very beamy yole, well built. They were hauled on land a lot – they were not built for harbours. They were broad and very strong.' He remembers being taught to sail. 'I know when I started in Stroma in 1960 I had nothing but a compass. You got to know the speed of the tide and you got to know how many degrees to allow for the speed of the tide, and you come in to the harbour maybe 20 yards or 50 yards off on either side – you wouldn't be that far off.'

George Gunn also remembers the yoles: 'You couldn't beat a Stroma boat. There were some good boatbuilders on Orkney too, but they were nowhere near half as good as the Stroma men. There's not a bad seaman amongst them – great seamen, the lot of them. Great pirates, too.' He misses the Stroma men and their shady skills. 'There used to be 250 people on that island. They made their living through the cod-fishing, but they were all pirates. When they left the island, they just up and walked away – left all their easy chairs and their plates and tables just lying. They wanted some relief from it.' Gunn was part of the syndicate which bought the *Pennsylvania*, though he says it was neither wrecking nor salvage which really engaged him. 'I wasn't really interested in the wrecks, not so long as there was a good living to be made from the fishing. There was a heck of a living to be made over at the [Pentland] Skerries. The fishing's more or less kaput here now, but we used to get a thousand a day of crabs – now you'd get days when you'd get six.'

Gunn is now nearly ninety, and lives on his own in a warm bungalow scattered with fishermans' flotsam overlooking the Firth. On the mantelpiece is the evidence of his life: ships in bottles, pictures of boats, cuttings and photographs tucked into the frame of the picture. One of the cuttings reads, 'Caithness Skipper Dies At Sea'. The skipper was his brother, who drowned by Duncansby Head while on a fishing trip with George. His brother had gone to pick up a heavy lobster creel. But a sudden swell and the weight of the creel pulled him overboard, and George could not save him. 'Before I got him back aboard,' says George now, 'I didn't know enough about resuscitation to revive him. These things happen.' He says it with stoicism, without pity or self-pity. His eyes are sunken now – so heavy-lidded he has to tip his head slightly to look at you, and he listens for the sound of the buses passing outside his window. Before I leave, I tell him I'm hoping to get over to Stroma in the next couple of days. George mentions the names of a couple of people who run trips over to the island during the summer. 'There's a fellow who might take you over, but I don't trust him,' he says disgustedly. 'He knows less about the sea than my backside knows about the Greek alphabet.'

The navigational skills of those who lived and worked by the Pentland Firth also provided another form of income. In the days of sail, ships unfamiliar with the Firth would wait near the entrance and signal for the services of a local pilot. The pilots acted as pathfinders for captains needing help in bad weather and as guides to ships coming into harbour. Since the service worked on a first-come, first-served basis, all the accredited pilots from the surrounding islands would race their boats onto the water as soon as they saw a ship's signal. The first on board would get the job, the last would get nothing but a wasted journey.

By local standards, piloting paid well and provided a useful supplement to their income from fishing. A straightforward passage could earn between 30 shillings and £5; more complex tasks could bring far larger sums, particularly in bad weather or over long passages. Payments could often be made in kind – whisky, tobacco and rum being, unsurprisingly, a currency as solid as sterling throughout the Highlands. But piloting had its hazards. Pilots could find themselves coerced into service as spare deckhands or pressed by the King's men. Tyrannical captains could hold pilots hostage or refuse to pay, though pilots usually found it easy to take revenge. There are tales – unsubstantiated, of course – of pilots guiding ships onto sandbanks or reefs, thereby ensuring not only that they themselves returned safe to shore, but that they also gathered the traditional wreckers' reward. It is also rumoured that the threat of an inadequate fee could also induce a pilot to salve his own payment from the ship's stores when the captain was distracted. Since most pilots' first target would be the stores of grog, this could have unfortunate results. There were pilots who got so drunk they became entirely incapacitated and could thus be transported as far from home as the captain desired.

James Simpson's family were Stroma pilots. 'There were pilots on Freswick, and there were pilots all over, but Stroma was the best site. It was in the middle and if there was a flood tide, they could be way out to the Pentland Skerries long before the fishing men, because they had the tide on the tail.' There were also some who made unexpectedly lengthy voyages. 'It has been known that the boat would sail on with the pilot on board and it wouldn't stop,' he says. 'One man on Stroma was taken away, and he couldn't read nor write. He was taken away to America, and no-one ever heard one scrap from him ever again. Some said, "Oh, the cannibals ate him." There was a lot of them taken on board in their slippers, and they made their way back through Europe. They'd be penniless too. If you got a man for piloting a ship, they'd be paid £5, and £5 was a lot of money – a schoolteacher year's salary was only about £6 or £7 a year. So if you got two or three ships a year, you had quite a good salary.'

But to imply that neither the pilots nor the wreckers had a scruple to rub between them fails to give the full picture. Wreckers had their own moral code, and if that code did not always remain true to the principle of honour among thieves, at least it adhered to an understanding of what was, and what was not, beyond the bounds of private precedent. And though there were undoubtedly instances of wholesale looting, things were different in cases where people had lost their lives.

The tragedy of the *Johanna Thorden* is still debated. Early in the morning of 12 January 1937, the Finnish motor vessel struck the Clett of Swona in almost exactly the same place that another vessel, the *Gunnaren*, had struck two years before. Like the *Gunnaren*, the 3,223-ton *Johanna Thorden* was carrying a 5,000-ton load of general cargo from America to Gothenberg which included cars, tractors, machinery, radio receivers, chemicals, tobacco bales, boxes of apples, paraffin wax, tinned fruit, and steel. The ship had already steered through a heavy south-westerly gale to reach Orkney, but on her way through the Firth, the wind shifted over to the south-east. It was dark, and the weather had come down so hard that visibility had almost reached zero. There was some subsequent dispute as to whether the captain had been confused by the recent construction of a lighthouse at Torness, which may have beguiled him into thinking he was heading for Dunnet Head in Caithness rather than directly for the rocks of South Ronaldsay. It is also possible that the large quantity of steel in the cargo pulled the compass needle away from its true course.

What is beyond dispute is that, of the thirty-eight people on board the ship, thirty-three lost their lives. The deaths included both the captain's wife, the wife of the chief engineer, and her sons aged six and four. The impact of the collision broke the ship's wireless, making it impossible for anyone to radio for help, and the storm-force conditions meant that both the nearby lighthouse keepers and the Rosie family, who lived and farmed on Swona, did not hear any of the distress calls despite over forty rockets having been fired. The first of the ship's lifeboat was launched with twenty-five people on board; nothing more was heard of them until the lifeboat washed up at Deerness the following day, empty and upended. The second lifeboat, containing the remaining crew and the captain, was launched just after the ship split in two and began breaking up. Having struggled through the wreckage and the boiling seas towards South Ronaldsay, the lifeboat capsized, tipping all thirteen men into the sea. Only five made it to shore alive.

In normal circumstances, the kind of cargo that the *Johanna Thorden* had been carrying would have been considered exceptionally desirable. Machinery parts, tobacco, food, radio parts – these were both the essentials of life and part of its great pleasures. But the circumstances in which the ship went down could not be considered normal. The deaths of so many when so close to help represented not only the worst disaster in the area since the First World War but something far deeper and more painful for the islanders.

Tom Muir, exhibitions officer at the Orkney Museum in Kirkwall, remembers his mother talking about the wreck. She had been living on Westray at the time and recalled parts of the cargo beginning to wash ashore. Some locals made use of the wreckage; his mother and grandmother did not. 'My mother said there was a lot of stuff washed up on the beaches of Westray – tins of peaches, paraffin wax – and in the late thirties, a tin of peaches would have been manna from Heaven. They wouldn't have been able to buy tins, and something like that would have been the most incredible, delicious thing that they'd ever tasted. A lot of people gathered them up and took them home, but her mother refused to have them in the house purely on moral grounds, because she said that women and bairns had died on that wreck, and she wouldn't have any of that in the house.' At the time, The Orcadian newspaper reported that beaches around Deerness on the eastern side of the mainland were strewn with wreck. 'A pathetic, unlifted reminder of the tragedy was a lifebelt, lying near the ship's lifeboat at Dingieshowe. Another five lifebelts were lying along the grassy land above the shore, unwanted by the Receiver of Wreck and neglected by souvenir hunters.'

The taboo on using the cargo would not merely have been that people lost their lives in the wreck, it was that women and children had too. Muir considers that, 'It's probably based on the way that society was structured at the time, where men did go out and do dangerous things to make a living. They went to sea, they went down coal mines, they would climb down cliffs to get birds' eggs. There was a lot of hazardous things they were doing, so the loss of a man was maybe not expected, but when it happened it wasn't treated as so much of a tragedy because it was just one of those things. And there would be a widow and bairns left, and folk would be genuinely sad about it, but it was God's will, and it was just the way things always were. Men did these dangerous things, and some were lucky and stayed unscathed, and some of them weren't so lucky and never came back. Women generally stayed at home with the kids, so it was less usual to have female passengers on ships until the emigrant ships started going.' But for women and children to die – that was a true horror, a reversal of the natural order. Who would touch the spoils of a ship from which children had been killed?

There is another story, very different in both form and conclusion, which illustrates an alternative side to Orcadian maritime ethics. This story has less sadness about it than that of the *Johanna Thorden*, and more of the sense of a tale enriched in the telling. During the winter of 1847, the *Lena*, a large Russian barque carrying many passengers, ran ashore on North Ronaldsay during the night. The islanders who went down to the wreck found some of the passengers lying dead or injured on the rocks, including the captain, half-drowned and knocked unconscious by the collision. The captain was therefore carried up to a nearby house in Sholtisquoy by the islanders, who roused the woman of the house – or guidwife – from her bed, and handed the captain over in the hope that she might be able to revive him. The guidwife placed the captain in her own bed and fed him a little brandy. The captain stayed senseless, and, since it was long before hot-water bottles were invented, the guidwife climbed into bed beside him, hoping that her own body heat might revive him. Her rough medicine worked and the captain revived, though, as one local wreck historian noted drily, 'How long she stayed in bed after he recovered, I never heard.'

Once restored to health, the captain realised he owed his life to the guidwife, and swore that when he returned home he would send her a gift as a sign of his gratitude. A few weeks later, a fine silk dress arrived from the captain's home town. This being the 1840s, all mail was routed through the landlord's factor on the island. Tom Muir takes up the story. 'There was this beautiful silk gown turned up, and the [factor and his wife] thought: that's far too nice to waste on a crofting woman, so they substituted it for a cheap, printed cotton dress and kept the silk one. I can't remember if it was the man's wife or his daughter who was then seen at the kirk the following week with this beautiful dress on, and everybody knew where this had come from – they put two and two together, and also nobody trusted the guy. So his reputation, which was probably black before then, was blackened even further by the fact that he'd stolen this dress.' Orcadians have long memories, and that factor's reputation has never recovered since.

The constancy of connection between Orkney, Caithness and the sea has also inevitably provoked superstitions. All mariners, whether fair-weather sailors or foul, are by nature and practice superstitious. To take to the sea means taking a bet on the future, and in the seas around these parts, the sea frequently wins. The local understanding of that gamble, and the atrocious odds it sometimes offers, gave them advantages and rewards in the days when there were plenty of fish to catch, and plenty of ships needing piloting. Now, as the odds get shorter, the chances of making any living at all from fishing are minimal. Families who for generations have worked on the sea have turned back to the land instead, either looking to the mainland for more diverse forms of employment or taking up work recycling history in the tourist and service industries.

But if the days of the wreckers have passed, many old practices still persist. Between them, Orkney, Stroma and Caithness
sailors managed more taboos than a coven of Victorian
spinsters. At one time or other, there have been superstitions
against rats, cats, pigs, rabbits, ministers, women, knives, Swan
matches, whistling, going to sea on a Friday, and the naming of
fish – if you called a fish by its proper name, so the thinking
went, then you would never catch it. But as Tom Muir points
out, there were elements of practicality in some of the superstition. Many fishermen refused to learn to swim, partly because
the seas in this area are freezing and secondly because if a crew
member on a fishing boat did fall overboard, they had very little
hope or chance of being rescued. 'So,' as Muir says, 'if you
could swim, all you were doing was prolonging your death and
stretching out that agony when you didn't have a hope anyway.
You might as well just get it over quick, and go straight down.'

On his trip through Shetland and Orkney in 1814, Walter
Scott also made note of another variant of the same superstition:

A worse and most horrid opinion prevails, or did
prevail, among the fishers – namely, that he who saves
a drowning man will receive at his hands some deep
wrong or injury. Several instances were quoted to-day
in company, in which the utmost violence had been
found necessary to compel the fishers to violate this
inhuman prejudice. It is conjectured to have arisen as
an apology for rendering no assistance to the mariners
as they escaped from a shipwrecked vessel, for these
isles are infamous for plundering wrecks. A story is told
of the crew of a stranded vessel who were warping
themselves ashore by means of a hawser which they had
fixed to the land. The islanders (of Unst, as I believe)
watched their motions in silence, till an old man

reminded them that if they suffered these sailors to come ashore, they would consume all their winter stock of provisions. A Zetlander cut the hawser, and the poor wretches, twenty in number, were all swept away. This is a tale of former times – the cruelty would not now be active, but I fear that even yet the drowning mariner would in some places receive no assistance in his exertions, and certainly he would in most be plundered to the skin upon his landing. The gentlemen do their utmost to prevent this infamous practice. It may seem strange that the natives should be so little affected by a distress to which they are themselves so constantly exposed. But habitual exposure to danger hardens the heart against its consequences, whether to ourselves or others.

As Muir explained it, if you save a man overboard, 'You've deprived the sea of its prey. And the sea will take you, or one of your family, in place of the person you've saved, because you've cheated it.'

In Orkney, those who did drown were also treated with caution. 'There was also a tradition that drowned mariners weren't buried in the kirkyard, they were buried by the shore,' says Muir. 'The belief here was that if you buried a sailor who had been washed ashore, the sea would try to claim its prey back. It was like taking a mouse off a cat – the cat would want it back. If you buried someone who had been drowned inland, the sea might flood the kirkyard trying to get them back, and you didn't want all your nice dry ancestors getting soggy because of some bloody sailor. So they were just pulled up the shore and buried on the banks by the shore.'

In some areas, this superstition had a religious element – the fear of burying an unknown and possibly heathen sailor in a Christian kirkyard. That fear mattered less in Orkney than in many areas, though by the nineteenth century there were very definite traditions about where exactly in the kirkyard people should be buried. 'The tradition in Orkney was that the south side of the kirkyard was reserved for the most important members of the community,' says Muir, 'and the north was reserved for paupers' burials and shipwrecked mariners – when they did start burying them in the kirkyard, it was at the north end. In Westray, I mind when I was a kid going there visiting my auntie, there was a new extension to the kirkyard, and they were starting to bury folk against one wall – the top end or something. And then down at the bottom end, there was just this one grave by itself, down by the shore. It was an old sea captain, and that was his request – he had wanted to be buried as close to the sea as possible. Not because of superstition, but just because the sea was his home. That's where he was happy, so he wanted to be buried as close to it as possible. Nowadays they've filled up all the edges, and so he's got company, but in those days, it was just this one. It was almost like somebody in a huff – there just by himself, not speaking to anybody.'

The days and times of superstition have not faded completely, but they, along with the wrecking, are not the things which are now uppermost. Scapa Flow has become the richest dive centre in Europe, attracting people from all over the world to examine – and, unfortunately, loot – the wrecks of the scuppered German fleet. Older men like Willie Mowatt regard the fading of a few old traditions with unconcealed disgust. What, I ask, would happen if a general cargo vessel went down in the Firth tonight? 'Oh, there would be boats going to the ship right enough,' he says, 'but it ain't what it used to be. By no means, because in no time at all there would be the lifeboat there, then if there would be any hopes of looting or anything, there would be the customs and police and coastguards and all that. The pirates now doesn't have a bloody chance – these [SAR] helicopters, they just swoop down and lift like bloody eagles out of the heavens. This is the trouble now – the water's got too small. There's no right thrill attached to it now, like what used to be. How are you supposed to defend yourself if there's a helicopter come right out of the sky?' He gets visibly irritated at the thought of it all. 'It's changed the whole bloody place, and you're photographed from above, and the first you know you're up before the court or slung in jail or every damn thing, that's what happens.'

So no-one would bother wrecking now? 'Oh, they're still bothering, yes, because the pirates was very helpful with salvage work and all, you see. They worked both ways. They was wanting to be paid a salvage award as well.' But, as he says, 'It wasn't easy doing the pirates either. Oh no, it wasn't. But with these helicopters and that now, you might as well stay home. Unless it was genuinely saving lives. But as far as loot was concerned, you'd just be inside in no bloody time, that's what it's come to, you know.'

Does he think that's the end of the wreckers? 'Oh, it will happen again, nothing surer than that, it will all happen again. It will not die out in a hurry. It's just a piece of wild human nature, that's what it is.' He laughs ruefully. And then takes me next door to the parlour to show me some of his finer spoils, and his MBE.

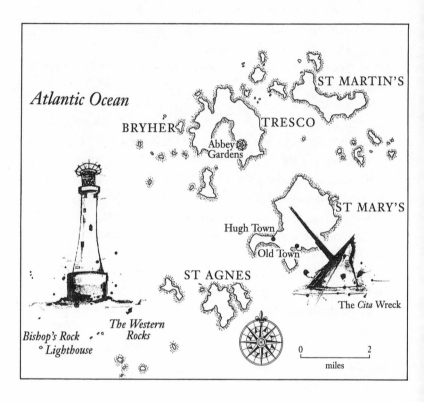

Atlantic Ocean

ST MARTIN'S

BRYHER

TRESCO

Abbey
Gardens

ST MARY'S

Hugh Town

Old Town

ST AGNES

The *Cita* Wreck

*The Western
Rocks*

*Bishop's Rock
Lighthouse*

0   2

miles

Scilly Isles

FOUR

Scilly Isles

On a nondescript day in March 1997, the bulk carrier *Cita* left Southampton docks and set sail for Northern Ireland. A solid, ugly vessel of 3,000 tons, the *Cita* was carrying a mixed shipment of containers to Belfast. Each container had been hired and stocked by separate freight carriers, and each was carrying goods ultimately intended for shops in Dublin. The *Cita*'s eight-man crew – all Polish – regarded the journey as a routine one: a short passage through populous sea areas. To reach her destination, the vessel had to round Cornwall's southernmost tip, keep well clear of both the Wolf and the Seven Stones, and ensure she was travelling north of the Scilly archipelago before heading up through the Irish Sea to Belfast.

The first part of that journey went according to plan, but as night fell on 25 March, fog began to creep round the Scillies. Though the weather initially remained calm, the short-range forecast promised worsening conditions. Unperturbed, and confident in the *Cita*'s ability to ride out all but the most severe weather, the crew made their arrangements for the night. By midnight, the barometer had fallen sharply. Though nowhere near gale force yet, the sea was jumpy and disruptive, and would need careful watching. Winter gales around Cornwall and the Scillies are notorious, and the area has always been known as a hazardous place to navigate. When most of the crew went below to get some sleep, the mate remained alone on the bridge. At around 1 a.m. he switched on the autopilot and adjusted the

Cita's course by a few degrees. A radar alarm, which would have warned him and the rest of the crew of any local hazards, was not activated. Shortly afterwards, he too nodded off.

In the small hours of 26 March the *Cita* ran full-tilt into the rocks of St Mary's. At the time she struck, she was travelling at 14 knots and no-one on board was awake. St Mary's is the largest of the five main Scilly Isles and home to its capital, Hugh Town. Like most of the islands, it is comparatively low lying and has a coastline frilled with beaches and rocky inlets. Conveniently for the Scillonians and the local RNLI, the *Cita*'s autopilot had selected an inlet a mere ten minutes or so from the town centre in which to run aground. The lifeboat and an SAR helicopter found her quickly and took off all eight members of the crew, including one man with a broken leg.

For a while, the *Cita* remained above water. To begin with, it was thought that it might be possible to refloat her, tow her to a place of safety, and repair her as necessary. But as the day wore on it became evident that the *Cita*'s injuries were going to prove fatal. The force of her arrival in the Isles had lodged her bow and bridge fast onto the rocks, leaving her stern hanging over open water. The position was placing an unsustainable strain on her hull, and it was evidently only a matter of time before the continuing high seas broke her back. Initially, what most worried the coastguard and many Scillonians was not so much the prospect of 3,000 tons of steel cluttering up one of their most beguiling coves, but the threat of environmental disaster. By cargo-carrying standards, the *Cita* was a comparatively small vessel loaded with only enough fuel to carry her safely to her destination. But the Scillies rely heavily on the tourist trade, and the consequences of any fuel spill, however slight, could have been catastrophic for the local economy. It was thus with considerable ambivalence that the Scillonians watched the *Cita* list heavily to starboard, shrug off her load of containers, and began to sink.

Not everyone was interested solely in the fuel oil, however. By the time the *Cita* began to submerge, much of the local interest had shifted from the contents of her fuel tanks to the contents of her containers. Throughout the morning, those gathering on the shoreline watched her cargo come ashore with the tide, and listened to the shriek of overstressed metal. Bobbing on the swell, many of the containers floated briefly around the bay as the air inside dwindled away and then vanished from view. Many of the containers split open as they reached the shore, some sank, and the remainder scattered themselves around the nearby inlets. Almost all of the accessible containers had originally been tied shut with plastic strapping and proved easy for either the sea or the Scillonians to open. By mid-morning, word had spread around the islands, and the surrounding headlands were crowded with locals picking their way over the littered rocks. Those containers which remained afloat long enough to arrive ashore proved to be the stuff of salvor's fantasy.

For a fully-laden general cargo vessel to run aground in an accessible position on an island in winter is more or less like having Selfridges crash land in your back garden – a Selfridges with all the prices removed. It is an event, a treasure hunt, a rare and splendid opportunity. Spilling out into the daylight was everything the Scillonians never knew they needed: a divine lucky-dip of random consumables. For householders, the sea gave out laminate flooring, wooden doors, barbecue sets, bathroom accessories, washing-machine spares and toilet seats. Farmers could take their pick of car engines and power tools, Land Rover and tractor tyres. For the mechanically-minded, there were multiple brake cylinders, wing mirrors and exhausts. For the underdressed, the *Cita* dispensed Marks & Spencer dresses and nighties, Ascot trainers, Ben Sherman shirts, workmen's clothing, and bright baby clothes. Even the children were not forgotten. Among the treasures on offer were several tons of toys, including Action Men. Lastly, for those who only required a souvenir or two, there were a million plastic supermarket bags (all printed with the instruction to 'help protect the environment'), computer mice, twenty tons of tinned water chestnuts, and a million pounds worth of raw tobacco in bales.

The islanders did not hesitate. Some people waded into the water, grabbing bagfuls of clothing and computer equipment. Those who owned boats or dinghies took to the sea, motoring out to the more inaccessible containers and stuffing their vessels to the gunwhales with tyres, doors or golf bags. One man noted sourly that by the time he got down to the beach: 'All that was left was one damaged computer mouse, a vast amount of plastic wrapping and sodden cardboard containers.' The local museum has a small display of *Cita* memorabilia, and a sign beside it noting that, 'from [a cargo of] thousands of tyres, the museum managed to obtain one inner tube.'

Though the one thing that the ship did not contain was alcohol, it was not long before the wreck of the *Cita* became known as Scilly's own *Whisky Galore*. Walk through St Mary's now, and it is remarkable how many of the islanders can be seen wearing Ben Sherman shirts or Ascot trainers, and whose houses boast piebald laminate floors. In the view of one islander: 'We had a bit of fun out of it, that's all. That's what most of that type of salvage were – it were just . . . Most people don't take much. You might get two shirts or something like that. The thing is, the stuff she had aboard, the firm wouldn't have accepted it anyway. What good is it if it's been in salt water? They'd never be able to sell it, and even if they were able to sell it, the cost of transporting it back, having it cleaned and so on . . . I mean, God, it would be dearer than buying a whole new outfit!'

But as the locals arrived at the scene, so too did the authorities. By fortunate coincidence, the local customs officer and coastguard had both recently retired, so the only people left on duty – and thus the only people left to represent the lonely might of Scillonian law enforcement – were two full-time police and two special constables. By tradition, the Scillies are quiet islands with an elderly population and relatively little criminal activity beyond traffic offences and domestic disputes. The police did initially try to prevent looting of the containers, but having found themselves significantly outnumbered, settled instead for a strategy which could be described as pro-active information management. They began by handing out salvage forms, and moved on to giving directions – 'Children's clothing? Porthcressa, sir. Golf bags? Watermill Cove.' As one island resident noted, directing traffic, 'was the most sensible thing to do. At first they tried to stop it, they tried to say, well, you shouldn't do this. But then there's two policemen, what the hell can they do when this stuff is coming in all along the shore? There's blokes running past them, and while one of them's talking to one man, the others are passing them with a load full of stuff. There was nothing else they could do.' As a cutting from *Lloyd's List* in the local museum put it, 'to the evident joy of the inhabitants of the Isles of Scilly . . . the cargo from the wrecked container feeder *Cita* is being salvaged in a refreshingly traditional fashion. The Receiver of Wreck will be having an exciting Easter weekend.'

In fact, the islanders were doing nothing illegal by taking items from the containers. Technically speaking, what they were doing was not wrecking, but salving, and between the two words lies a world of difference. As the law sees it, wrecking is conducted with malice aforethought, but salving is a more self-less pursuit. Any policeman who tried to obstruct the islanders would himself have been breaking the law. What is illegal is not the act of finding and rescuing cargo, but the failure to declare those findings to the UK's Receiver of Wreck. In theory, every islander should have filled in a form detailing everything they took, sent it off to the Receiver in Southampton and waited to find out if she could trace the cargo's original owners. If those owners were found and did demand their goods back, the salvor would then be compelled to hand it over in exchange for an award. If the owner remained untraced, or proved to be un-interested in the goods' return, then – and only then – it would become the property of the salvor. In practice, many wreck forms were either filled in facetiously (the Scillies suddenly acquired a large new population of Donald Ducks and Mickey Mouses) or not filled in at all. As the subsequent Marine Accident Investigation Branch's report delicately expressed it: 'After the accident, many finders and temporary possessors of containers or their contents were unaware of their statutory obligations.'

Mike Collier, who in 1997 was the Maritime and Coastguard Agency's spokesman on the wreck, recalls that, 'I had a very good conversation with John Humphries on Radio 4 about this. He said to me, "They're stealing it." I said, "They're not, they're looking after it." "Oh, come on," he said, "they're stealing. There's pictures of them on the television trying clothes on." I said, "Well, what they do with it is entirely up to them. They're looking after it – they're taking it away, they're telling the Receiver where it is and if the owner of that cargo wants to come and get it, fine, he can come and get it. But they're entitled to charge for their time and danger in recover-ing these things. And they could charge the owner storage time as well, if they wanted. If you do it properly, it's not looting, you see, it's recovering and holding wreck until the rightful owner comes along".'

Giving people directions to the wreck wasn't exactly official policy though, was it? 'You might just as well, because you've got all these people strolling around on the rocks, and it's a lot easier to keep it as a controlled mob than have people wander-ing around willy-nilly and fighting over stuff. There was some amazing scenes – there was people picking up pairs of shorts, trying them on, and going, "No, don't think these look right," and putting them back; kids walking around with a pair of trainers on and another pair of trainers around their neck; tractors with flat-profile racing tyres on them . . .' He trails off, laughing.

The islanders' case was also helped by the fact that the Receiver found it almost impossible to trace and notify the owners of such a large and varied cargo. Many owners were outside the UK, and most were uninterested in reclaiming a few size 12 salt-damaged nighties. As the Scillonians saw it, all they were doing was clearing up. If no-one else was prepared to mount a salvage operation, then they would evidently have to do so themselves.

They also had a strong environmental point to make. Amongst the useful items, there were also many which were either so damaged they could not be re-used, or which posed an active threat either to the ecology of the islands. In addition to the fuel oil – tackled mainly by the Coastguard's Marine Pollution Control Unit – five of the containers held pallets of polyester film ultimately intended to be used for cassette and video tapes. When the *Cita* sank, so too did the polyester. Once wetted, the film became useless, and was left abandoned on the sea bed. Over time, the sea began to break up the rolls of film and send them shredded ashore. For a while, the island was decorated with an impromptu confetti of translucent plastic. To the islanders' considerable irritation, the clear-up operation took months.

The Scillonians were also helped by two other factors. Faced with the *Cita*'s vast and unexpected riches, a group of islanders got together to collect children's clothes for charity. Six builders' skips' worth of clothing were eventually sent to charities on the mainland and in Romania and Africa. Finally, the locals could – and did – claim that they were doing no more than resurrecting a traditional island art. 'We all went wrecking!', one man was later reported to have jubilantly declared. 'First time since 1938. We could have got an EU grant for revitalising an ancient industry!'

The daily helicopter shuttle from Penzance to St Mary's passes over some of the prettiest death traps in the world. As well as guiding the novice passenger through some of England's most desirable tourist destinations, it also completes an unintended survey of almost every one of the south coast's worst sea hazards. Flying south-westwards over Land's End, the helicopter passes the final tip of Britain and its three unmythical guardians: the Longships, the Wolf and the Seven Stones. Standing at the axis of three major shipping routes, each watches over some of Britain's busiest waters.

The Longships are a ragged cluster of rocks rising up out of the sea like the doodles of some bored celestial mapmaker who forgot to polish off the Cornish coastline properly. The largest of those rocks is topped off with a lighthouse, shining photogenically in the early September sun. The Wolf, eight miles further south-east, guards the entrance to the Channel. Its light is often the first sight of Britain that returning sailors see, though it was not until 1870 that the reef was lit. The Wolf was supposed to have taken its name either from a corruption of an Anglo-Saxon word, or from the legend that the rock on which it stood contained a cavern which, when the sea rushed through it, gave out a deep lupine howl. There is a story – too good to be true, and too credible to be fictional – that local wreckers, aware that the sound of the howl alerted ships to the rock's existence, sailed out from Cornwall and stopped up the Wolf's mouth.

The Seven Stones (named by someone with a good sense of alliteration, if not of arithmetic – there are actually eight stones) rise seven miles from the Scillies. It was on one of those rocks that the oil tanker *Torrey Canyon*, laden with just under 120,000 tons of crude oil, ran aground in 1967. The ship had been doing 17 knots when she grounded, and the impact damaged her hull so badly that she began leaking almost immediately. At the time, it was the biggest maritime disaster in history. But even this unholy trinity of risks – Longships, Wolf and Seven Stones – are not the last of the hazards in this area. What Cornwall and the Scilly Isles gain in beauty, they pay for with danger.

Beyond the Seven Stones, and twenty-eight miles south-west of the mainland, are the Scillies themselves. There are five main inhabited islands, but over 140 smaller ones scattered across the oily sea, most of which are no more than small reefs populated by sea birds. Like the Hebrides, they form a rough and pattern-less archipelago, surrounded on many sides by a pale rind of sand. Seen from above, the sea that surrounds them is clear, the holiday-brochure turquoise of the tropics. Closer to ground level, three-dimensional details appear – the steep rise of a cliff face, trees and woods, tidy striped fields; the usual postcard views. It is not until well beyond the airport doors that the difference between Scilly and the mainland becomes properly apparent. Initially, the most notable thing is the absence of municipal outbuildings and an almost startling sense of fecundity. Hugh Town is a small-scale place, its centre pinched to slimness by the bays on either side, and still blooming fit to burst. Along the side streets, the sun shines down on front gardens full of plants so stiffly disciplined they look as if they have been grown with rods up their backs.

September is peak tourist season, and the roads are occupied by squads of patrolling geriatrics squinting at the un-British sun or making occasional dignified lunges for the park benches. Like the Channel Islands, the Scillies are a haven for old folk; warm, pleasant, almost entirely free of the irritations of modern life, and modelling a version of Englishness which died with

Winston Churchill. This is a wish-fulfilment version of Britain, an island with all the bad bits removed. The Scillies' greatest success has been in turning erstwhile disadvantages into assets. By restricting the quantity of accommodation available and by setting prices high enough to make your eyes water, they have cultivated exactly the right sort of tourism – retired, respectable and respectful, interested in horticulture and history, traditional, affluent. The husband likes boats and the wife likes flowers or golf; both of them like being warm. Every year they come, and every year they book again a year in advance.

Over on the island of Tresco, all of the Scillies' selling points are vividly shown. There are plants in the Abbey Gardens which could not possibly exist anywhere else in the British Isles. Walking along the neat gravel paths, the passer-by is surrounded by the horticultural equivalent of post-surgery Californians: huge oozing succulents, looming mutants with razor-tipped leaves, brash spires of bright vegetation, ferns casting lacey black shadows, bruising grey-green shrubs with saw-toothed leaves. The colours are different too: bright, sharp pinks and oranges, primary reds, exuberant greens. In this small acreage alone there must be enough foliage to stock a continent's worth of garden centres. The Abbey Gardens thrive on a whole different scale to the few balding palm trees scattered around the promenades of Falmouth or Brighton. It seems at times like a dream of England, a digitally-enhanced reality in which all things familiar have been air-brushed by the sun into a better version of their normality.

But the Abbey Gardens also contain something else. Walk round a far-off corner of this strange English rainforest and there, suddenly, is 'Valhalla', a breeding ground for monsters of a different sort. Walk three steps in, and you are confronted by a huge golden eagle, with its wings half spread and a gilded snake in its beak. Beside it is a man in a frock coat and black buckled shoes brandishing a cobwebbed sword. And beside him is a vast flat salmon, a sad-eyed lady in an unseasonable frock, a friar wielding a cross above his head, a fish with a faceful of teeth, a Turk in a fez, and a soldier with a rifle, braced to run. The monk, the fish and the bird make an ill-assorted army, but all of them seem warlike enough. All strain forward, longing for the command to action, gazing towards invisible armies advancing over the horizon.

The thirty-odd ships' figureheads at the Valhalla exhibition were collected by Augustus Smith, a man who made even more of an imprint on the Scillies than the *Cita*. Up until the early 1830s the islands had been run by the Godolphin family on a lease from the Crown. When the lease expired, the islands languished for a while. In 1834 they were bought by Smith, a rich thirty-year-old bachelor from Hertfordshire with a yen for reformation. Throughout Britain, the 1820s and 1830s was the age of the Great Improvers – moneyed men who had absorbed many of the new theories of land management and wanted a patch of land to put them into practice. They felt that, with hope, money and benign autocracy, it would be possible to transform their new fiefdoms from a state of faithless sterility into vast roofless factories filled with sober, God-fearing peasantry.

In Smith's view, the Scillies made an ideal case for 'Improvement'. The islands themselves were fertile and had the potential to support one or two small-scale industries. But at the time Smith took the lease, the land was badly overcrowded. The prevailing system of apportionment divided land equally between all the children on the tenant's death. The system meant that the available land became smaller and smaller, and more and more impoverished. Titling himself the Lord Protector of the Scillies, Smith evicted those families he considered to be 'unproductive', introduced universal primogeniture to guarantee the size of each farm, and brought in compulsory education (including navigational classes for all children). He also constructed a quay and the 7 acre Abbey Gardens, as well as encouraging shipbuilding and developing the islands' reputation as a source of unusual horticulture. To foster a good and godly population, he built several churches and made strenuous efforts to eliminate the island's reputation for smuggling.

Up until his arrival, the Scillonians had made a good, if erratic, income from bartering goods to passing ships. On the arrival of a vessel on its way northwards to one of the west coast ports from Europe, the local fishermen would sail out with meat and fresh vegetables which they would exchange for payment in kind: silks, tobacco, rum. Though Scillonian smuggling was never on the scale of the Cornish and Devonian trade, Smith remained vehemently opposed to it, and – given his strong moral influence over the islands – managed to put a stop to it wherever possible.

So what was a man who disapproved of a bit of free-enterprise nautical barter doing building up a collection of salvaged ships' figureheads? Did Augustus Smith ban smuggling, but sanction wrecking? The collection at Valhalla does at least show just how many wrecks Smith had to choose from. As a general rule, he was a shrewd man who proved intelligent enough to adapt his passion for Improvement to local conditions. He realised that, aside from sunshine, the Scillies have two great lures for the tourist: plants and wrecks. In the past 150 years, it has been calculated that almost 400 vessels have met their deaths around the Scillies; in the age of sail, the casualties were considered too numerous to bother counting. Smith could either work against the sea, or he could work with it. He could either pretend that there were no wrecks, or he could – like his subjects – reap their benefits. A figurehead from a ship which had already been destroyed represented an eloquent souvenir, and if the sailors no longer had use for it, then he might as well transform it into a bit of horticultural statuary.

Smith began his collection of figureheads in about 1840, shortly after he had bought what remained of the abbey and began establishing a garden there. Most of the items were taken from small merchant vessels wrecked on the islands. Figureheads could support a multitude of meanings: as forms of identifying shorthand for other shipping, as quasi-religious sacrifices to the sea gods, and as mascots in which the crew could place their faith. Over the centuries, they went from being the slaughtered head of a real animal to a kind of wooden daemon or familiar, personifying the spirit of a ship. Elizabethan warships went to sea as much to show off all the wealth and strength of England as to engage the enemy, and were often so over-dressed they resembled churches turned inside out. By the 1700s figureheads were only part of the passion for decorating every available surface of a ship from the gun ports to the gunwhales. As the passion for expensive decoration diminished during the eighteenth century, the navy began shaving away the more ornate embellishments around the hull of warships, but – though the figurehead often sat uneasily under the bowsprit or astride the stem post – they proved almost impossible to eliminate completely, since sailors felt that a ship without a familiar was a ship surely doomed.

Merchant vessels, meanwhile, fitted figures according to the size and splendour of their ships. East coast colliers and fishing boats usually had nothing more than an elegantly-painted name board, while East Indiamen and transatlantic ships could take their pick of animals, vegetables or minerals – the most popular image being, unsurprisingly, a nineteenth-century version of a page-three girl clad in not much more than a bit of skimpy symbolism. Wives, daughters and mistresses of shipowners were used as muses, and occasionally fictional characters like Tam o' Shanter or Ivanhoe echoed the name or nationality of the ship. Though clipper ships, with their sharp-angled bows, were ideal for figureheads, most did not carry them.

The figurehead vanished with the first puffs of the steam age, and by the early twentieth century, none but the oldest ships wore them.

Smith's collection at Valhalla was therefore only a response to the facts. He might have been able to put a stop to smuggling, but he was never going to be able to prevent shipwreck. Though the Scillies are not the most prolific area for wrecks in the country – with 800 known wrecks over the past 800 years – the Scillonians are unquestionably the most ingenious at dealing with them. Nowhere else in Britain, not even Cornwall, has made such triumphant commercial success out of so much destruction. Even now, nearly 200 years after Smith first came here, the business of wreck is still going strong. It would be entirely possible to return from St Mary's to some dry corner of Britain carrying half a household's worth of flotsam. There are books, pens, trays, candlesticks, two or three shops doing a flourishing trade in trinkets; Irish linen tea towels depicting the most significant wrecks; mugs emblazoned with images of the naval flagship the *Association*, fridge magnets, posters. The local pub, the Bishop and Wolf, seems to have been the victim of some devastating flood during which every piece of nautical paraphernalia in Hugh Town Bay has been washed in through the doors. Every spare inch of vertical space has an old binnacle or a sea-marked piece of wood tacked to the beams.

Looking round at the beachcombings, John Troutbeck's assessment of the Scillonians comes to mind. They are, he wrote, 'by their situation, the sons and daughters of God's providence and accordingly are otherwise clothed and supplied out of wracks sent in by the sea, the spoil of their rich neighbours'. Given the poverty on the islands, Augustus Smith must have realised that, had it not been for wrecks, he might never have had a population there to reform.

The secret of the islands' disastrous allure is threefold. Like Stroma and the islands of the Pentland Firth, the Scillies are low lying, the highest point of St Mary's being only 54 metres above level. The islands spread out in a confusion of reefs and tiny isles in each direction for almost ten miles, and stuck directly in the centre of three major shipping lanes. But all of these factors and more are true of other parts of the British Isles. Several of the Hebridean islands are also low lying and surrounded by heavy sea traffic, but they have not spent quite so much time since the advent of lighthouses collecting flotsam. It is a fourth factor which makes the difference to the Scillies. It is the Western Rocks.

On a bright summer's evening, I walk over the hill from Hugh Town to a house called 'Nowhere'. The tarmac on the lanes is still warm, and the hedgerows boom with busy insects. Beyond the trees, the halyards of the visiting yachts plink unrhythmically against their masts. The land may be calm, but the water is not; there is a heavy swell, and a sense just at the edge of consciousness that something ominous is moving this way. 'Nowhere' has a small iron canon as a door knocker, and a walk of fifty yards from the house to the sea. Mark Groves has a broad, tanned face, and the unfeasibly blue eyes of the habitual sailor. While I explain what I've come looking for, he presents me with a pair of gumboots and an assessing stare.

Groves is a local dive expert who has spent half a lifetime peering under the secrets of the Scillonian waters, and who knows the islands and their subterranean history better than almost anyone else on the islands. So show me this place, I say: I want to understand which way the water lies. Groves smiles. He could sail round the islands for two weeks or more, he says, and still never see half the Scillies' wreck sites. But he'll try; it's a good evening with perfect visibility, and the boat is ready. We row out to the *Zodiac*, take a last glance at Old Town and depart.

As the *Zodiac* accelerates away, I realise something. Time and many years of research has taught me that there are very few men on this earth who, when presented with a whey-faced woman with a notebook, won't take it as a God-given chance to find out how shipshape she is. Put a woman to sea, and suddenly every sedate Sunday sailor turns into a boy racer and their boat into a watery TVR. Groves glances at the rising swell, whacks the outboard up to full throttle, and howls out of the cove: from 0 to 30 knots in 2.7 soakings. Pluming exhaust fumes over the rocks, we belt southwards, round the point at an angle of 45 degrees, and – with a splashy handbrake turn – stop dead in the cove at Porthcressa.

Wiping the water off my face, I look about me. The low evening light has backlit the boulders around the edges of the bay, emphasising their size and darkness. The stones are strange around here liquid-looking curves of gneiss, big lump-ish squares with their edges softened off, boulders with deep wrinkled fissures running all the way through their length. Some look as if they have been poured like pumice into the sea, and most have something almost stagy about their shape, as if they were really made of light fibreglass, and all of this – the rocks, the light, the town beyond – is just a temporary film set. The sea slurps around the coastline, plucking weed from the rocks and making the seabirds scatter. Groves glances backwards at me. I'm okay, but my notebook isn't.

'There,' says Groves, pointing to the right-hand side of the bay: 'That's where the *Cita* went down. Right over the site of another wreck.' What did he make of it? 'People go on about it,' he says, shifting defensively in his seat, 'but it was just a bit of fun. It was a great day out for everyone, everyone enjoyed themselves, everyone got something, and there was no harm done.' It was not those who took things from the containers that bothered him, but the police who tried to enforce what they considered to be the law. 'No-one was doing anything illegal,' he says. 'It's illegal to stop someone from collecting wreck as long as they report it. It was the police, not the people, who were breaking the law that day.' And what of those who never had any intention of declaring their findings to the Receiver? Groves snorts. How is one woman sitting in an office in Southampton supposed to police the whole of the British Isles? How is she supposed to know what really happens when a ship goes ashore?' Both of us peer silently into the translucent waters for a minute or two. Groves revs the motor and we howl south-westwards, trailing panic in our wake.

Out to sea, the swell is deeper. As it slops over the half-submerged rocks, the water catches the last of the sun in an unbroken cascade of light. Belting past St Mary's and towards the island of St Agnes, several things about the Scillies become clearer. Firstly, this place must have more lighthouses than any other part of Britain, each of them hunkered behind their thick sea walls and shining white in the perfect visibility. And where there is no lighthouse, it seems there is always something to mark position – a church, the ruin of a tower, the blackened entrance to a cairn, a radio mast.

But although it is possible to see 360 degrees in every direction just now, ships do miss their bearings, mislocate the islands, or believe themselves to be out in the safety of the Atlantic when only inches from disaster. Just past Peninnis Head, Groves points out the site of the wreck of the *Minnehaha*. An 845-ton wooden vessel carrying a cargo of guano from Falmouth to Dublin, she struck the rocks on January 1874 during a gale, having mistaken a light on the island for the lighthouse on the Wolf. With her sails still set, she, like the *Cita* over a century later, ran full speed onto the rocks and ploughed such a hole into her bow that she was almost entirely under-water within two minutes. The captain and those of the crew who survived took to the rigging. For reasons still best known to himself, the captain then stripped off his clothes, shouted

'With God's help I will save you!' and plunged into the sea. It was not until the following day that the futility of such a leap was made clear. The darkness and gale-force winds had obscured the fact that the ship was inches from the shore, and the majority of those crew who had remained on board were able to climb along the rigging and over the jib-boom onto the rocks. The captain, sadly, was drowned.

Although the Scilly Islands are low lying, they are not flat or featureless like the islands of the Pentland Firth. Though there are plenty of elements here which serve as a reminder of the more northern islands, the one conspicuous difference is the vegetation. In addition to the un-English flowers and shrubs, the Scillies have trees, woods and coppices. Though the islands may at times be just as windy and exposed as the Hebrides, the balmy climate and sheltering coves give trees the chance to flourish in a way that no blasted northern moorland could ever afford. So, given that they had timber, fertile soil, and plants which self-seeded in their enthusiasm to grow, why did the Scillonians acquire such a reputation for wrecking?

Daniel Defoe – who went no further than Cornwall's edge during his tour around Britain – had evidently been deterred by the islands' notoriety. According to him, 'those excrescences' had the worst record for shipwreck in Britain. 'How many good ships are almost continually dashed in pieces there,' he wrote, 'and how many brave lives lost, in spite of the mariners' best skills, or the lighthouses, and other sea-marks best notice.' The Scillies, he claimed, were inhabited by, 'a fierce and ravenous people; for they are so greedy, and eager for the prey, that they are charged with strange, bloody, and cruel dealings, even sometimes with one another, but especially with poor distressed seamen when they come on shore by force of a tempest, and seek help for their lives, and where they find the rocks themselves nor more merciless than the people who range about them for their prey.' Did they wreck because they needed to, or just because they wanted to?

The light has taken on a brassy, artificial quality now, and the wind has risen slightly. The swell is building, its perpetual restiveness at odds with the sight of so much silence on shore. Once in a while, a car putters slowly up one of the lanes, its windows flashing back the evening light. Cows graze in the fields, tourists on bicycles stop at the summits or by the beach. Over there, it's just a slow summer's evening. But out here, there's unceasing motion: the boat hurtling in and out of the lengthening troughs, the water breaking in on itself, the wind plucking at the collar of my jacket.

I have been looking down for a few moments, preoccupied with trying to keep both myself and my notebook dry. I'm aware that we're passing the edge of St Agnes and heading south-westwards, and I know from maps what we are heading for. But it isn't until I look up again that I realise why it is that these islands so profoundly alarmed Defoe. Seeing the Western Rocks for the first time seems like that moment in films when the plane flies over the edge of the mountain range or plunges the viewer over the side of a cliff. A chord, a sudden thunderous sound, the first gigantic notes as all-consuming as the view. Something immense and deep; a sound as huge as a cathedral. A mass, perhaps, or a requiem. Whatever the music was, it would have to be melodramatic, because the Western Rocks are melodramatic.

Up ahead, there is nothing but the sea and an immense black semi-circle of rocks. The first rises up quite close to St Agnes and the last stretches off almost beyond the point of visibility. These are not the softened, liquid-looking stones of the bay near St Mary's. These are savage-looking things, a giant hell-mouth ringed with black-tipped fangs. Many are large enough to stand well clear of the water, close enough to each other that any ship unwary enough to become entangled among them would be sliced to splinters within seconds. Alongside the larger reefs, there are little ones poking only a few feet out of the water like archetypal sharks' fins, rocks with ridges so sharp you could slice meat with them, enormous squared-off lumps of granite, whole islands without a single horizontal surface. This is an Alcatraz, and these rocks are the everlasting version of bullets and razor wire. The brassy light gives them all a strange burned beauty, and within that beauty, a deep sense of menace.

Seen on a map, the Western Rocks form an incomplete circle, a perfect, naturally occurring security fence stretching for three and a half miles to the south-west of the Scillies. Like Scapa Flow at the other end of the country, the rocks are outriders to the islands shaped to form a perfect bay, and have become a place of pilgrimage for wreck divers all over the country. Unlike Scapa Flow, they offer no safety at all. The largest of the rocks are those furthest to the west – coincidentally the point which would be closest and most hazardous to shipping coming up from the Bay of Biscay. Though their vertical spikes make them seem immensely tall from a small boat, none can be much over 20 metres above sea level. On a rainy or a foggy night, these rocks must be all but invisible. If a ship was caught within this circle, it would have found it almost impossible to manoeuvre out again. Smaller boats – gigs and fishing vessels – might have been nippy and shallow enough to negotiate their way past the various hazards. But a large sailing vessel with the wind in the wrong direction would never have had the leeway to get free. Once in, they were trapped. Small wonder that two-thirds of the Scillies' wrecks are buried here among the Western Rocks.

In the past, sailors could rely on nothing more than the light on St Agnes and the Bishop, and the sight – too close, and too late – of white water breaking on the rocks. Navigational aids did not help much. Before 1750, charts quite often depicted the whole Scilly Isles archipelago as being ten to fifteen miles further north of its true position. And, just in case the rocks themselves are not enough to frighten off even the most steady-headed sailor, the Scillies have a few more tricks for the unwary. Right in the centre of the western circle, in the one space which seems clear, is another rock, Luitreth, which lies just under the surface of the water, submerged by only a metre at low tide but imperceptible from above. The same goes for the reefs to the north-east of Great Crewabethan, which also never quite emerge from the water. Just outside the main circle are four further rocks – Crebinicks, the Retarrier Ledges, the Gilstone and the Bishop. Some measure of their unpleasantness can be gauged by the fact that, in medieval times, they were used as sites of execution for felons. Once convicted, criminals would be rowed out past the islands and abandoned. Having been given a jug of fresh water and two loaves of bread, they would be left to starve, drown or die of exposure; whichever came first. Each of these rocks has been responsible for horrific losses. The Bishop – which either took its name from its supposed similarity to a bishop's mitre, or to an early shipwreck in which a man named Bishop was one of the only two survivors – is the westernmost of the four, and thus the one on which Trinity House constructed a lighthouse.

The Retarrier Ledges were the site of one of the worst peacetime disasters in maritime history, when the SS *Schiller*, a 3,400-ton passenger steamer, hit the Ledges in May 1875. The *Schiller* was heading from New York to Hamburg via Portsmouth with 254 passengers and 101 crew. Though built as a 'high-speed' transatlantic liner, the *Schiller* was moving comparatively slowly as she neared the Scillies, since a thick fog had recently descended. At 9.30 p.m., the captain ordered a change of course designed to take the *Schiller* further out into the Channel and thus well clear of the islands. As it was, the change was already too late. Unknown to him, the ship had already been carried by the complex currents far further north than he anticipated, and at 11.40 p.m., she struck the half-submerged Ledges. As the seas rose, the *Schiller* began to sink. Confusion, the destruction of two lifeboats, the fog and a bitter spring gale all conspired to form a tragedy. In the end, several hours after she grounded, it was neither the lighthouse keepers nor anyone from the Scillies who reached the Schiller's survivors first, but a boat from Sennen Cove in Cornwall. Despite the rescuers' attempts to reach the ship, 311 people lost their lives in the disaster.

These rocks are also the scene of the best known of all the UK's wrecking incidents. In 1707, four naval warships under the command of Admiral Sir Cloudisley Shovell were on their way back from fighting in the Mediterranean. At 8 p.m. on the evening of 22 October, all four struck the Gilstone Reef. Like the *Schiller* two centuries later, the flagship *Association* had mistaken her position, and was sailing far too close to the Scillies. She was blown by a gale onto the rocks, and the rest of the fleet followed her: 1,630 soldiers died that night. It was subsequently rumoured that Sir Cloudisley had been warned that he was steering a course for disaster by one of his own sailors, a native Scillonian. Sir Cloudisley, incensed that a subordinate should question his instructions, ordered the man hanged at the ship's yardarm. The condemned man's last request was that Psalm 109 – probably the loveliest curse ever written – should be read out to the Admiral

> Set thou a wicked man over him: and let Satan stand at his right hand ... Let his days be few, and let another take his office. Let his children be fatherless, and his wife a widow ... Let there be none to extend mercy unto him: neither let there be any to favour his fatherless children. Let his posterity be cut off; and in the generation following let their name be blotted out ...

Because that he remembered not to shew mercy, but
persecuted the poor and needy man.

Sure enough, no sooner had the man been hanged than the
weather turned foul and the *Association* struck. Some time later,
the Admiral was washed up – alive, but only just – on the beach
at Porth Hellick on St Mary's. He was found by a local woman
who was said to have mutilated him, stripped him of a valuable
emerald ring and then buried him on a patch of the foreshore
where, to this day, no grass will grow. Later, on her own death-
bed, the old wrecker was supposed to have confessed to the
crime, 'declaring', according to Sir Cloudisley's grandson Lord
Romney, that 'she could not die in peace until she had made this
confession, as she was led to commit this horrid deed for the
sake of plunder'. Whether or not the stories are true, they have
stuck, and now remain as part of the Scilly's folklore.

Groves steers the boat a little northwards and switches off
the engine. In the sudden silence, there is nothing except the
slurp of the swell against the hull and the sound of the sea birds
endlessly resettling. We are encircled here, the closest spikes
only a few metres away. The light has become heavier and
because we are pointing almost directly westwards, the inward
circle of the rocks are cast in deep shadow. When the sea breaks
against their sides the sun catches the water and shines through
it, making every droplet iridescent. For a second or so, it looks
as if someone is hurling up handfuls of diamonds from the deep.
This combination – high swell, angled sun, still air – doesn't
occur often, but when it does, it can sometimes make even the
baldest patch of sea look both beautiful and sinister. Here, with
the silent islands in the background and this vicious geology all
around, even the sea birds seem threatening.

Despite the summer temperatures, I am starting to feel very
cold – and not just physically, either. Up until now, researching
this book has been about the facts of shipwreck – the tides, the

currents, the hours, days, dates, the endless statistics and names of ships I'll never see, the vessels which might, at best, have one or two old newspaper photographs as their final commemoration. Pursuing the wreckers was a fascination, but until now a comparatively abstract one. Out here, surrounded by the black water and this strange light, the whole concept of shipwrecks and wrecking has suddenly moved from the abstract to the real. Below our feet, there are ghosts in the water – the unsettled suggestion of people who lost their lives slowly in fear and in pain. This place is eerie, and it does not seem as if one would have to be particularly suggestible to find the sheer physical facts terrifying. I asked to be brought out here. Now, seasick with destruction, I want to go.

Groves, however, has got into the swing of things. He fires up the outboard again, and we fly round the bay, spraying to a halt inches from yet another monstrous rock. He points southwards. 'Out there,' he says, 'that's where the *Association* went down, and all the other ships with her. They're diving the site at the moment. With recent shifts in the sand and improvements in dive technology, they're finding parts of the lost fleet they could never have expected to locate before. Over there' – further westwards, just beyond the visible horizon – 'are the Retarrier Ledges. Somewhere over here are also the remains of seven East Indiamen who went down at different times. And here' – pointing backwards towards St Agnes – 'is the wreck of the TW *Lawson*, one of the largest sailing vessels ever built. She broke her back among the Western Rocks.'

Being the closest of the inhabited islands to the Western Rocks, St Agnes had such a ferocious reputation that the islanders acquired their very own patron saint of wrecking, St Warna. To the south of the islands are the Lethegus Rocks, where two ships lie, one on top of the other – the first of which, the steamship *Plympton*, sank while looters were still stripping her insides. We set off again on a breezy tour of the rocks to the

north-west of St Agnes: Moinnow, Hellweathers and the Old
Woman's House. Further east, the rocks are lumpier again, as if
the land had been beaten into giant cobbles. Whirling round
and round from reef to reef, I feel disorientated, unsure any
longer which island is which and which rock hides which wreck.
Seen from different angles, the reefs all look the same, each
spike the colour of dried blood. The land is all pale, sandy
coloured and flat, and the rocks are all hostile. I cannot work
out which island is St Agnes, or Annet, or St Mary's. As he
points out one wreck site after another, Groves's voice takes
on a lugubrious note, a kind of doleful satisfaction in all this
demolition. If I feel lost on a sunny day, I wonder, what did the
people who had sailed across the Atlantic feel when they found
themselves trapped here?

On the way back, Groves races the boat right up close to one
of the coves on St Agnes and stops. 'This was our most recent
wreck,' he says, and points over towards a narrow shelf of rock
overlooked by a looming great lump of squared-off granite. 'It
happened a couple of years ago. Cornish fishing boat, at night,
bad weather, and the man on watch couldn't disengage the
autopilot. There were four crew and the others were all asleep.
The lookout realised they were heading straight for the rocks at
full speed, but by the time he discovered it, there was nothing
he could do and there was no time to issue a Mayday call. They
struck the coast just here. The boat sank so fast the crew had
to swim upwards to get out of it. A couple of the crew didn't
survive.' I look at the rocks and think about that Cornishman,
alone on watch, unable to disentangle the electronics. He knew
what was about to happen and he must have been aware of the
Scillies' reputation. What must he have felt, watching his own
destruction approaching him at 15 knots? And how many men's
bones already lay beneath his feet?

By the time we have belted back to Old Town, and I have
unstuck my notebook from the soaking boat, the Scillies have

begun to feel infected with these deaths. Walking back through Hugh Town, the light catches the water and throws flickers of sunlight onto the walls of the houses, making the whole place seem as if it were just on the verge of floating away. Seen with the Western Rocks still in mind, the holiday yachts still plinking at their moorings all look like shipwrecks that haven't happened yet. Perhaps that is my fault for expecting the past to be a comfortable place, and for believing that clear-cut divisions could exist between the sea and the shore.

Gibson & Kyne stands on a sunny side street in the centre of Hugh Town. It's a quiet place with an old-fashioned 1960s fascia and operates as bookseller, stationer and gallery. On the wall at the back of the shop are a series of black and white photographs, each showing a shipwreck with the name and date of its demise written underneath. Most are of sailing ships, which – given that sails had been almost entirely eliminated in the larger vessels by the early years of the twentieth century – makes most of the photographs impressively ancient.

Many of the photos have evidently been taken by a large-format camera with a long exposure in difficult conditions. In one or two, the camera seems to have been shaken by some unseen force. The sea has been blurred to a silvery softness, sails have slapped back at just the wrong moment, and in one print the entire body of the ship seems to have been caught just at the point of dissolving into the water. In others, everything is crisp and coldly detailed. Ships with their decks almost entirely submerged sail into bays above which wait crowds of sightseers in bowler hats and pelisses; ships with their sterns already submerged; ships embayed; ships half-drowned in sand; ships apparently sailing straight into the base of lighthouses. Some look at ease in their unintended resting places, as if they'd just taken a brief stop in an unexpected mooring. Others are torn and piecemeal, their masts snapped midway, their sails slopping over the decks. What is striking about the pictures is not only their cumulative effect – enough shipwrecks to fill a wall – or what they depict, but their loveliness.

Shipwrecks in other parts of the country generally end up with nothing more than a grainy, indeterminate shot taken in bad weather from a difficult angle by the local newspaper's resident snapper. Usually there are rocks in the way or the storm has obscured the detail, or the ship itself is too far away to be clear. Even when the pictures do reveal more than just storm-force conditions, most twentieth-century shipping would hardly inspire poetry. But these photographs are unquestionably beautiful. Not, one supposes, that the crew and the passengers of these wrecks cared much for looks as they sped towards their graves. But in showing these ships and the people surrounding them with such care and veracity, the photographs do give them back some final dignity.

Reaching round the wall is a much more recent picture, taken in colour and evidently of the *Cita*. A man is standing in the open-ended doorway of a container. He is holding a bunch of trainers by the laces and passing them over to a group of waiting women. In the picture, he is smiling. When I look up at the man behind the till, the smile is the same. He nods. 'That's me,' he says, pulling out a large box from under the desk, opening it and flicking through a stack of prints. All the pictures are of the *Cita*, of islanders waist-deep in waterlogged clothes, of cracked containers, and of the hull itself before it sank. He did well from the wreck. He managed to find a load of laminate flooring, but – since it was dark when he collected it – it was not until he came to install it that he discovered that he had picked out two different types, one of which was darker than the other. Still, a two-tone new floor is better than nothing. 'We were just tidying up,' he says equably. 'Nobody else seemed to want the stuff, so we took it.'

The man behind the desk is Peter Kyne, son-in-law of the man who took many of the photographs. Frank Gibson is the fifth member of four generations of Gibson photographers. His great grandfather John Gibson, who lived into his nineties, was a fisherman who taught himself how to use a camera. By 1866 he had learned enough to leave the sea and set up his own business as a general photographer who took pictures of shipwrecks where and when they occurred. His sons Alexander and Herbert joined him in the business, and in time Alexander's son James took over the studios in Penzance and St Mary's. Frank, James's son, succeeded him, and has in his turn been succeeded by his daughter Sandra.

Each member of the Gibson family photographed far more than wrecks, though it has become the wreck pictures for which they are best known. In person, James's son Frank Gibson is small, wiry, and vivid. At his house in the thin strip between Hugh Town and Porthcressa, he waits on the doorstep with a sailor's sense of punctuality and leads me through to the lounge. There is a clutter of tripods and filters in one corner, but otherwise the room is neat and sunny, without any of the detritus of the habitual wreckers' den. The shelves are filled with pictures and souvenirs, things collected on his many post-retirement travels around Britain and Europe. He is evidently a strong man, with sharp blue eyes, and a pair of eyebrows so large and lively it seems he's got a couple of cairn terriers strapped to his forehead. He is also clearly a man at ease with being interviewed. Every time there's a wreck in Cornwall or the Scillies, every news organisation in Britain contacts the Gibsons. Their reputation goes before them: both John Fowles and John Le Carré have written introductions to books of Gibson photographs.

When the Gibsons first began taking photographs, they used

the wet collodion process, a method which often proved cumbersome and wasteful in the field, but which also produced some of the most striking images of the sea ever taken. The first John Gibson built up a network of friends and informers who would let him know when and where a wreck was likely to take place. He and an assistant would set off up the coast in a pony and trap, or set sail in a four-oared boat, taking an old-fashioned glass plate camera, a tripod, and a small wheeled cart to serve as a portable darkroom. If they were lucky, they would reach the site of the wreck before darkness, and before the ship sank.

'Our people in those days had a business in Penzance,' Frank explains, 'and that was how they were able to get all those Cornish wrecks. It was quite a lot of work. They had these great tripods, these great massive cameras, the boat would be rocking around. Amazing photographs for those times. And the quality – these days, you use a 35 millimetre or something, there's no comparison between ours and what they did. These modern cameras doesn't stand it like these old ones would. Those old ones didn't have these intricate shutters, and that's what gets damaged with salt water. They were primitive – all they had was a bellows and a back screen, and a lens stuck on the front.'

Even when conditions were good enough to get a clear shot, the Gibsons' work would only be half done. Because the silver nitrate would begin to ionise in the fresh air, the exposed plates would have to be developed within an hour, otherwise the image would fade. 'I've still got the original glass plates, and I used to have to hand-print them,' Frank continues: 'The old photographic process of hand-printing required an awful lot of afterwork with the brush, and painting over spots and everything. This is where the art comes into it – you get the picture that you envisaged when you took it. You're there taking this picture and you see this dramatic sky and everything. Well, from a straight print, it looks nothing. You've got to work on it, you know, with dodging, and printing and so on, until it's your idea of what you saw.'

Once finished and retouched, the prints would then be sent to the relevant organisations. 'Being down this part of the world, you were a long way from civilisation as such, weren't you? Now, my daughter, if she gets a picture which is worthwhile, she can email it just like that. In my early days, I couldn't do that – I had to get it over to Penzance to catch a train . . . you know, you were twenty-four hours out of date before you even got the thing to the right people.'

But why did the Gibsons start on the wreck pictures in the first place? 'I've been told but I don't quite know if it's right, that the shipping companies were interested from an insurance point of view. That's what I've been told, but I begin to wonder – I think they were just interested in that sort of thing. You know, if you're born in an island or around the sea, anything around the coast, it's the first thing you notice. I think one only has to look at the number of people on any coast who will just go along to see a wreck. Not necessarily to go and pick it over, but just to go and see it. It seems to create an awful lot of interest in people.'

Frank's grandfather, Alexander, and great-uncle, Herbert, were the family members who got the most impressive shipwreck images. Though capable of using steam, many ships were still designed and built as sailing vessels during the second half of the nineteenth century, and the sheer volume of shipping passing the coasts of Cornwall and the Scillies ensured a steady level of casualties year after year. Add to that the persistent hazards of faulty instruments, erratic charts, human error and a dark coastline, and it was small wonder that to the Gibsons, they were, 'a different world. The [ships] were so beautiful, they were. The unfortunate thing about those sailing ships in some of the pictures we got – they were 100 days out of Australia, and that was their first landfall. What a terrible experience . . . You know, sailing for 100 days to get to England, to Falmouth and end up on the Lizard.'

Frank himself has not seen many wrecks. 'There's been very few major wrecks in my time, there really hasn't. Our photographic collection was built up in my grandfather's time, from the 1880s upwards, and wrecks were ten a penny then ... I've photographed the *Torrey Canyon*, the *Poleaire*, a Russian fishing boat up on the Seven Stones ... What else? God, I'm getting old, I'm forgetting.'

And what of the wreckers? The Gibsons must have been aware of them: those black-clad watchers in many of the photographs were not always just sightseers. 'In the 1800s, I don't say it gave them a living, but by gosh, it was essential, you know, because they were very very poor in these islands in those days. Before Augustus Smith came, these islands were extremely poor, so shipwrecks were terribly important to people. I don't believe the story that they attracted them to shore, I don't believe that one bit. But if a wreck occurred, they were there as quick as lightning.'

He remembers being told the story of the *Schiller* disaster, though it was many years before his time. 'They salved a lot of cargo, a lot of American green banknotes, but nobody knew the value of them. All these green notes were coming ashore, dollar bills, and one particular man paid kids a shilling a bucket for them – "You go round, pick up all these, I'll give you a shilling a bucket". Well, the kids were enjoying themselves, they thought they were wealthy with a shilling, I suppose. He built houses and God knows what on the strength of that. Oh yes, that's a nice little story, that one.'

Two streets away, Matt Lethbridge and his wife Pat are contemplating a quieter retirement than Frank Gibson. When I call round the door is opened by a man with white hair, a half-moon smile and a pair of eyebrows even more extravagant than Frank Gibson's. (Perhaps, I think, this is the pure-bred Scillonians' defining physical characteristic: a pair of eyebrows as wild as gorse. It certainly runs in the family; some years ago, Matt's brother Richard wrote a volume of memoirs simply entitled *Behind the Eyebrows*.) Matt shows me into the front room, where his wife Pat sits smiling in one of the armchairs. The room is packed to the eaves with watery memorabilia – family photographs, cups and tankards, a cabinet-full of flotsam, pictures of storms and boats, and laid into a folding coffee tables, a series of expertly painted ships. On the pelmet above the curtains is a row of small china cats.

Matt guides me over to the sofa on the other side of the fire, and I explain my mission. Both Matt and Pat look at me with caution, but not with unkindness. Sitting side-by-side – Pat nearest the fire, Matt nearest the door – they touch each other's hands on the armrests occasionally; a quick, open gesture of affection. Matt is younger than his voice on the phone; only his hands and a faint whitening round the irises of his eyes betray his age. Several people have told me that Matt is not a man to suffer fools, and I have come prepared for a sharp exit. As it is, both he and Pat are far more generous and forthcoming than I have any right to expect. 'Won't you,' says Pat after five minutes, 'take off your jacket?'.

For three generations, the Lethbridge family have been involved with the Scilly lifeboats. Matt is the third of four brothers, three of whom have worked alongside each other on the St Mary's boat – at one time, with their father and uncle, there were five Lethbridges in a crew of eight men. Did he choose to volunteer? 'I didn't want much choice,' he says, laughing. He was taught to sail by his father and his uncle, and learned navigation the old-fashioned way, through trial and error. 'In Dad's time, in my early days, a lot of the navigation and things like that were just rule of thumb. I mean, in around the islands, we wouldn't use a chart at all, no matter how dark or how foggy the night was. It was all in your head, you know,

South Goodwins Light Vessel, wrecked during a 1954 gale on the Goodwins.

The wreck eventually came to rest on the very sands she was designed to warn other ships against.

OPPOSITE

Above The abandoned island of Stroma in the Pentland Firth.

Below Interior of one of the semi-derelict crofts on Stroma.

Right Willie Mowatt MBE, 'Chief Pirate of the Pentland Firth'.

Below One of the largest abandoned crofts on Stroma. The wreck could be hidden in the kirk, the fields, or the sea, but never within the crofts themselves.

Above Figurehead in Augustus Smith's Valhalla Collection on Tresco in the Scilly Isles.

OPPOSITE
Above Figureheads in the Valhalla Collection.

Below The Western Rocks.

Above A still from
Whisky Galore:
Captain Paul
Wagget discovers
the stash of
contraband whisky.

Right Compton
Mackenzie.

A selection of whalebones washed up and left on Stroma.

Whalebones in the Natural History Museum's collection.

The Portrait of
PATRICK COLQUHOUN ESQ.re J.L.D &c
was painted A.D 1802. and placed in this House
by the Committee who superintended the
building thereof as a mark of respect for his
character and a token of the grateful sense
entertained of his services to this Parish.

Left Portrait of Patrick Colquhoun in the Marine Police Museum in Wapping.

Below A plaster model of a dolphin in the Natural History Museum's collection. Because of the difficulties inherent in preserving cetacean specimens, the museum originally made life-sized plaster models. These have now been superseded by lighter, fibreglass versions.

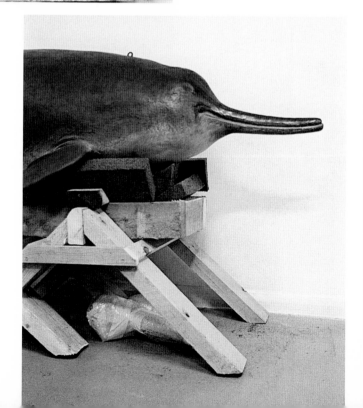

Richard Sabin, curator of the Natural History Museum's
cetacean collection and UK strandings co-ordinator, with
a mummified sperm whale's heart.

Above Models of the
Victorian river police in
the Marine Police
Museum.

Right A river policeman's
cutlass.

Opposite RMS *Mulheim* on
the rocks at Land's End in
April 2002.

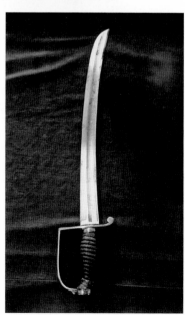

OPPOSITE
Above Local historian Joe Mills.
Below Mike Pearce.

Above The *Mildred* struck Gurnard's Head in Cornwall in April
1912 while carrying a cargo of slag from Newport to London.

The *Seine*, a French bounty clipper which ran ashore in Perran Bay in 1900. Two weeks after she grounded, the little that remained of her was sold for £42.

OPPOSITE
Above One of the shipbreaker's recycling stalls at Alang in Gujarat. The scales are used for weighing scrap steel.

Below Old navigation lights and porthole glass on a shipbreaker's stall at Alang.

Old deck lights and mattresses found on a shipbroker's stall at Alang.

and you were safer using your own knowledge than you were working on the chart.'

Matt started out lobster fishing around the Scillies. The fishing alone taught him all he needed to know about island waters. At one stage, he had ten strings of pots, all in different places and each tied together with hemp rope. When the rope became waterlogged it would sink and only rise again when the tide slackened. Matt would have twenty minutes to find the rope and haul the pots. 'So you had to know exactly what time to be in that area, what time that tide was going to change in that area, and you had to know that for each one. The best local knowledge of anything is an inshore fisherman. You can't beat that knowledge.' Having learned his ropes, he then graduated to the lifeboat.

Inevitably, once working for the RNLI, Matt was involved with many of the area's most notorious shipwrecks. 'To be honest, the bigger they are, the better as far as the lifeboat's concerned, because you've got more chance of getting a sheltered spot and more chance of being able to get people off from a bigger ship than you are a smaller one. The larger ships draw a lot of water. You've got to know the area yourself as well, and the angle the ship is lying and whatever, but you can say, with a ship that size, you're going to be able to get alongside it somewhere.'

To make such bold calls, he must have had considerable faith in his own judgement. 'Oh yes, you've got to act confident,' he says with equanimity. 'But there again, anybody who grown up in that area, who's been working on the sea all their life, now, who's got more confidence or a better judgement? Alright, some of them will make mistakes, but their judgement is the best judgement of anyone in the world, isn't it?' To this end, 'I never drank. None of our family ever drank. My dad always used to say that booze and boats don't go together. Another thing he used to say, well, if anything happened to the boat –

the lifeboat and the crew – at least they would know it wasn't through drink. Lives wouldn't have been thrown away because the captain was drunk. There was three of us, two of my brothers with me in the boat, and none of us drank. We went out on a New Year's Day, one o'clock in the morning, something like that, and everyone on the boat was sober because it was a dirty night and they knew it was possible that the boat would be wanted.'

It is this, and what he regards as the monolithic ignorance of the present-day lifesaving services, which most exercise him. Take salvage, for instance. From its beginnings, the RNLI has always allowed lifeboatmen to claim salvage, but never encouraged the practice. Those who do wish to claim it have to ensure both that they pay for the use of the lifeboat, and that they claim for a lower value than a dedicated salvor would receive. 'As I say, salvage in general was a laugh. I mean, we towed in lots of boats and so on like that, but most of the time the lifeboat didn't claim salvage anyway. Well, to be quite honest, this is the stupid part again, the courts never give lifeboats a fair salvage.' Why not? 'Well, because they just expected them to do it for nothing. Simply because the lifeboat didn't usually claim salvage, they thought they never should, you know. But they were all men earning their living, and they got to give up their time to go in the lifeboat anyway. I mean, many of the yachts won't take a tow from a fishing boat because they can get it for nothing from a lifeboat, you know. But you would still have to pay for any damage you done to that lifeboat, you would have to pay for all the fuel, and so on. You'd have to pay for the cost of using the boat. But the Institution itself wouldn't support you on a salvage – in fact, they would punish you for it rather than support you.'

What about the theory I've heard from other lifeboatmen that the lifeboats were once crewed by wreckers? 'Yes, yes,' he says, 'wreckers were saving lives before the Institution was formed. The reason the Institution was formed was to provide them men who were losing their lives in their own boats with a better boat to do the same thing as they were already doing. I don't care how big a wrecker they were – you might get a very odd one who just don't care at all – but 99 per cent would save lives first. Life would come first, no matter how big a wrecker they were.'

There would also be good pickings to be had simply from wandering the foreshore. Since wrecks were so frequent, the Scilly Islanders maintained a strong and long-established sense of beachcombing decorum. 'In those days it was respected law – it was unmade law, but it was a respected local law – that if you picked up a plank and you stood it up against the cliff or something, nobody would touch it. If you couldn't get it above the cliff, then you pulled it above high-water mark and you put a stone on it to say, this has already been found. And nobody would pinch it, or very few people would in them days.'

And did the 'finders keepers' rule also extend to corpses? 'Well,' he says, 'with bodies sometimes, the person who picked up the body was probably saddled with the job of burying it. Around these coasts, around here, there's lots of bodies around the sandy shores and things. There is an awful lot of super-stition. Luckily, in that respect ...', he leans over, raps the wooden table and chuckles, '... touch wood, that sort of super-stition never worried me. I was only sixteen when the war broke out and I worked under the Navy then. Part of our job was to collect bodies from torpedoed ships, or anything that washed inland from the islands. So I become immune from superstition in that respect. I mean, a body can't hurt you, can it? All you can do for a body is to show respect in the way you handle it. I mean, I didn't like handling dead bodies, nobody likes bodies, you don't want to see them and you've got every sympathy with them, but it didn't mean a thing to me as regards superstition of finding a body in the water. I mean, I'd rather have it aboard the boat than leave it there in the water.'

It is not just superstition, but old law which affects attitudes to bodies, however. 'The laws and that were a bit funny – they still are,' Matt continues. 'If I was fishing three and a half miles off, and I picked up a body and brought it in here, I would be responsible for burying it. I would be forced to have it buried properly, in a church, a coffin, everything. But if I picked it up within three miles, the national line or whatever, then the council's responsible for burying it.' And there's another thing, he says. 'This is going back years, but if I picked up a body, I would be awarded five shillings for picking it up. There's an old story of one bloke picking up a body, and it was too dark to bring it down to report it, so he put it in his boatshed, and he slept in the boatshed with it in case somebody stole it!' The story is true; in nineteenth-century Cornwall – which at that time included the Scilly Isles – a bounty of five shillings was offered for those who recovered shipwrecked corpses.

And what of those infamous Scillonian traditions? Does he think that the islanders ever deliberately caused wrecks? 'I'm not saying they couldn't arrange a wreck. There have been cases of it happening.' Would it, I ask nervously, have been something that he took an interest in? 'Like I say, as regards that, what we call salvaging from boats itself is just, um . . . When we went out in our own boats, that was salvaging. I've never got a bloody bob out of salvage, not that sort of salvage, not really. Very little.'

How about the general cargo vessels? 'Oh yes, you got a lot of fun out of that. There was at the beginning of the war, the Longships. She was a good wreck, she had everything. The lighthouses were all gone out and she run on the Seven Stones. She had everything, she had suits of clothing, bolts of material – suiting material, dress material, just ordinary sheeting material – and she had bundles of sheets and blankets and clothes, barrels of apples and there was a lot of drink, bottles of all sorts, and there was potatoes . . . I don't know, everything. All the islands was clothed, all the washing lines was full, the bushes was full of drying clothes.' He laughs. 'But she stayed afloat out there, which was very rare, so the boats had a go at her. I've always said that the first long trouser suit I had was from the Longships.' 'There was another man,' he recalls, 'who went out on one of the boats to the Longships. And when he came ashore – he was a bit rough really, he never dressed up or anything – but when he come ashore, he had three suits on! Never looked so smart in his life. He had the shoes with it.'

He stops for a minute, and then adds reflectively: 'It was good fun really, an awful lot of it was good fun. But I mean, really, in our case there was a lot to be gained, because people couldn't afford much in them days.' What was the best thing he ever found? 'I salvaged a clock once. It was a beauty. It had the three minutes' silence on it. I just took that for a souvenir really. So I had this, and it worried Pat so much, I said, alright, I'll get rid of it. So first time, I took it down the fishing store, and then Pat knew I hadn't really got rid of it. So then I said, alright, and I took it out to our allotment where we used to keep the chickens and I put it in the chicken house.' He laughs, and she smiles. 'Eventually, she gets it out of me, because she knew I wouldn't tell a downright lie, you know, so I had to admit I still had it and I'd put it in the chicken house. "Oh, that's too bad," she said. In the end I got so fed up I went out one evening and threw it over the parapet of the bloody quay!'

But as he points out, he could have had much larger prizes. 'I've had chances to have stuff which were illegally salvaged by divers and things, and I never take it, because I always used to say, well, what's the good of it? I can't show it to anybody without taking the risk of being summonsed. So there was just no point in it. I mean, there were stupid little things – bits and pieces I used to take as souvenirs, like a pair of dividers. I had one or two of them off a chart table. That brass lamp up there, that come from the Longships. It's of no great value or anything like that. That little pot there come off a ship, and the little jug. One of the other wrecks, there was serviette rings, that was the Captain's serviette ring. My next brother down, Harry, he had the mate's ring, and the other brother had the engineer's. These here,' – he points to two large brass engine telegraphs by the door – 'they weren't actually salvaged, these come off a boat we towed in one time, a big steamer. The captain gave them to Pat – I said I didn't want them. So they're hers really. They are nice, aren't they?'

They are nice. Both have been polished to a high shine and show the Lethbridges' house pointing full steam towards France. All these things – the paintings on the tables, the tillers, the serviette rings, the lamp – are no more than the ornamental evidence of a life spent surrounded by water. Nothing about them, or in Matt's conversation, indicates that he was at one stage the most highly decorated lifeboat coxswain in the country, or that he has been the recipient of three RNLI silver medals for gallantry. Some time after I meet him, a poll in the Scilly News voted him the 'Greatest Living Scillonian'. When he mentioned the fact that the lifeboat crews risked their lives every time they took the boat out, he does so almost with a sense of squeamishness, as if saying such things amounted to melodrama or sentimentality.

Walking back through the thin streets of Hugh Town, past the flocks of old folk, I think of Scilly's two extremes. Nothing in this place ever seems to match up. The Abbey Gardens and the Western Rocks; the *Cita* and the *Schiller*; Defoe's allegations and Lethbridge's courage. Creation and destruction; fertility and death. Does anyone ever really find out what's going on under these waters and beneath those eyebrows? Standing on the quay, looking at the sea slopping softly against the stones, I think what a lovely place this is for a visit, and how little I would like to sail by on a dark night.

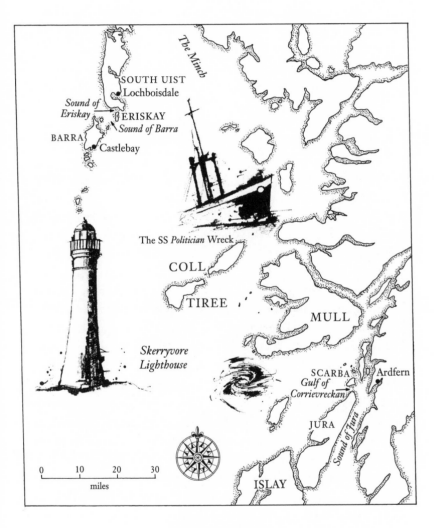

The Minch

SOUTH UIST
Lochboisdale

*Sound of
Eriskay*
ERISKAY
Sound of Barra

BARRA
Castlebay

The SS *Politician* Wreck

COLL

TIREE

MULL

*Skerryvore
Lighthouse*

SCARBA
*Gulf of
Corrievreckan*
Ardfern

JURA

Sound of Jura

ISLAY

0   10   20   30
miles

West Coast

FIVE

West Coast

I n 1947, the writer George Orwell rented a place on Jura, a
Hebridean island shaped like an elongated raindrop overlooking some of the filthiest seas in Europe. Barnhill, a
farmhouse tucked right up on the island's north-eastern edge,
satisfied Orwell's desire for distance. It is five miles down a
track impassable to anything but tractors, and twenty-five miles
from the nearest shop. Anyone wishing to get in or out of the
area would either have to walk or take a boat across the Sound
of Jura to the mainland.

While he was at Barnhill, Orwell began work on the novel
which was to become *1984*, his apocalyptic fable of the individual within the totalitarian state. During the summer months,
Orwell spent time with his son Richard (then still a toddler), his
sister Avril and his nephew and niece Lucy and Henry Dakin.
For much of the time the group pottered about the island, tending the land, mending boats and wandering out on occasional
picnics. In August, Orwell proposed a camping expedition over
to Jura's western side for a couple of days. On their way back to
Barnhill, he took Henry, Lucy and Richard with him on the
boat and set off for home, skirting along the island's northern
tip. It should have been a brief and unexceptional trip; as it was,
Orwell met the Gulf of Corrievreckan.

Many years later, Henry Dakin gave his version of events to
Orwell's biographer, Bernard Crick:

When we turned round the point, there was already a fair swell, the boat was rising and falling a lot, but we were not worried because Eric [Orwell] seemed to know what he was doing . . . But as we came round the Point, obviously the whirlpool had not receded. The Corrievreckan is not just the famous one big whirlpool, but a lot of smaller whirlpools around the edges. Before we had a chance to turn, we went straight into the minor whirlpools and lost control. Eric was at the tiller, the boat went all over the place, pitching and tossing . . . so much that the outboard motor jerked right off from its fixing. Eric said, 'the motor's gone, better get the oars out, Hen. Can't help much, I'm afraid'.

Henry unshipped the oars and they made their way unsteadily over to a small island nearby.

Even though that bit of it was very frightening . . . Eric didn't panic, but nobody else did either. Indeed, when he said he couldn't help you very much, he said it very calmly and flatly.

Having arrived within touching distance of the island, Henry leapt out of the boat and onto the rock with the painter rope in one hand. As he did so, the boat capsized, pitching Orwell, Lucy and Richard into the water. Orwell swam back, and managed to rescue both children from beneath the boat. All three hauled themselves onto the rocks, righted the boat and secured it. According to Henry, Orwell remained unperturbed.

We were left on this island . . . with the boat, one oar, a fishing rod and our clothes. Eric got his cigarette lighter out – never went anywhere without it – and put it out on a rock to dry. We had not been there for three minutes when he said he would go off and find some food. A slightly ridiculous thing, it struck me afterwards, because we had had breakfast only two hours before and the last thing that any of us was thinking of was eating or of hunger . . . I thought we were goners . . . He [Orwell] almost seemed to enjoy it. We waved a shirt on the fishing rod about, and after about one and a half hours a lobster boat spotted us and picked us up.

Orwell's own account of the incident is laconic:

On return journey ran into the whirlpool and were all nearly drowned. Engine sucked off by the sea and went to the bottom. Just managed to keep the boat steady with the oars, and after going through the whirlpool twice, ran into smooth water and found ourselves up abt. 100 yards from Eilean Mor, so ran in quickly and managed to clamber ashore . . . Most of the stuff in the boat lost including the oars . . . We left Glengarrisdale at abt. 10.30, which was abt. 2 hours after high tide, & must have struck Corryvreckan at abt. 11.30, ie, when the tide had been ebbing about three hours. It appears this was the very worst time, and we should time it so as to pass Corryvreckan in slack water. The boat is all right. Only serious loss, the engine and 12 blankets.

Orwell's insouciance was misplaced. Corrievreckan is not for absent-minded writers in small boats. In fact, it is not really for anyone at all. Corrievreckan is the largest whirlpool in European waters and the second largest whirlpool in the world, superseded only by the true Maelstrom off the Lofoten Islands near Norway's west coast. Sailors have always considered it one of the great maritime dragons, up there with Portland Bill, the Alderney Race or the Men of Mey in terms of risk and challenge.

The whirlpool runs between the islands of Jura and Scarba and is formed both by the pressures of a 9-knot tidal bottleneck and by two significant underwater obstructions. The flowing tide pulls water northwards from the Clyde estuary and the Irish Sea into the narrow gap of the Sound of Jura. As all the accumulated weight of water races north-eastwards up through the Sound, it gathers pace. By the time it enters the channel between the two islands, it is moving at 9 knots or more, and as it rounds the corner into the Gulf it runs directly into four major opposing forces: the two islands themselves (no more than two-thirds of a mile apart at their narrowest point); a large submerged rock stack to the north of the channel, smooth-sided and vertical on its eastern edge and rising up to within 29 metres of the surface; the current running in the opposite direction round the coast of Scarba, and lastly, a deep sub-aquatic pit hollowed out by the movement of water reaching down 219 metres below the surrounding sea bed and known as the Gateway to Hell.

The pit sucks water down and the stack throws it upwards, creating vortices which rise to the surface as pulses. In a heavy wind, the standing waves directly above the stack can reach 10 to 15 feet high, and during the autumnal equinox, when the whirlpool runs in fullest spate, it can revolve at up to 10 knots, pushing the water up at the sides to 30 foot above the surrounding sea level. In those conditions, the water roars. They say that Corrievreckan's thunder can sometimes be heard ten miles or more inland. As the old *Statistical Account of Scotland* put it: 'Three currents, formed by the islands and mainland, meet a fourth, which sets in from the ocean. The conflux is dreadful and spurns all descriptions. Even the genius of Milton could not paint the horrors of the scene. At the distance of twelve miles a most dreadful noise, as if all the infernal powers had been let loose, is heard.' Those who do emerge – including Orwell – have earned the right to call themselves lucky. Pilot books warn sailors to avoid the area if possible and to venture into Corrievreckan only at slack water. The Royal Navy judges it to be entirely unnavigable except by vessels over a certain tonnage and horsepower.

Alex Renton, a journalist who knows the western sea well and who has sailed through the area several times, observes that Corrievreckan has a strange effect on the mariner's psyche: 'You first realise what's happening because the coast is moving far faster than it should be – the knot meter will still be showing you whatever leisurely speed you were at, but if you check the GPS, you find that you're going two or three times faster in real terms. It begins to dawn on you what's going on, and you become instantly aware of the fundamental misconception about what you and boats do at sea. Usually you think of yourself in a boat as progressing over the surface of a stable planet as you do in a car or on your own two feet. This is of course completely wrong. The surface you are on is not stable at all. You're a very small force hitching a lift on something with infinitely greater energy and purpose. Where the water wants to go, so will you, like a clockwork toy in the bath. And at the mouth of the Corrievreckan you get a very clear demonstration of what happens when the plug is pulled out. Very soon after this rather challenging notion settles, you begin to realise, physically, just how powerful the force is. Though it's talked about as the great whirlpool, I've never been conscious of there being a single monster ready to suck you down. But the boat will suddenly spin 60 degrees before you can regain control – and you'd have to wrestle the tiller to do it. The water looks like it's being stirred from below. The best effect is the swellings that come up, as big as the boat; muscles of water thrown up to the surface. The boat will lift with the water lumps, shudder a bit, and spin again. Out of control is quite relaxing – you've got on the fairground ride and there's no point fussing until it stops. There's no way out except the way out.'

Since Corrievreckan is such a narrow channel, and since there are alternative routes up the Sound of Jura or the Firth of

Lorn, the whirlpool is comparatively unfrequented. Those vessels that do use the route are generally local with knowledge-able crew. One of these is the *Sea Leopard*, skippered by Lindsay Johnson, who has sailed this part of the world for over thirty years. And so, on a balmy day one spring tide away from the vernal equinox, a small group of day trippers collect on the pon-toon at Ardfern. Johnson greets us and gives a quick safety drill: keep hold of the guard rails, expect to get wet and if you're daft enough to fall overboard no-one's going to bother coming back for you. He also assures his passengers that the *Sea Leopard* is both more powerful and more skilfully skippered than Orwell's little clinker-built boat. It is capable of a maximum speed of 18 knots, which should in theory be strong enough to outstrip even the worst of Corrievreckan's races.

We gaze down at the water. It looks exactly as it should do: slack and placid, as untroubled as the sky above. Over our heads, an occasional lonely cloud passes by and the sun beams down like mid-July. Johnson's dire warnings of races and capsizings sound overdone; surely on a day like this nothing can go wrong. We can hear no watery roarings, no Miltonian hordes. By the time the boat leaves the dock, most of the passengers have begun wondering if all this maelstrom stuff is no more than tales for the tourists. Besides, I had read the other day that Corrievreckan has even been swum. In 1981 Orwell's brother-in-law, Bill Dunn, who once farmed Barnhill and who had lost a leg during the war, decided that he would attempt the crossing to raise money for charity. He chose the calmest pos-sible conditions: a neap tide with the flood running from east to west. He made the crossing in August, dressed in a sleeveless wet suit, a woollen semmit, and as much lanolin as he could smear on his exposed skin. Watched by a crowd of 300 or more, he swam slowly across the Gulf on his back. 'The swim itself was uneventful,' he wrote later. 'In fact, it was rather boring.'

We motor down towards Crinan, watching the slow play of

shadows over the mountains. The sea remains calm, no more than the occasional ruffle of wind darkening its surface. But once the boat turns the corner and heads into the Sound of Jura, things begin to speed up. The water coming up the Sound is moving fast, and where it meets the opposing currents travelling south and eastwards, there are signs of disagreement. To begin with, the change doesn't look that profound: a few small over-falls, a patch of peaky water to starboard, an area full of small circular boilings up ahead. Then suddenly, something plucks at the rudder. The boat turns 90 degrees or so, spinning slowly on its axis. The passengers catch an unasked-for panorama of the further sea isles and stop talking for a second or so. The engine, untroubled by the interruption, chugs onwards towards the Gulf. Everyone starts talking again.

A couple of yards further on the odd circular tugging begins again, almost like something rather large beneath us has reached up and given the hull a quick turn between forefinger and thumb. The sensation makes the sea seem slippery, as if we're sailing not on water but on something more tenuous. Not that the *Sea Leopard* seems much bothered by these subterranean proddings. She rights herself and we sail on. The northern coastline of Jura looms up ahead, Barnhill and Orwell's near-nemesis down to the left.

Lindsay steers the boat northwards, right in close to the coast of Scarba. In a couple of minutes we are no more than a few metres from the shore. 'You'll notice,' he says, 'that on one side of the boat, the current is moving one way and on the other side, it's moving the other way.' He's right. On the starboard side, the water is travelling eastwards. On the other side, it's going west. On both sides, it is moving fast, the pace not of a normal sea current but of a river in spate. And that water doesn't look like any water I've ever seen before. It's completely flat and it shines with a bright reflective calm, like beaten panels of tin. Parts of its surface have acquired an odd ripped edge, as if each section of ocean had somehow separated itself out into different liquid islands. Around the borders of each island are hundreds of small plughole eddies, endlessly forming and vanishing as they pass by. The water on the Scarba side gets glassier, smoother, brassier. The little plugholes expand. When I look straight down at them, there is nothing at their centre but blackness.

And then the bumpings start. For a second, it feels as if the hull has hit a small submerged log that then rolls under the boat: a faint but palpable jerk. The tiller twitches. A second or two later, there's another one, a bigger log this time. Again that sense of something absolutely solid underneath, thumping against us and rolling down the boat from bow to stern. As the logs roll by, there comes from time to time that odd lazy tugging at the keel again, the twitch of something plucking at us from below. It feels exactly like the first faint tremors of a fish on the line. Except that this time, we're the fish, and something else is controlling the line. Abruptly, the boat starts to spin again, turning away from the coast of Scarba and towards the Gulf. As we move, the tugging continues, harder this time, as if whatever's there beneath us has stopped being mildly curious and is now actively interested. Johnson guns the engine and we speed up, trying to outstrip our underwater inspector. We roll over a few more logs, each a little heftier than the last. Bump. Bump. Bump. By now, I'm gripping the guardrail as though my life depended on it.

Then – and Jesus this is weird – I look at the land, and I realise that some parts of it are higher away from the water than others. The water is not all at the same level. The tidemark on the rocks directly ahead is around a metre high. The tidemark a little further away is 4 or 5 metres high. The sea is rolling like a lowland hill. This particular patch of ocean has hummocks and contours, and a one-in-four gradient. At the moment it is also doing its very best to carry us somewhere where we do not want to go. To distract myself I look westwards to where the islands separate out. Rolling in from the Atlantic are waves: big ones. Waves breaking with the same force and weight as if they'd just come all the way from Canada and hit the solid granite walls of Jura. But they're not breaking on land. They're breaking on ... well, nothing. Breaking on water. On themselves.

A couple of hours ago, I thought I understood the laws of physics. I thought I understood that water remains level, that waves do not appear without wind, that boats cannot hit liquid obstructions, that cold water cannot boil. But Corrievreckan is taking everything I know, and rendering it wrong. Normal laws do not apply here, because there is no normality. The water in Corrievreckan is not normal water. This is not a normal place.

Someone who knows Corrievreckan as well as Lindsay Johnson had told me earlier that he'd been out on the whirlpool one day, and a pit had opened up in the water ahead. There was no other way to describe it; one minute he was sailing across level water and the next minute he was staring into a 10-metre abyss. Small wonder that the whirlpool has taken its own dark place in local legend.

But Corrievreckan is not alone. There is something about the western sea which fits comfortably into a world of myth and fable. Fingal's Cave, Cape Wrath, the Torran Rocks, the cavern on Eigg, part-time islands, the Dutchman's Cap, Suilven, the abandoned island of St Kilda; this is a place where every stone has a name and a tale attached. That legendary edge is due in part to the shape of the landscape. This place is not the comfortable, domesticated shape of the lowlands, but is formed on a more inhuman scale – a place of cloudy mountains, monstrous geology, wild exaggerations. It can be both beautiful and hostile, but it is never ordinary.

Even a glance at a map shows the west's peculiarity. Here, the coast does not follow the tidy line of the east, but takes a ragged meander from one side of the country to another. Some parts of the shoreline point in for miles, some stab outwards, blocking the path of what would otherwise be a safe passage. Some parts of the coast turn almost invisibly into islands, some ought to be islands but have stayed as peninsulas instead. What should be land is water and what should be water turns out to be a reef, a sandbank or a wreck. Look at the place, and it dissolves; a ripped confusion of earth, rocks and water. It seems impassable, uninhabitable, unnavigable, 'a region without people, disquiet without cause, a road without a goal', as the writer Karel Capek put it. Scotland has 5 million inhabitants and more than 10,000 kilometres of coastline, half of which is either part of the sea lochs or skirting the country's 790 islands. Small wonder that this place has always been notorious, or that even now it remains impossible to effectively light or police.

Which, predictably, makes the west perfect for wreckers. To start with there has always been plenty of traffic through the Sea of the Hebrides, and much of that traffic has been valuable. These seas have seen everything from Clearance ships carrying reluctant emigrants from the Highlands to the New World, to cargo vessels laden with tobacco, cotton, sugar and manufactured goods heading back from America to the Old Country. Whether it be shipping on its way from Scandinavia to Newfoundland, liners running the transatlantic race between Liverpool and New York, or merchant vessels with their armed escorts on the North Atlantic convoys during the Second World War, this stretch of water has seen a greater variety of traffic than almost any other area of Britain.

But if the surrounding seas were cosmopolitan, the islands within them were not. In the eighteenth and nineteenth centuries, travel to the Western Isles was still perceived as a risky business. Until Queen Victoria popularised the idea of the tartanised Highlander, very few Englishmen had ever travelled north of Perthshire for pleasure. Those who did make the trip did so either for professional reasons or for the advancement of science. Defoe's journey in 1700 was intended as part of a wider intelligence-gathering mission, while Martin Martin's trip in 1695 was made in order to search out new material for science and anthropology. According to James Boswell, even Samuel Johnson's trip to the Highlands in 1773 was designed as a kind of patent cure to Johnson's anti-Caledonian prejudices. (Even after Boswell had persuaded Johnson to make the journey northwards, their friends regarded both of them as mad. 'When I was at Ferney, in 1764,' Boswell noted, 'I mentioned our design to Voltaire. He looked at me as if I had talked of going to the North Pole, and said, "You do not insist on my accompanying you?" "No, sir." "Then I am very willing you should go".')

Unsurprisingly, those travellers who did make the trip returned with stories which made Scotland and the Scots sound as aboriginally exotic as shark-eating Eskimos or man-eating pygmies. Their accounts of 'seal people', second sight and old women who sold winds to sailors perpetuated an image of Highlanders as wild seafaring men with an aptitude for survival and an almost total indifference to matters of personal hygiene. Most travellers were simultaneously disgusted by the crofters' living conditions and astounded by their scholarship. Almost all usually returned to their native lands with a fondness for Gaeldom's greatest liquid export, whisky.

By the late nineteenth century, Scotland had crept closer to England. Better transport and communication between the countries had lowered the image of the Highlands from being one of heather-clad savagery to something closer to a bunch of ginger-haired trolls with a fearsome interest in sheep. Writers, however, still found the place fascinating. The west's stock of ready-formed stories enchanted everyone from Sir Walter Scott to Virginia Woolf, Stevenson to Orwell. The west left its mark on them, and their writing has left its mark on the west. Much of the tartan-and-teacake tourism around the Highlands is still based on Robert Louis Stevenson's image of Argyll in *Kidnapped* – an image which was, in turn, based on his own time as a reluctant apprentice engineer on the isle of Earraid. And Compton Mackenzie's tenure on Barra led to the ultimate wreckers' text, *Whisky Galore.*

Briefly, *Whisky Galore* is the comic tale of two small Outer Hebridean islands during the Second World War. Great and Little Todday live according to the timetable of the sea, in which everything – birth, death, work, relationships – is dictated by the ferry schedule and the intermittent arrival of supplies from the mainland. Like most islanders, the inhabitants of the Toddays have also become skilled at making the best of unscheduled deliveries. 'There was hardly a house on Little Todday which did not contain a certain amount of undeclared treasure trove from the sea,' Mackenzie writes. 'Turpentine, cheese, lard, tinned asparagus, salt (very salt) butter, tyres, pit props, paper, tomato juice, machine oil, lifebelts, in fact almost everything that could be thought of except spirituous liquors.' This being wartime, the island's inhabitants are subject to the same strict rationing as the rest of the country, and despite their desultory attempts at temperance, are now down to the last few drops of whisky.

Matters on the island have reached crisis point when, fortuitously, the SS *Cabinet Minister* runs ashore in the Sound of Todday while en route to America. On board are 50,000 cases of whisky for export. The islanders react predictably, working night and day to 'liberate' the whisky before either the official salvors or the mainland customs officers can stop them: 'It may be doubted if such a representative collection of various whiskies has ever been assembled before . . . there were spherical bottles and dimpled bottles and square bottles and oblong bottles and flagon-shaped bottles and high-waisted bottles and ordinary bottles, and the glass of every bottle was stamped with a notice which made it clear that whisky like this was intended to be drunk in the United States of America and not by the natives of the land where it was distilled, matured, and blended.'

Some they drank immediately, some got sold off to friends on the mainland, but most was hidden around the two islands: 'Peat stacks became a little larger than they usually were at this time of year. Ricks suggested that the cattle had eaten less hay than usual this winter. Loose floorboards were nailed down. Corks bobbed about in waters where hitherto none had bobbed. Turf recently disturbed was trodden level again as carefully as on a golf-course.' Meanwhile, the island's sole law enforcer, the humourless Captain Waggett, did his utmost to ensure that the looting was stopped and the offenders prosecuted. Sooner or later, the peat stacks had been drunk dry and Captain Waggett had exacted his legal hangover.

The story, of course, is based on truth. At 7.40 a.m. on 5 February 1941, an 8,000-ton cargo vessel called the SS *Politician* ran aground on a reef in the Sound of Eriskay between Barra and South Uist while en route to New Orleans. Though subsequent attention has focussed on only one particular part of her cargo, the Politician was in fact carrying a mixed load including Jamaican banknotes, cotton, motorcycle parts, tobacco, medicines, and various other items including school exercise books and baths. But cotton or schoolbooks were never going to be as appealing as the 264,000 bottles of finest malt whisky from two bombed-out warehouses in Leith and Glasgow stacked in Hold no. 5.

In the confusion of wind, rain and conflicting chart data immediately following the grounding, the *Politician*'s captain lost all sense of place. When radioing for help, he initially gave his position as south of Barra instead of north. Pounded by heavy seas and by now immovably lodged on a submerged reef, the ship was in imminent danger of breaking up beneath his feet. The captain gave the order to abandon ship and made his way with the crew across the Sound to South Uist. Having reached safety, he made a full report both to the Admiralty and to the insurers, who sent out a group of Glasgow salvors to inspect the damage. Having concluded that the ship itself was now a write-off, the man in charge of the salvage operation, Captain Kay, took off as much of the general cargo as possible. He refused the request of local customs officers for an armed guard to protect the whisky left on board, believing it to be both contaminated and irretrievable.

Kay was wrong. It had not taken long for news of the grounding – and of the cargo – to be transmitted across both islands. Within a few hours, small parties of 'liberators' began visiting the stricken *Politician*. Within a couple of days, everyone on both Barra and South Uist knew what Captain Kay did not: that the whisky was not only salvageable, it was drinkable too. So drinkable that it was soon rumoured to possess almost magical qualities. It was said that whisky from the '*Polly*' did not cause hangovers, that it was a sure-fire cure for rheumatism, and that it would sort any disorder in cattle from croup to warble fly. With or without the aid of magic, the *Polly*'s fame spread fast. Within days of the grounding, boats were arriving not just from those islands closest to Barra but from Lewis, Mull, and the mainland. For a few sublime weeks, there was so much whisky to be had that people drank themselves to stupefaction and the hold still did not run dry. In fact, the sheer quantity of whisky gave the islanders a new difficulty: there were simply not enough hiding places for it all. Raiding parties were taking off thirty or forty cases at a time and hiding them as best they could in the fields and barns back home – down rabbit holes, round the backs of matchboard walls and propping up the centre of corn stooks.

John Macleod, an ex-RNLI coxswain who still lives on the edges of Barra's main town, Castlebay, is eighty-four, with clipped grey hair and a voice half-sunk by age. One eye is blind, and the thumb on his left hand is lopped off at the knuckle. For much of his day, he sits watching the cars turning off the road towards Vatersay outside his windows. The flotsam around the house tells the tale of a life lived on water: gateposts topped with fading pink plastic buoys, fish boxes used to store firewood, a coven of cats waiting by the door.

Macleod remembers the *Polly* well: 'There was a terrible shortage of whisky in the war. If you went into a bar in Castlebay, they had only about a dozen wee tots a day, first come, first served, and that was it for the night. So they were in short supply. And oh, the *Politician* was a godsend! It was meant to be going to New York for to improve the American's morale in the war. But it was much more needed to improve Scots morale!' He laughs long and happily. The day the *Polly* grounded 'was at the beginning of the war, like, and I happened to be at home at the time. I came from being at the fishing at the time, and there was all the fishing boats there from Eriskay. There was a lot of excitement when they realised it was whisky, you see. Aye. She had all kinds on her – rayon, tyres, all kinds of general cargo. There was rolls and rolls of rayon. And there was the Jamaican money there, swilling around.'

Were people interested in that? He shakes his head. 'Ach, no, they were just pushing it out of the way. They were mostly after the whisky. We got such a lot we were giving it away. There was people giving it out on the mainland, people sending it to their friends, you know, as a Christmas present. It was a great cargo, indeed aye. My gosh yes. But it was hard work, taking the whisky off. The boat was full of oil, she was holed, and she'd burst her tanks. Heavy duty fuel oil, you see – she was a steamship with the boilers, and the bottles were bobbing about in this thick stuff, like tar, like treacle. Oh, ho . . . what a mess!' He laughs again. 'So everyone who went down to look got covered in the oil. So people knew when you'd been down to her, because you were covered in the stuff. You were well prepared, though, with oilskins and sea boots and all that. You could clean the oilskins, but the other clothes, you couldn't. You just threw the lot over the side.'

So how much did he personally manage to take off her? 'Loads. And I wasn't drinking then.' Really? What, none of it? 'No. I was giving it away. I was only twenty, twenty-one at the time. No, wait, I was twenty-four. Now I would, I'd have maybe a pint of beer or suchlike, but at that time, no, I was over twenty-four before I went into a pub. My father was never in a pub in his life, never smoked in his life. It wasn't a religious thing; he just couldn't be bothered with it. That's the way we were brought up, like, and three of my uncles too, they never touched the drink.'

But surely he must have tried some of the *Politician*'s stock? 'Oh, yes. You shared it out. And when I tried it, I didn't like it at all – I'd drink it now, I'd take a shot of whisky now, at night time before I go to bed. And I'd take a pint of beer in the pub now. But when I tried it first, oh gosh, I mind I couldn't believe it what the hell they were drinking that for!'

Macleod's temperance marked him out. As with the rest of the Highlands, Barra's affection for whisky has been a theme throughout all its histories. The geologist John MacCulloch's account of the Western Isles, published in 1819, notes that, 'It is a drawback on the merits of the Barra men, that they are addicted to the use of whisky ... the quantity of this strong spirit which they could drink without apparent inconvenience is incredible ... A damp climate is considered not only a justification for the morning dram, but as the disease for which whisky, whenever it can be got, is the only remedy.'

Dr Jeremy Hidson, who works both as one of Barra's local GPs and as an auxiliary coastguard, still considers the drink to be a major part of island life. Hidson has customised his surgery in Castlebay with a bright Victorian rug, a selection of prints and an old tin spinning top. The impression given is one of both officialdom and informality, which is exactly how Hidson comes across himself. He is a rumpled, middle-aged man, with a habit of closing his eyes when he's speaking and of absently brushing his hair back into place across his forehead. The gestures are all those of a shy man, though Hidson, when he speaks, is not. He has been living and working on the island for twelve years, and his fondness for both the place and the people are palpable.

So does Barra have any unique medical problems? Hidson nods: 'I think the further west you go in Scotland, the more people drink. I used to work in the Borders, and there was never nearly such a big problem with it. And it's not just the men; it's the women, unfortunately, who we don't come across – it's more hidden. But if you did blood tests on people to see what their liver function was like, the women would be not that far behind. It's difficult to tell what proportion of people are drinking seriously. But if you try to find fit, reliable people for things like the lifeboat crew, the coastguard, the airport fire crew, that's ten of us, twenty for the lifeboat, it can be a struggle.' By fit and reliable, presumably he means sober? 'Yes. I mean, everyone will have a drink – I'm not saying that, but to be rendered incapable . . . And if you're not capable of driving a vehicle, then you're not going to be capable of any emergency services. You spend half your time thinking: can't have them, because of the drink. And then of course there's all the drink-related accidents. We know that there are ten deaths on the road in the UK per day, but because everyone knows each other here, it's more focussed.' Does he think the high level of alcoholism is connected to the hard winters and the early nights? Hidson rubs his forehead. 'Er . . . they don't usually wait till it gets dark.' He smiles. 'When I first came here, I think people were a little bit reluctant to say they were bored here, but if you actually talk to locals here in February, they're bored out of their minds. They really are. They've had Christmas, the weather's still bad, it's a long time till Easter – people will admit that they're bored. It's hard going.'

There is an old rule – backed up by statistical evidence – which states that the further north one goes, the higher the incidence of alcoholism and depression. Summer in the Highlands is enchanting enough to make even the most fundamentalist urbanite run away to a lonely sea isle, but the endless confining nights of winter can be hard. The twenty-first century has made the outside world more accessible, but that accessibility has not meant that life on the islands has got either easier or cheaper. Which, of course, provides an extra incentive for the locals to get hold of materials by more creative means. What does Hidson think Barra's inhabitants would do if a general cargo vessel struck the rocks tonight? 'I suspect that if they thought there wasn't much chance of being found out, they would go for it. One can see why, really. I think it's a long distance from the centres of power, and if they knew that something was there I don't think people would have any qualms at all. And other people would turn a blind eye. I think at the moment we've only got one policeman here, and he may well be doing something else – he can't be on duty all the time. So it would be easy enough to do things, especially when you've got Barra, Vatersay, and the islands south of it, which is a fair-sized bit of coastline that people could go down to.'

In the past, visiting officials have usually taken one of two attitudes to the islands. Either they have embarked on puritanical vendettas against Highland debauchery, or they have gone native. It was just Barra's bad luck that the customs officer who eventually dealt with the *Politician*'s cargo was one of the first type. The islander's bacchanalia was interrupted by Charles McColl, who, like his fictional equivalent Captain Waggett, comes across in print as a scrupulous, honest and entirely humourless man. Furious at Captain Kay's refusal to remove the contents of Hold No. 5 and having recruited the help of Ivan Gledhill, his customs superior on Skye, McColl began hunting down the whisky liberators. McColl galvanised a second salvage company into re-examining the chances of retrieving the whisky and eventually recovered 13,500 cases of whisky. Several cases were sent over to the mainland to be stored in customs warehouses; some were drunk by the salvors themselves. McColl arrested as many wreckers as he could round up and handed them over to the mainland police, insisting that they should be charged under the punitive terms of the Customs and Excise Act.

The police, who had better things to do than prosecute men for having a drink, ignored McColl. McColl persisted. In total, nineteen men were eventually sentenced to between twenty days' and two months' imprisonment. So passionate was McColl's one-man temperance campaign that he insisted on having what remained of the *Politician* blown up in order to ensure that no-one could retrieve the few stray bottles left from the second salvage attempt. The zeal with which McColl and Gledhill had sought to apply the law turned the final chapters of the *Politician*'s saga into something far more rancorous. Even now, some residual anger still lingers against McColl and Gledhill and still inclines the most law-abiding West Highlander to doubt the wisdom of officials.

But once in a while, it is possible to feel some sympathy for those officials charged with preventing wrecking. Part of *Whisky Galore*'s success was its expression of a wider truth. Life in the Hebrides was – and is – hard, sometimes unbearably so. As Hidson points out, the costs of importing almost all goods and raw materials puts a heavy premium on island life. 'If you think of the amount of money it costs to transport anything here . . . you have a small box that you want on a carrier here, it will probably cost you £5 just for the carriage. I've got a small lawnmower I've just ordered from Argos in Oban, and that's

£11.50 carriage charge extra. The mower's only £30. There's a big extra whack on everything. All food, all materials, everything. There's not much to be had for a living here – natural resources are fairly low, and everything has to come in by sea. If you go into the local shops, you'll probably find that the prices are the highest you've seen anywhere in the UK.'

And though the land may look bewitching in the summer sunlight, it is stony and difficult to work while exposure to the Atlantic winds makes it almost impossible for trees to grow. Those plants which do survive skulk close to the ground, gripping the clefts between rocks and taking shelter in gullies rather than facing the full salt fury of the sea. Lack of anything from which to build boats, roofs, fence posts, window casements, floorboards or carts would alone have been enough to turn most people into wreckers; poverty and resourcefulness did the rest. And so the Hebrideans became adept at turning their disadvantages (remoteness, delays in communication, high cost of raw materials, a small population) into advantages (adaptability, secrecy, a tight community, seafaring skill). Everything that could be used, would be used. Seaweed made good fertiliser, driftwood became fuel or fencing, sand and seashells turned into concrete and mortaring. Ships carrying heavy deck cargos – timber, containers, ropes, pallets – would often lose them overboard during rough weather. Whatever then washed up on Hebridean beaches was, as far as the islanders were concerned, theirs for the taking.

Those who attempted to prevent local communities from picking off occasional loads of deck timber or stripping a wreck had a hard task. Not only did they have to contend with the difficulties of policing an immense area of remote coastland but they were forced to deal with a population who had more right than most to regard shipwrecks as a God-given bounty. Some sense of the difficulties can be gained from a nineteenth-century list outlining the areas of responsibility for the Receiver of Wreck for Greenock. As well as dealing with all wreck on the Clyde, the Receiver also had to cover Arran, Tarbert, Skerryvore, Tiree, Ardnamurchan, Sunart, Lismore, Appin, Bute, Mull, Coll, Islay, Jura, and 'all other islands, bays, lochs, rivers, harbours, creeks, roadsteads, sounds, and channels, lying or being within the said limits respectively'. Undermanned, underfunded and underequipped, it was probably not the officials' faults that many of their attempts at enforcement came closer to comedy than to law.

Thomas Gray, an official at the Board of Trade's Wreck Department, paid a visit to the Outer Hebridean islands in August 1866. On his return to Glasgow, he submitted the following report:

> I regret to have to report that matters relating to wreck and salvage in those islands [the Hebrides], especially in South Uist and Barra, are as unsatisfactory as they can be. The inhabitants are mostly very poor; they frequently live in huts with their animals and subsist from hand to mouth. They look upon a wreck as a common right, and do not fail to appropriate what they can ... Some of the highest class, the tenant farmers, are, I learn, but little better than the poorest class in their dealings with wreck. It is true that they proceed in a more indirect manner to obtain any benefits likely to arise from wrecks, but they work towards the one end, of making the most they can. There are no Customs or Coastguard officers in South Uist and Barra: there is only one policeman in Barra, and he works with the inhabitants, and the coast guard cruisers have, so I am informed, only visited the islands three times in ten years ... From what I have seen, and from what I have heard, I am satisfied that an occasional visit by the coast guard would have a great moral effect.

As it is, the people might, so far as the authority of the Board of Trade is concerned, be in Greenland or the Cape of Good Hope. Wrecking in Barra far exceeds anything reported of wrecking in the Bahamas, or anything arising out of the wreck laws of Heligoland.

Matters were not much helped by the apparent ignorance of captains and locals alike in the duties of a Receiver. When giving evidence to an enquiry at the Board of Trade in 1866, the shipmaster Alexander Coulter, whose ship the *Bermuda* had been wrecked on Vatersay, claimed that, 'It was only a day or two before … that I ever heard of there being such an official, through Mr McLellan (a local farmer), and I then said, "I don't see he would be of any use".' Worse even than local indifference was the difficulties posed by traditional bureaucratic enmities. Coastguard officers would argue with the police; the police would argue with Customs and Excise; Customs would argue with Board of Trade officials; the Board of Trade would take issue with the Receivers, and the Receivers would fight with the Lloyd's agents. Two undercurrents run through much of the official correspondence: firstly that tackling the enemies within took up more time than investigating shipwreck, and secondly that each official department believed that every other official department was either in league with the wreckers or too stupid to know one end of a ship from the other.

After the wreck of the *Harmony* on Vatersay in January 1866, Thomas Gray made another journey out to Barra. 'It is a good pull to the nearest land,' he wrote later,

> And it became quite evident to me that no plunder could have taken place if the slightest attempt had been made to stop it. In the first place, anyone at the wreck can be seen from the adjacent land and islands, and anyone coming away from it could be intercepted before he

had time to make off with property. On examining the vessel, I found her to be very large, and to have an old wooden sheathing over the greater part of her hull. She was evidently an oldish vessel from the way in which she was built, and the copper in her was very valuable ... The labour in getting the copper bolts out of this vessel must have been considerable. They all had to be hammered out from the outside with driving pins and sledge hammers. To do this the men at work must have stood conspicuously on the hull. It must also have been a work not of hours or days, but of weeks. Some of the driving-pins are left about the wreck by the people who stole the bolts ... As I came along from Vatersay, I saw a man running about and shouting, and was informed that he was a watchman employed to look after the remains of the *Harmony*; he was two and a half miles away from her.

Worse even than mad watchmen was an older, more familiar problem. In his deposition to the Board of Trade during the enquiry into the *Harmony* wreck, William Burnie, factor to a local landlord, reported that the island's only policeman had been of little help, since at the time he was 'in liquor'. Below was a footnote from Thomas Gray: 'These definitions puzzled me a little. As far as I can make out, it appears that in Barra a man is not "drunk" unless he falls down and cannot get up. When he is abusive and violent, and does not know what he is about, he is only "in liquor".'

The official correspondence also makes clear just how many Receivers faced a choice between turning a blind eye or becoming Charles McColl. Angus Maclean, Receiver of Wreck on Tiree between 1946 and 1960, chose the former course. A comfortable, round-faced man, he sits in the sunlit front room of his house in Scarinish, surrounded by ornaments and ticking clocks, and balances each question carefully before answering. When he does reply, it is always with courtesy, but never with more information than strictly necessary. So what did he do when he heard of a wreck ashore on Tiree or Coll? He smiles. 'I wasn't going about looking for things like that, I was waiting for somebody to come to me with a report of whatever they'd got. And if they didn't come, that was OK.' The smile gets wider. 'There was an awful lot of stuff like timber washed ashore, but most of it really was pretty much useless, saturated with thick black oil, and nobody wanted to touch that stuff.' So the job required some diplomacy? 'Oh yes, yes, yes. I turned a blind eye to many things. You had to, really, you had to. I don't think it would be possible to do it any other way. If you tried to be strict about the whole thing, you'd be liable to get lynched some nights.'

He has a point. Born and bred on the island, Maclean had to balance his status as the only official on the island responsible for enforcing the wreck laws with his role as part of a small local community. Should he have upheld the letter of the law and inform on his friends, or should he have remained quiet, as a native of the islands? Besides, if a major shipwreck incident had occurred on his patch, he had few options available to him. He could have summoned the aid of the island's one policeman or sent for delayed reinforcements from the mainland. But long before some notional troop of 'the Receiver's dragoons' arrived, he would have been outnumbered and overpowered. Worse than that, he would have been ostracised by his own friends and relations. The wisest course of action, as he points out, was to sit safely at home watching the ships pass by.

It wasn't just the Hebrideans who took a good wreck for granted. Further down the west coast, other local communities proved equally enterprising. So enterprising, in fact, that witnesses at the 1839 Commission, appointed to consider the establishment of a rural constabulary, alleged that the wreckers of Cheshire made the efforts of those in the Scillies, Norfolk and Scotland look like polite little trifles. Successive witnesses gave an image of a coastline populated by corrupt magistrates, indifferent shipowners, petrified Lloyd's agents and murderous locals.

Why this should be so is not immediately evident. True, the coastal communities around Liverpool and the Wirral were poor, remote, and believed they had a perfect right to the 'sea's bounty', but so did Orcadians and Cornishmen. True, they had plenty of shipping to choose from and few lawmakers to prevent them, but so did both the Hebrideans and the north-eastern wreckers. And true, they lived on a hard coastline with plenty of hazards and a seascape full of sandbanks, but so did the Deal men and the beach companies of Norfolk. At first glance, there was nothing singular in the geography or environment around Hoylake, Wallasey and Liverpool which should so explicitly have marked it out for lawlessness.

Part of the answer to their ferocity lies not by the shore, but in the nearby city. Like many other coastal areas, the area around Wallasey and Hoylake was populated by a small number of close families bonded to one another through many generations. After taking the evidence of one witness from among 'the lower classes of population' from the area, the commissioners reported that, 'They intermarry, and are nearly all related to each other . . . The[y] pretend to be fishermen, but though the witness has been at Hoylake for some time, he has not seen or tasted any fish.' As elsewhere, the locals made most of their living from wrecking. But unlike anywhere else in Britain, the Cheshire men lived right next to a major city. Not only did Liverpool's port provide plenty of shipping to plunder, it also provided an excellent marketplace for selling off whatever could be stolen. Whereas in Cornwall a salvaged grand piano would end up gracing the wrecker's own house, in Cheshire, that same grand piano would have been flogged off through a network of fences within hours of a ship running aground.

According to the commissioners: 'Much of the property is sold in the villages and adjacent districts, but most of the plunder is taken to Liverpool and there sold at the marine store dealers. A great quantity of plundered property (indeed, nearly all the unsold portion) is concealed underground . . . Strangers come from all parts and deal with them, so that there is no occasion for them to run the risk of taking it to Liverpool, as they might be stopped.' In other words, the Cheshire men had the best of both worlds: they wrecked among friends and sold among strangers.

And there were plenty of strangers. By 1800, the city was handling 140,000 tons of shipping a year, much of which was travelling to or from America and much of which was laden with valuable raw materials and manufactured goods. Since journey times across the Atlantic were fastest from the north west, the vast majority of cargo vessels disembarked from the Mersey.

But it was not freight which made up the bulk of Liverpudlian traffic. It was the Irish. Out of the 4,000 ships a year entering or leaving Liverpool by the end of the eighteenth century, 2,300 were on their way to or from Ireland. The numbers of migrants coming to Liverpool in search of work or a passage to the New World inevitably meant that many got caught between ship and shore, unable to find a job, unable to pay for a passage, and thus unable to contemplate much more than a life of beggary and a punctual death. Unsurprisingly, criminality flourished. Destitution and anonymity gave the lawbreakers' work a barbarous edge, exacerbated by territorial disputes between Cheshire men and Liverpool incomers. John Taylor Gregson, formerly a master mariner and then a Lloyd's agent, stated in his evidence to the Commission that: 'If a Liverpool man were to go to assist, there would be jealousy directly; they do not wish to have those people among them. When the Sophia was on shore, two or three boats' crews used to go off: they were very insolent wreckers from Liverpool; they would go and take the copper off the vessels' bottom . . . I said, "You must not do this, this is plunder." "We are not taking anything." I suppose every man has a right to take what is here, as much as another.'

Not that wrecking was a new phenomenon in the area. It was said that seventeenth-century Liverpool shipowners had protested against the planned construction of a lighthouse near Hoylake on the grounds that the wreckers would only create false copies and thus lure even more ships to a premature end. Like many parts of the country in which both smuggling and wrecking were endemic, there was supposed to be a network of tunnels leading through the soft local sandstone of the beaches to nearby roads or safe houses from which the criminals could make their escape. Over time, the Cheshire wreckers' methods had also become more extreme than in other parts of the country. An unnamed local witness to the Commission declared that:

> On many occasions when wrecks have taken place he has known the produce of their plunder to have been openly hawked about for sale; butter 2d. and 3d. per lb., rum 4s. and 5s. per gallon, fine gown prints 3d. and 4d. per yard, and many other articles in the same proportion; and the bodies of the drowned persons are almost invariably stripped of every thing valuable, money, watches &c. About three or four years since, the 'Grecian,' Captain Salisbury, was wrecked off the Cheshire coast; Captain Salisbury was drowned, and when his body was found it was stripped of every thing,

and whilst on the shore waiting to be conveyed to some house for holding an inquest, his finger was cut off to secure his ring. The body of a female was washed on shore, when a woman at Moreton [a nearby village] was proved to have bitten off the ears to obtain the earrings.

This was wrecking of a different order entirely. Pilfering things from grounded general cargo vessels was one thing; gnawing dead women's ears off was quite another.

Matters reached crisis point in January 1839 when three large first-class packets bound for America and carrying both general cargo and emigrants were driven into the soft sand of the Burbo and West Hoyle banks during a hurricane. The Hoylake lifeboat was despatched to the scene and managed to rescue many of the survivors. Despite the numbers of corpses washed ashore over the next few days and the presence of the Liverpool police, the local wreckers were out in force. The *Liverpool Mercury*, suspicious about the circumstances surrounding the wrecks and hinting that the light vessel guarding the East Hoyle bank had come adrift at the vital moment once too often for credulity, noted that:

it is scarcely two months since she parted her moorings before a gale and came into port. To us this is very extraordinary and inexplicable ... We lament to find that those infamous wretches, the wreckers, have been at their fiendlike occupation, both on the Lancashire and the Cheshire shores, plundering what the elements had spared, instead of seeking to alleviate the calamities of their fellow creatures ... about a score of police officers were sent over to protect property and to disperse the ruffianly marauders ... Twenty-five or twenty-six of the wreckers were taken into custody, but, from having been lodged in an insecure place, twenty of them contrived to regain their liberty.

And elsewhere, it was noted that:

> The wreckers who infest the Cheshire coast were
> not long in rendering the catastrophe a source of
> emolument to themselves. The property of the pas-
> sengers and crew were plundered by them to an
> alarming extent. The steward, who had in his trunks
> sixty watches and other articles of jewellery, found on
> regaining the vessel that the whole had disappeared.

During the hearings it also transpired that the Commissioner
of the Liverpool Police did not have a very high opinion
of those whom he was supposed to serve. Asked if the wreckers
had any respect for the existing law enforcement methods,
Mr Dowling was unequivocal. 'A wreck takes place, and the
wreckers, unless prevented by the assistance of the police
from Liverpool, plunder and do as they please . . . if the vessel
is sufficiently injured to form a wreck, the accumulation of
wreckers is the most instantaneous thing you can imagine. They
see from their residences what is likely to happen when a vessel
is on the coast. They look out for it and they are there before
we can possibly get to them.'

As successive witnesses made clear, effective policing had
proved impossible. Since Wallasey possessed no local force of
its own, it was the constabulary from Liverpool who made the
journey over the Mersey every time a ship ran aground – a trip
which took time, organisation and expense. If the police were
lucky enough to reach the scene before every last rivet had been
stripped and hidden, then they were usually undermanned and
overwhelmed. Unlike other areas, there was no provision for
backup to be provided by the army or the coastguard. Faced
with hordes of feral locals, the police had occasionally applied to
local magistrates to create one-off 'special constables', a process
which only took up more time and which did not, in the long
term, prove particularly effective since the local Cheshire

magistracy resented the incursions onto their turf. On the rare occasions when the police had been able to make arrests, the local magistrates threw the resulting cases out of court. As Dowling put it:

> On the occasion of a man having been taken into custody for stealing a tarpaulin which was found in his possession, a magistrate of the county of Cheshire came to me while the man was in custody, and said that it was a trifling thing, and asked to look at it. It was shown to him. He said that the man ought not to have been taken into custody; that he was a very good man, generally speaking, and that it was too trifling a thing to take a man into custody for, and endeavoured to persuade me that I ought not to proceed against the man for it.

In theory, the police should also have been assisted by Lloyd's agents, who were responsible for collating details of shipping casualties and for doing what they could to ensure wrecks were correctly salved. In practice, the local agent was often too terrified to step outside his front door. According to Dowling, 'the agent employed upon the coast there for Lloyd's ... has frequently applied to me, stating that it was perfectly useless his attempting to interfere; he was in danger of his life if he attempted to go out of his house. He was threatened that unless he retired, he should be marked. He said it was no use interfering even with a number of men, unless they went armed. Such was the state of things, that he resigned the agency.' Given the chaos of existing law-enforcement methods, it was small wonder that the wreckers treated the police with such contempt.

Matters altered slowly. Over the course of the nineteenth century, communication, transport and law enforcement around the Wirral area did improve, even if human nature did not. When the brig *Elizabeth Buckham* was driven ashore in November 1867 with a cargo of rum and coconuts, events took the traditional course. According to a local witness, one woman who lacked any receptacle from which to drink the rum removed her own shoe and used that. Most of the wreckers became so drunk that many fell unconscious on the beach. The combined might of the new Wallasey police force (all five of them) spent the evening hauling them out of the way of the rising tide.

In many parts of the west it was not the intervention of the police or the coastguard which prevented wrecking, it was the lighthouses. Until the 1840s, wreckers on Tiree had the additional advantage of the Skerryvore Reef, eleven miles off the south-west tip of the island and the most efficient shipwrecker on the whole of the west coast. When Robert Stevenson, the National Lighthouse Board's chief engineer, conducted a preliminary survey of the reef in 1830, he found that rents on the side of Tiree closest to Skerryvore were higher than those further away. Wrecks were so frequent and their cargos so lucrative that wrecking had become an accepted part of the local economy. Robert's son Alan calculated that at least thirty vessels had been wrecked on the reef between 1804 and 1844, and that, 'It is also well known that the Tyree Fishermen were in the constant practice of visiting the Skerryvore, after gales, in quest of wrecks and their produce, in finding which they were but too often successful.'

The Duke of Argyll owned Tiree and his factor was responsible for setting local rents. For those tenants who lived closest to the reef, the sum included a premium for the benefits of any wreck from Skerryvore. Often, however, the factor also claimed that wreck for himself or for the Argyll estates, and squabbles could break out between tenants and factor over the extent of the rake-off. It took Alan Stevenson four years to build the lighthouse on Skerryvore and a further two years before the lamp was lit. Almost immediately the numbers of wrecks around Skerryvore slowed. From being an island considered so closely associated with wrecking that half the houses were built of ships' timbers, Tiree became an island with one of the lowest accident rates in the Hebrides.

For a while, the lighthouses did the wreckers out of a job, though two world wars did make a significant difference to local casualty figures. Between 1939 and 1945, 3,500 British and Allied merchant ships were sunk in the Battle of the Atlantic. The British merchant navy lost over 32,000 men, and the Royal Navy almost 51,000. Only a small percentage of those losses occurred around the Scottish coastline, and escorted vessels always had a better chance of surviving the journey than unescorted ones. But the casualties remained appalling and the cost was always too high for comfort.

In many parts of Britain, there is also the suggestion that the various lighthouse authorities were instructed to dim or extinguish their lights at moments when it was thought German warships would be lurking around the Minch or the Hebridean Sea. By 1941, the British had broken the Enigma code, and were thus able to provide some advance warning of German intentions to crews making the journey. In theory, the lights would be dimmed every time enemy ships were likely to be approaching and then turned back on to full power when the Allied convoys passed.

James Taylor, chief executive of the Northern Lighthouse Board, remains unsure of exactly what went on, and points out that much of the information remains classified even now. 'As I understand it, the lights didn't operate normally, they operated on reduced range. But if you knew a convoy was coming – and that was something the lightkeeper was told – then you put the light back on to full beam. We've still got those lights. If you've ever been to a lighthouse and there's a little plastic lamp in the corner, that's them. They're still there. The emergency light in the corner was called the Scheme R Light, and every now and again, the Admiralty, the Western Approaches command, would say to the Commissioners that this was the light that they wanted to use, and it had a range of about four miles as opposed to 24. That's what you'd normally use. But then when a convoy was coming, you'd put the big light on.' Was there ever a point when the lights were totally switched off? 'I don't think so. The short answer is, I don't know. They may well have been.'

With so many additional shipping casualties during the war, there was also plenty of extra wreck. Sigurd Scott, then the young son of Skerryvore's principal keeper, remembers what happened when an American liberty ship was blown up in Bunnessan Bay off the western edge of Mull in 1942. The keepers had a 14-foot Shetland yawl equipped with both sails and oars, and broad enough to allow two men to sit abreast of one another. For several evenings after the explosion, the keepers made frequent trips to the stricken ship. 'I have the clearest memory,' Scott wrote,

> of their coming back in the bright light dawns to Earraid pier, the boat laden with an exotic miscellany of plunder, the gunwhales only a few inches above the water. Everything was transferred to the Lighthouse store near the pier. The variety of the loot was extra-ordinary. There were bales of calico, bags of white flour, packets of dried eggs, oranges, plywood, shellac, tools of all descriptions, hammers (magnetic and claw), planes, nails . . . It was my father who was appointed quartermaster. The spoils were divided out into piles, one for each family, their contents depending on the size and constitution of each household. After several days we were summoned to uplift our ration. Mothers,

fathers, boys and girls all spent a day bringing home their haul, traipsing up and down the rocky road from the pier. Wheelbarrows, pails, sacks, bowls – every type of container served. I did my duty pulling a toy lorry my father had made for me on the rock. There were no dire repercussions, no sudden appearance of customs officials or police, but the ladies did suggest that a large hole be dug in the garden for the disposal of all contraband should authority threaten to pounce! For months we lived off the spoils in a style few could enjoy in those days . . .

The fact that lighthouse keepers were explicitly banned from doing anything that might bring the Lighthouse Board into disrepute was beside the point; this was war, and no-one was counting. 'Of course,' Scott admitted,

> where beachcombing was a natural part of the way of life, we were always picking up the fruits of war. My father scarcely ever came ashore from the rock without some object, toy, stool, chair, carved ornament, which he had wrought out of the flotsam and jetsam swept by the Atlantic Westerlies on to Skerryvore, mindings of the high price paid by our merchant seamen on convoy. Not everything beached was useful or harmless. In school, a poster depicted an assortment of dangerous weaponry which we as youngsters were sternly warned to leave alone. Not that we paid heed . . . until a rogue floating mine exploded on the rocks a hundred yards below the houses!

The lighthouse authorities were also aware that normal human impulses would occasionally override the keepers' sense of duty. In theory, a reputation for temperance and probity was a vital prerequisite for the life of a lighthouse keeper. James Taylor considers that there are no verifiable cases of the keepers ever tampering with the lights because any desire to do so should have been vetted out of them when they were first employed. 'There are no cases of tampering that we know of. Of course, one of the reasons there is this puritanical view of the light-keepers – they weren't to drink, they were to be upright and sober men of good character etcetera – was, in the early days, so they weren't corruptible and so they couldn't be bribed to put the light on or off. But there are so many stories, mostly from the Western Isles, about ships running aground, and you're never sure whether it's all *Whisky Galore* – whether truth follows art or what.'

Sigurd Scott made the point that, along with most other coastal dwellers, the keepers considered beachcombing to be a good example of the invocation to 'waste not, want not'. To have ignored the detritus which landed on their rocks or beaches would almost have been regarded as a kind of moral profligacy. Most Scots are by nature suspicious of waste; most are inclined to believe that all things perishable should be husbanded with care, whether it be food or love. To ignore what appeared on their doorsteps would thus be considered as much of a psychological failing as to leave the children uneducated or the errands unattended.

Alasdair Maclean, whose father ran a croft on Ardnamurchan, explained something of the local philosophy in his memoirs: 'In theory, presumably, all flotsam and jetsam is the property of the Receiver of Wrecks, working through his agents the police and the coastguard. In practice it is not so simple. If you found, for example, a washed-in dinghy you would expect to report it. A tragedy might be involved; in any event the boat would be valuable and its owner would wish it returned. Mere firewood, on the other hand, the authorities would not thank you for wasting their time with. It is what lies between these extremes that can cause problems.' Maclean also remembered the local etiquette attached to beachcombing. 'In Ardnamurchan of old, if you took your beachcombing finds well clear of the high-water mark, so eliminating any possible ambiguity about their status, they were there till you chose to fetch them or, if you did not choose, till they mouldered where they lay. Generations might pass and no-one would touch them. I have seen some handsome pieces of timber disappear into the ground almost, through decay, after having been put up by someone who had died before managing to retrieve them.'

Alasdair Sinclair lives on Tiree and helps to run the small local museum. He's a thin, trim man, with scraped grey hair lifted into tufts over his ears and the vitality of someone with an outdoor life and a well-nourished mind. His own house – one of the distinctive, low-lying island houses – was built partly from bits of wreck. 'There are partitions between one room and another upstairs which are an inch thick. They really are most beautifully figured wood – a sort of reddish, fairly hard type. I'm told that that stuff came ashore in big logs. They'd already been sawn, the best part of a foot square. That stuff would be regarded as a soft wood, but it's certainly pretty hard stuff and it has lasted all these years without being painted. I did put some clear varnish on it to seal it off a bit, but the figuring of it, the grain, is beautiful stuff.'

He also remembers the kind of things which came ashore during the war and the uses the islanders put them to. 'Of course, a lot of warships were being sunk and anything that would float off such a ship came ashore. Typically, there would be lifeboats and life rafts, copper tanks and the like. Quite often they were filled with kapok – a fibrey stuff – I think they were put into the tanks so that if they were punctured by gunfire, they wouldn't sink. And among the other odds and ends that might have been in lifeboats there were the cargoes of the ships themselves. There was a huge cargo of grapefruit that arrived on Tiree in the middle of the war, but that was unfortunate to an extent. Had they been sweet oranges that would have been fine, but they were grapefruit, and the last thing that you could get during the war was sugar. Any of us who were around at the time could remember the shortage of sugar more than anything else, so the grapefruit weren't a great success.'

From the islanders' point of view, perhaps the most successful wreck during the war was the *Nevada 2*, a 3,500-ton general cargo steamship on her way to join a convoy heading for West Africa which ran aground off the northern tip of Coll in 1942. She was packed with all kinds of supplies, including vehicles, food, cement, cigarettes and clothing.

The islanders fell on her. As Sinclair recalls it: 'Word got round of this wonderful bonanza of stuff there at the far end of Coll. So off went everyone to find out, as many as could get a boat round the corner down there. But of course the salvage people and the Receiver of Wreck – not just the local chap in Coll but the official one, and the customs officers and everyone – they were in on it too, so it was a battle of wits as to who would get what. And it was quite remarkable what that ship had. She had lots of whisky, and a good proportion of that was picked up by expeditions from here and roundabout. She had an immense quantity of cigarettes; in fact, so many tins came ashore that you could have chain-smoked all day long. And cloth – great rolls of very brightly coloured cloth. I remember seeing this rather old-fashioned-looking cloth, different from all the rest. Perhaps it had been in a store for a very long time and then bought and put on that steamer. This stuff was quite dark; shiny, but not silk. It was perhaps some kind of printed cotton, but it had machine embroidery all over it, like something which had been made in late Victorian times. One of my aunts was a dressmaker, and she used to have people from here and the other islands coming in and saying, I want you to make me a dress, I'm going to a wedding, or I need this or that. They would duly get measured and if they had a piece of cloth, that was fine, and if not, she would get something from her own stock. This woman, she got all measured up for a dress, and then she said to Annie, "You can make it out of that," and she produced a roll of this cloth on a wooden stick. It was maybe not a complete roll, but there was still plenty of it. And she said, "You can take as much as you want of that, and take some for yourself while you're at it".'

Even now, there are still things to be found for those who look. Go for a walk around many Hebridean beaches and you could probably return with enough inessential household objects to stock a small ironmongery. A representative wander round Tiree yields several car tyres, a section of vinyl flooring, two tins of paint, a loo seat, infinite quantities of rope and plastic twine, an excellent stock of undamaged driftwood, several shoes (suitable mainly for the one-legged and fashion-free), twelve plastic buoys, cattle-feed bags, light bulbs, oil cans, three large car batteries, an exhaust pipe, and a large colour television apparently in full working order. It is also possible to see the uses to which this flotsam and wreck has been put. Look closely at much of Tiree's fencing, and you may note that the strainer posts could once have done duty as a mainmast. Several farm gates have a bespoke quality; one of the uprights has a curve on it very much like the curve on a small boat's stem post, and the crossbar is surely the spitting image of a wooden tiller. Once in a while, you may pass a post holding up a washing line formed from high-quality hardwood and about a foot in diameter, or note that the lintel above a doorway is thick enough to support the weight of a small castle.

Here among the sea's twice-a-day leavings is a silent record of the ways in which we currently use the sea. Against the cautious monochrome of the stones and the sand, the plastic flotsam stands out with discordant clarity. Welly boots and washing-up bottles, rope and old feed bags. These things won't rot, they'll just remain, rolling around the rocks until the next big storm throws them out on a different beach. Every creek and gully has been made a resting place for twenty-first-century detritus: plastic fishing boxes, bright rope, rubber gloves. Looking at these, it is difficult not to see something melancholy. All of this everlasting garbage just serves as a reminder of the mainland's indifference to the consequences of their consumption. Much of the litter will have been hurled overboard from boats and trawlers; some will have been surreptitiously dumped from cliffs and outfall pipes. None of it will go away.

But even this rubbish has something interesting to say. Among the flotsam left above high-water mark on Tiree are a Danish apple-juice carton and a plastic Norwegian milk bottle. Were they dumped overboard from Scandinavian trawlers fishing in this area? Or have they somehow drifted all the way from their native makers round the east coast, through the Pentland Firth and into the west? What great journey did those inconsequential things make in order to end up here? Scientists have already begun to use the transoceanic movements of plastic litter to study the patterns of currents. They've read the messages in bottles, watched the migrations of Lego blocks or plastic bath ducks and used their trajectories as a way of understanding the behaviour of the Gulf Stream and the North Atlantic gyre.

An American website, www.beachcombers.org, collates stories of curious things found on the world's beaches and the uses they have been put to. The majority of the objects were lost from container vessels which shed their loads during storms. Around 10,000 containers are lost overboard every year and though many sink immediately, some burst open, releasing their contents out into the sea. In 1992, some 29,000 yellow plastic bath ducks and 'bathtub friends' were lost overboard from a ship in the Pacific. Having sailed in a complete circle around the North Pacific, the ducks are now nearing their final nesting place.

If some of this plastic flotsam can be reused to tell us something useful about the habits of the ocean, then it should also find other purposes as well. Looking back inland from the beach on Tiree, it is possible to see the way in which these leavings have found other lives as fencing or furniture or just as beautiful sea-washed objects existing in their own right. They also act as commemorative proof that, though the west may be a more peaceable place than it was in the days before lighthouses and ear-chewing thieves, there are parts of this place which will always stay dark.

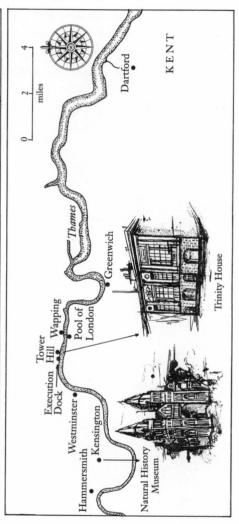

Thames Estuary

Southend-on-Sea

Canvey Island

ESSEX

KENT

Gravesend

Grays

0 2 4
miles

The Thames

Hammersmith
Kensington

Westminster

Execution
Dock

Tower
Hill Wapping

Pool of
London

Greenwich

Thames

Dartford

KENT

0 2 4
miles

Natural History
Museum

Trinity House

SIX

———⊶◉⊷———

Royal Fish

S
omewhere in the lost corners of the Natural History
Museum, Richard Sabin passes me a jar of pygmy sperm
whale's eyeballs. As they bump against the walls of their
transparent grave, the eyeballs look like strange fruit – giant
rotted lychees, perhaps, or some weird deep-fried kiwi. Parts
of the soft tissue around the cornea have begun to unfurl, and as
the eyes come to rest again, they squint at me darkly through
the glass. After the first shock has passed, it occurs to me that
what seems surprising is not that a pair of disembodied whale's
eyes are rolling around at the bottom of a jam jar in central
London, but that they are so small. These things once belonged
to a beast twice the length of Sabin's office, but they are not
much bigger than the eye of a sheep. I put them down, and look
around. Sabin's office has plenty to hold the attention: two jars
of noodlish-looking nematode parasites; a giant pair of antelope
horns; a squid beak; a whale's rib honeycombed with age and
wrapped in tissue paper; two or three posters describing the
various species of cetacean; a computer, and a framed copperplate document listing exemptions to the 'Royal Fishes' Act.

It is that Act which explains the eyeballs. Royal Fish – or,
more correctly, Fishes Royal – are those cetaceans (whales,
sturgeon, porpoises, dolphins, and 'generally whatsoever other
fish having in themselves great or immense size or fat') which
were once claimed by the Crown. These were not whales or
porpoises killed during commercial hunting, but those which

183

had stranded themselves along the shores of Britain either deliberately or accidentally, dead or alive. It is one of the many anomalies in Britain's salvage laws that, along with all flotsam, jetsam, lagan and derelict, cetaceans are also classified as wreck and have exactly the same legal status as a container full of trainers. In the twenty-first century, the psychological leap from a ship spilling its cargo of whisky or car parts to a decaying minke whale on a Hebridean beach is a sizeable one. But until fairly recently, the leap between animal and mineral was less extreme.

Until well into the 1960s, the British hunted whales not just to eat them, but to strip them of everything they offered, since almost every part of a whale could be used for something. Baleen (a rigid, horn-like material from the upper jaw of certain whale species) could be moulded in the same way as plastic, and would either be cut into strips to be used for the splinting in Victorian corsetage, or used as the guard plates at the back of military helmets. Teeth could be decorated with scrimshaw (a form of engraving considered no more than an old whaler's novelty until recently, but now beginning to command high prices among collectors). Tendons could be threaded into surgical catgut, bones supported furniture, skin became boot-laces or bicycle saddles. In several places, whale bones were used as a traditional building material. There is evidence in Orkney of whale rib and jawbones being used as rafters in houses, and there are arches formed from sperm whale jawbones in Shetland, Harris, North Berwick and North Yorkshire.

Whale and porpoise meat – considered by one early consumer to be of 'very hard digestion, noysome to the stomack, and of a very grosse, excrementall and naughty juice', was nevertheless considered a delicacy in mediaeval times. Ambergris, found in the stomachs of sperm whales and used as a fixative in the perfume trade, was to cetaceans what pearls are to oysters. Sperm whales feed on squid and octopus, and since the beaks of the squid irritate the lining of whales' stomachs, they produce a thick sticky resin which coats the beaks, reducing the irritation. Over time, the resin builds up and is eventually expelled in a lump. Those lumps can be immense; one of the largest single pieces of ambergris ever found weighed 926 lbs. Initially, the ambergris is pale in colour, though it will darken to a heavy golden orange shaded with bands of black and grey, and with the squid beaks still visible inside. Its rarity, and its usefulness, made ambergris exceptionally valuable in the past. A single lump once saved an entire shipping company from bankruptcy, and at one stage it was worth more than its weight in gold.

Perhaps most crucially of all, spermaceti oil is ambergris' liquid equivalent. It is produced and stored in a large chamber in the heads of sperm whales, though zoology has yet to explain why exactly one particular breed of cetacean needs a vast internal fuel tank. A single animal can yield over 500 gallons – part of the reason why sperm whales were hunted with such intent for so long. Once extracted, that oil has exceptional properties. Unlike most animal fats, which burn with too much smoke and not enough fire, spermaceti produces a clear, bright white light. It freezes only at very low temperatures, and it can be stored for years. For many years NASA used spermaceti oil in preference to all other oils because of its low freezing temperatures, and because of the clarity of its light. It was also used as a waterproofing material, and was the fuel which lit the Scottish lighthouses for almost a century. Unfortunately, spermaceti oil has one other quality. It reeks. It is the smell to end all smells; olfactory Armageddon. Many of the old Scottish lights have rooms in which barrels of spermaceti oil were stored. Nearly two hundred years after the oil was phased out in favour of paraffin, those rooms still stink like the grave-pits of Hell.

Because the by-products from whales had such value, the law honoured them with the same treasured status as other forms of wreck. And since the Crown had the authority to appropriate whatever the sea provided, it appropriated dead whales too. The 1324 Statute de Praerogativa Regis not only established the Crown's claim to all wreck on British foreshores, but extended that claim to include 'great fishes'. If a whale was washed up on a British beach, the Queen was supposed to get the tail and the King the head, it being (erroneously) considered that the tail yielded more whalebone for corsetage than the head. By the mid-twentieth century, however, the British found far fewer uses for a dead whale. Baleen had been replaced by plastic, spermaceti oil by electricity, and whale meat by foods that were actually edible. Dead cetaceans came to be regarded as useless for anything other than zoological research. In 1913 the Crown handed over its prerogative to the Natural History Museum in London, giving them first refusal on any future strandings (though in theory, the Queen could still assert her legal right to demand a portion of humpback or minke for herself. According to *Kennedy's Law of Salvage*: 'It has not infrequently happened ... that a captor has offered a sturgeon to Her Majesty the Queen and that her Majesty has been graciously pleased to accept such a gift.') Though the logic behind the practice of treating whales as wreck has long gone, the legal connection remains.

It remains a matter of debate why cetaceans beach themselves, but they always have, and they continue to do so. Since no-one really knows why a whale would voluntarily leave its native element to die in a hostile one – and to keep returning there despite repeated attempts at refloating – the explanations have been varied and imaginative. It is thought that beached cetaceans may have been chased ashore by predators, disorientated by sonar interference from ships and military installations, or harried away from their natural feeding grounds by drilling and fishing. Strandings can occur singly or en masse, and there have been occasions when over fifty dolphins or whales have simultaneously chosen to commit hara-kiri on Britain's un-welcoming coastline. Unlike those deaths caused by human malpractice – dolphins trapped in nets, porpoises tangled in long-lines – those cetaceans which do strand themselves tend to be in good physical condition when found, and are therefore of interest to zoologists trying to identify the whys and where-fores of their behaviour.

Which is how Sabin – a gentle, wry man with an evident passion for his job – came to be responsible for 7,500 assorted cetacean parts, several jars of nematode worms, and a pair of sperm whale eyeballs. Any whale, dolphin or porpoise washed up along British coasts is reported to him, logged on the Natural History Museum's strandings database and then either claimed for science or disposed of. All of which sounds quite straightforward in print, but is less so in reality. There are some very interesting logistical difficulties in getting, say, a 16-ton, 40-foot fin whale from some stormy cove in the Outer Hebrides to inner London. In the early days, says Sabin, 'Most of the big animals were brought back here. How, I've no idea, but they brought humpback whales, sperm whales, into central London and de-fleshed them.' By what means, exactly? 'We've got photographs of humpback whales being lowered into a pit in the ground at the back of the museum where the Darwin Centre is now. They'd be left in the ground to rot for a few years, then the bones would be pulled up, cleaned, pinned and put on display in the whale hall.' So the museum had decom-posing whales on site in the middle of Kensington? He smiles. 'Yes.' In fact, whales were buried and left to rot in the grounds right up until the outbreak of the Second World War. In the aftermath of the war, the museum began to use less challenging methods of preservation. Either full-scale models would be made out of plaster or fibreglass, or the bones would be buried where they had been found. It may or may not comfort any Kensington residents to know that the museum has recently began stripping the corpses of some of its specimens with the help of flesh-eating beetles – though this does not, as yet, include whales.

Sabin leads me off into a large ante-room filled with locked metal cabinets containing a few of the museum's several million specimens. On a trolley by the door are two large skulls. One, weirdly asymmetrical and punctured by a cancerous hole, belongs to the same pygmy sperm whale as the eyes. Below it sits the lower jawbone, which looks at first sight like a rare and elegant flower; two graceful flutes of translucent bone joined by a pale stem. The other skull is older and in less good condition, worn almost to lacework by age. The skull belonged to a bottlenose dolphin who found her way up to Tower Bridge on the Thames three years ago. She was sick, malnourished and very much weakened by several weeks in fresh water. When she died, Sabin and the River Police retrieved the corpse. 'The police,' says Sabin, 'were quite upset by the process – we used a body bag that would normally have been used for a human retrieved from the river. They said, "Well, we're used to pulling people out of the river, but dolphins are a different matter".'

He personally deals with only those strandings (like the dolphin) which present problems, or which, because of the rarity of the species, most interest the museum. The rarest are the whales – sperm whales, minkes, killers, sei whales and fin whales – which occasionally turn up in British waters. 'If you look at the total number of UK strandings each year, you'll find that 50 per cent of all the strandings reported to us are harbour porpoise, and that the Scottish strandings normally account for 30 per cent of the total. We don't get that many from Northern Ireland – that's not because they're not reported, it's just that the geology of the coastline is such that most of the animals get washed away from the coastline when they get into difficulties. We tend to see sperm whales off the north and east coast of Scotland, but rarely do you get those big, big animals in the North Sea. Things like common dolphins you see along the south-west coast of England, harbour porpoise in Cardigan Bay, bottlenose dolphins around the north-east coast of Scotland – particularly the Moray Firth area – and things like white-sided and white-beaked dolphins around the north and west coasts of Scotland. But it does depend on the time of year.'

Having either recorded the details of a stranding or retrieved the carcass, Sabin will log all the information onto a database: height, weight, size, condition, area, evidence of disease or injury. Ultimately, he hopes that hidden within those cautious statistics will be the image of something bigger and bolder; an explanation of why strandings happen in the first place.

Once in a while, however, he finds that he and the museum have got competition. Just as there are ship-wreckers, so there are whale-wreckers too. During both world wars, the numbers of reported strandings decreased, not because fewer cetaceans were beaching themselves, but because more people had begun eating them again. In peacetime, Sabin occasionally finds that what was reported to him as a 2.5-ton whale has been reduced to a 1.2-ton whale by the time he has raced to the beach. 'I was called out to a 60-foot fin whale stranded on the Pembrokeshire coast in 1995. It had been dead for about three or four weeks and was really badly decomposed, to the point where the skin and blubber of the animal had started to get quite tough and split, and the skeleton and skull had started to slide out of the skin. I got a phone call on the Friday to say that this thing was on the beach in a fairly inaccessible cove that you needed more or less to abseil down to get to, and I couldn't get a team together until Monday. We jumped into the Land Rover, drove up there, and by the time we got to the cove, the skull had gone, most of the vertebrae had gone, virtually all of the ribs except one had gone, and one of the scapulae had gone. I discovered that a local fisherman had backed his boat up as far as he could into the cove, tied a rope around the skull, and used his boat to pull the skull off.'

Why on earth did he want it? 'He took it across the bay and around the headland over to the National Museum at Cardiff. He called them and said, "I've got this whale skull, how much will you give me for it?" They said, "That's a Royal Fish, you've broken the law, mate; we can't do anything for you." They told him to contact the Natural History Museum, but he just cut the rope and the skull went down.'

Sabin also found there had been other visitors to the site. 'Most of the bones had vanished by the time we got there. I ended up with one rib, one scapulae, and about six of the tail, the cordal vertebrae, and that was it – the whole thing had gone. It just amazed me how resourceful people can be, but also how much these things still mean to people, and the risks that people are prepared to take. We heard all these stories – there'd been a pregnant woman and two children sitting down there next to the carcass having a picnic. And when they'd finished, they took a couple of the vertebrae, stuck them in a couple of bin liners, and went back up the cliffs. Rod Penrose, who does all of the recording work for us in Wales, said that there were people with the bones in their gardens, that one of the scapulae appeared hanging up outside a workshop. It had been cleaned and sign-written; traditional things to do with them, but a bit annoying as far as we're concerned.'

But it is with those strandings unwanted either by science or by wreckers where the biggest problems arise. Since the Natural History Museum already has most of the specimens it needs, someone has to find a way of disposing of the surplus. Unfortunately, trying to find a way to get rid of a putrefying minke presents a whole new set of problems. Which is why a young woman sitting in a dank Southampton office block is empowered – or compelled, depending on your point of view –

to deal with dead dolphins in the same way that she would deal with looted Saabs.

When I ask Sophia Exelby, the UK's Receiver of Wreck, about whales, she smiles. 'Yes,' she says, 'it's one of the less salubrious parts of the job.' When Sabin and the Natural History Museum can't put a stranding to good zoological use, Exelby is responsible for ensuring its removal. Which, it turns out, is more complicated than it sounds. 'Now, of course, whales are what's technically termed a "managed waste-product" under EC regulations, which means that you can't do what might be considered to be the most sensible thing, which would be to tow them back out to sea, weigh them down and sink them naturally. So you then have to think of other methods of disposal – incineration, burial – either in situ or on a landfill site. Certainly in the past various methods have been tried, such as blowing them up and burning them; things that don't prove terribly successful. The dolphins are so small that it's no problem for someone just to put them on the back of a pick-up truck and drive them to the local landfill site. They're easy to deal with – it's the big whales that are the real problem.'

Those of a ghoulish disposition may find it educational at this point to type the words 'exploding whale' into an internet search engine. In 1970, a 45-foot, 8-ton Pacific grey whale stranded itself on a beach in Florence, Oregon. The US State Highway Division decided that neither burial nor dismemberment were suitable options, and that the best method of disposal would therefore be to blow it up. The final clear up would, they hoped, be completed by seagulls and scavengers. News of the stranding had got around, and by the time the Division had stuffed the whale's belly with half a ton of dynamite, a large crowd of spectators and a local TV news crew had gathered on a beach nearby. The resulting video shows the detonation, accompanied by an admiring murmur from the crowd. Then there is the unmistakeable sound of curiosity turning to fear. Blasted high into the air by the explosion, half-ton lumps of decomposing whale blubber began to rain down on the spectators and their cars. No-one was badly hurt, but the seagulls kept their distance. In the end, the Highways Division was forced to bury the remains.

Since dynamite is evidently not a possibility, those responsible for British strandings often find themselves confounded. In isolated parts of the country, cetacean carcasses are often left to decompose naturally. But in more populous areas, there is no chance of waiting for time to do its work.

Down on the seafront at Deal in Kent, Andy Roberts mans the coastguard station. But the crisis he dealt with three years ago was not of human devising. A whale had been spotted, stranded alive on a beach at Sandwich. Initially, it was thought to be a minke whale – the most frequently stranded of all whale species. Roberts got in touch with the RSPCA, a local marine-life organisation, and the local vet. When the vet arrived, it transpired that they were dealing not with a minke, but with a humpback whale – in fact, the only humpback to have stranded in Britain for the past hundred years. Humpbacks are filter feeders between four and six metres long at birth, and up to 19 metres long when fully developed. This particular humpback was around ten metres long, and, 'not well – not well at all,' Roberts says. 'I remember standing next to the whale and asking the vet what the prognosis was. The vet put his arm around my shoulders, led me about 40 yards away from the whale, and whispered, "not so good, I'm afraid". It was odd, that thing of leading me away – I think he felt very emotional about it, almost as if it was his granny dying, and that you wouldn't say anything about her condition in her presence.'

Since it was evident that the whale would not survive to be refloated, the decision was made to have it put down, or – more correctly – to 'euthanase' it. Unfortunately, 'euthanasing' a whale was evidently going to take something far stronger than the barbiturates commonly used to put down dogs or cats. 'They used a drug called Imobilon,' remembers Roberts, 'which is ten thousand times more powerful than morphine. Most vets only carry enough to kill a horse, so the vet had to contact all the other vets in the area and see if they had further supplies. He ended up with enough to kill an elephant, but that still wasn't going to be enough, so then he contacted Howlett's Zoo nearby. They've got elephants, so they need to keep supplies of Imobilon, but they wouldn't come out because of the foot and mouth outbreak. So in the end, the vet injected all the Imobilon he had into the whale. Gradually his breathing and heart rate slowed, and he died.'

Once dead, the responsibility for the whale passed from the RSPCA to the Natural History Museum and HM Coastguard. Having completed a postmortem on the whale, the Museum vets established that the humpback was a young male, 10.66 metres long and 16 tonnes in weight, malnourished, and suffering from a kidney disease – the most likely reason for the stranding. Having completed the tests, the various different organisations then had to find a way of disposing of the body. It was generally agreed that neither burial nor incineration were possible, and because of EU rules it was necessary to take the whale's remains to a nearby landfill site. Matters were further complicated by the risk of contamination by Imobilon, and the difficulties in keeping the public away. 'You don't really have that much chance of disguising a 30-foot humpback whale, do you?', Roberts points out. 'His flukes were about 15- to 20-foot across, and this whale had to be driven through the historic town of Sandwich with a bit of plastic over it, without anyone seeing it – it was tricky, believe me.'

Tess Vandervliet, Roberts' colleague at the coastguard station, remembers the difficulties they had in wrapping the whale and lifting it onto a low-loader. When they did finally complete the loading, Vandervliet went with the truck to the landfill site. It was then that the organisational difficulties of the stranding gave way to more profound considerations. Throughout the conversation, Vandervliet refers to the humpback as 'she', despite knowing that it was male. Listening to her, I realise that there's a kind of logic to this switch of gender – 'she' not only rescues the whale's identity but softens it, rescuing the humpback from being just a lump of intransigent blubber to a creature which once had a far richer story than the one which ended on a Sandwich beach. As Vandervliet says, 'I found it quite upsetting, the way she was disposed of, just pushed into a huge hole like that. It was such an undignified end, so ungainly. The landfill site was the only possible option, but it was still terribly sad; I cried while it was happening. You look at humpbacks and they're such wonderful, elegant creatures in the water. But when they're dead, they're just this huge lump to be disposed of.'

In the past, whales were too useful for their own good. Now they have no use at all, except as souvenirs, specimens, or jokes. Which, you wonder, is ultimately the worse fate?

A few miles further down the river in Wapping, Bob Jeffries deals with some equally malodorous aspects of the past. Jeffries is a part-time curator at the Thames Police Museum, in which the best and worst of London's liquid history is preserved for the edification of interested members of the public.

To get to the museum you walk through the police station, out into the central courtyard, up an iron staircase and in through a locked door. The door divides this world from the next. On one side are all of London's current policing troubles – surveillance, terrorist threats, politicisation – and on the other are its criminal dead. The room has the look of an historian's pet project, a small local museum evidently maintained with more enthusiasm than money. Two long display cabinets run the length of the room, containing an assortment of old policing equipment: a rattle – used for summoning help before whistles were introduced – a cutlass, a book of punishments, and an eighteenth-century map of the river. Ranged around the side are several portraits of ex-superintendents, a copy of the official directions for the funeral of Winston Churchill (all lifting cranes along the Thames to be kept at half-mast until the procession had passed by), a seek-and-search lamp stamped with the words 'Do Not Remove – Needed for Marchioness Enquiry', a Schermuley line-throwing rocket apparatus, two crossed standard-issue swords and several models of police and coastguard cutters. Two male mannequins in waterproof boaters stand guard in sealed cabinets, sagging under the weight of black coats made of such heavy material that they must have taken an effort of will to put on, let alone run in. Jeffries unlocks the cabinets and holds them open. We both gaze at the figures. 'I'm not sure these two know which side they're playing for', Jeffries says eventually, pointing to the dummies' hands. Both have bright red painted fingernails. 'Nowadays, I suppose they'd call that diversity.'

He crosses to the other side of the room and opens the top half of a divided wooden door. We look down at the river directly below. The smell of the Thames (mud, diesel vapour, salt, something animal) rises up to meet us. On the opposite side of the river London's history basks in the sun: docks, half-renovated warehouses, office blocks, a church, a couple of disused landing stages. Launches plough a muddy path upriver, rocking the boats moored alongside the police pontoon and leaving a brief flicker of white in their wake.

It is low tide, and directly below the doorway the shore lies exposed. All the way along the banks, the decrepit evidence of past business lies drying in the sunshine. Seeing it is a reminder of the Thames's erstwhile significance. To the majority of Londoners now, the Thames has been reduced to a tourist attraction, a slime-grey demarcation line between north and south. The river doesn't matter any more than Buckingham Palace or the London Eye matter; it's just a part of the scenery. Most people could spend their whole lives in London and see no more of it than the angular blue ribbon flowing through the Underground map. But those who look beyond the water see more than just a costly stage set. The Thames provides the clue to the capital's existence, its reason for being, its good fortune and its bad luck. It gathered up all the prizes of empire and distributed them along its shores; from here, Englishmen, Scotsmen and Irishmen sailed out to the four corners of the world searching for trophies to bring home. It represents the history of England's relations with the outside world, its strength as a seafaring nation and its skill for money-making. Along the banks is the evidence of all the river's pasts; the banks and wharves and warships, the trading places, the seats of government, the places of power and of power-generation, the law courts, a couple of palaces and enough churches to satisfy a multitude of schisms.

For many people, the Thames also represented a final resting place. Jeffries points downwards. 'This,' he says, with only a trace of relish, 'was probably once the site of Execution Dock. And there, over by the bend in the river, is Cuckold's Point.' I look down into the mud and the soft slop of the water. For over four centuries, convicted pirates were brought here from Newgate Prison, laid down on the banks, and staked – still alive – to the foreshore at the low-water mark. When three tides had risen and fallen over the newly drowned man, he would be taken up, tarred, strapped into an iron bracing and hanged from one of the gibbets at Cuckold's Point. Those who were lucky would be hanged before they were staked to the foreshore. The point of all this ghoulish ceremonial was not so much to avenge the state – though the state did regard the loss of revenue from piracy with particular bitterness – but to act as a deterrent. Sailors passing up and down the river were meant to see the corpses bound and tarred, and to reflect again on their choice between a brutal legality and a worse fate. In his novel *Heart of Darkness*, Joseph Conrad's hero Marlow acknowledges the river's ambiguous history. '"And this also," said Marlow suddenly, "has been one of the dark places of the earth".'

Jeffries, meanwhile, turns back from the window and begins showing me around the room. As he pauses by a musty portrait, someone appears from downstairs to inform him of a phone call. Jeffries vanishes, and I stand there looking up at the portrait. Patrick Colquhoun appears the model of an upstanding Regency gent: calm, sober-suited, with a temperate gaze and a strong jaw. He is wearing a black frock coat, a plain stock, and a forthright look in his eye. He doesn't look like someone who paid much attention either to clothes or to ceremony, but then nor does he look like a radical. Colquhoun looks like what he was: a man who could pass comfortably in both the upper-class law courts of London and the most degraded corners of the Victorian criminal world. He also looks recognisably Scottish.

Born in Dumbarton in 1745, Colquhoun built a business as one of Glasgow's tobacco lords before becoming its Lord Provost. In 1789 he moved to London to become a police magistrate. Galvanised both by the poverty he saw and by the indifference of the middle classes, he began by setting up a series of soup kitchens in Spitalfields. It did not take long for it to become evident to Colquhoun that soup kitchens were not – and never would be – enough to make a difference. Around the Thames in particular, crime had become a rich and settled way of life for a sizeable minority of the population. The rudimentary police force which existed at the time was inadequate and underfunded; Henry Fielding's establishment of the Bow Street Runners in 1748 had provided a first step towards curbing the capital's crime, but had made no special provision for river criminals or the particular types of low-lifes who existed round the shores of the Thames.

As Henry Mayhew did several decades later in his book *London Labour and the London Poor*, Colquhoun set out to interrogate his subject in person. Instead of providing a dry second-hand polemic culled from the account books of shipping companies, he walked down to the shore in search of his subjects. The result was his treatise on 'The Commerce and Police of the River Thames', first published in 1800. As he noted in the introduction, the interested reader would find within its pages, 'a species of systematic delinquency, which, in its different ramifications, exhibits a degree of turpitude as singular as it is unparalleled'.

Colquhoun began by detailing the numbers of people then working on the river: 'Journeymen Trunk and Box Makers – 450, Working Lumpers &c – 1,400, Pilots – 200, Bumboatmen – 155, Coal Heavers – 800, Fishermen of various classes – 1,250, total workforce 120,000'. Having calculated the total value of vulnerable property passing in and out of the Thames docks at around £75 million, he calculated the losses suffered by the major shipping companies to theft, fraud and embezzlement at £10 million over the course of the eighteenth century. He estimated that a quarter of London's population depended directly or indirectly on the river for its livelihood, and that some 10 to 20 per cent of those individuals had gone to the bad. Given that there were rarely less than a thousand ships moored in the Port of London at any one moment, and that Thames trade contributed a significant percentage to Britain's annual gross domestic product at the time, crime on such a scale was becoming a serious threat to the Empire.

The culprits were legion. As Colquhoun acknowledged, it was the Thames's very success as a port which made it so difficult to impose effective law and order. Existing resources –

customs houses, wharves, landing places – were often strained to and beyond breaking point. Since there was only 12 foot of navigable water from Gravesend to the Pool of London, large ships – including East Indiamen carrying the most valuable cargos – were forced to moor further downriver near Deptford. Smaller vessels would often have to wait days or even weeks for a berth to become available. With so many centuries of such heavy use, the Thames itself had become a foul trickle, regarded by all as London's open-air gutter. Its banks were pocked with grimy hiding places and smuggler's dens, while the shoreline still held the skeletal gibbets of another age. The water itself stank. Forty years after Colquhoun paced the banks, one writer claimed that:

> Whoever swallows it, quaffs what is impregnated with all the filth of London and Westminster, and charged with the contents of the great common-sewers ... the drainings from dunghills and laystalls, the refuse of hospitals, slaughter-houses, colour, lead, and soap works, drug-mills, gas-works, the minerals and poisons used in mechanics and manufacture, enriched with the putrefying carcasses of dogs, cats, rats, and men; and mixed with the scourings of all the wash tubs and kennels within the bills of mortality. And this is the agreeable potation extolled by the Londoners, as the finest water in the world!

The rich might wish to make money from the Thames, but they did so partly in order to be able to afford to live as far away from it as possible. The bankers and shipowners extracted gold from mud and then got out. It was the poor who actually co-existed with the river.

Unsurprisingly, the opportunities for lawlessness – both out on the water and onshore – were plentiful. According to Colquhoun, there were almost as many people profiting illegally from trade on the Thames as there were making an honest living. Every individual in contact with the river was, in some sense, a wrecker, since every inch of the Thames represented one vast vessel waiting to be robbed. In fact, the river's pickings were so rich that a complete sub-genus of wreckers had evolved. 'It is not unlikely,' Colquhoun speculated,

> that the disposition to pillage Commercial Property while afloat derived its origin in no inconsiderable degree from the habit of Smuggling, which has prevailed ever since Revenues were collected . . . the mind thus reconciled to the action, the offence screened by impunity, and apparently sanctioned by custom, the habits of pillage increased: others seduced by the force of example and stimulated by motives of avarice, soon pursued the same course of Criminality . . . New Converts to the System of Iniquity were rapidly made. The mass of Labourers on the River became gradually contaminated. A similar class upon the Quays and in the Warehouses caught the infection, and the evil expanded as Commerce increased.

Whatever the reason, river crime was running out of control. But before he began proposing any solutions, Colquhoun set about detailing the different criminal species with an almost zoological exactitude, parting the waters to reveal a thriving interdependent network of organisms previously unrecognised by science.

In addition to those with legitimate jobs who worked as criminals on the side – lightermen and game-watermen who received and transported stolen goods, and coopers, who took a cut of the contents of any barrel they were supposed to be repairing – there were also those who made a living solely from crime. Of these, Colquhoun particularly noted, 'the river pirates – the most desperate and depraved class of the fraternity of nautical Vagabonds'. Most operated by selecting a target, re-connoitring it by day and then returning at night. After dark, they appeared armed and en masse, overpowering the captain and night-watchmen and stealing everything the ship had to offer.

As often as not, the pirates would make straight for the anchor chains, aiming not only to disable the ship but to sell on the chains to maritime supply stores for a decent mark-up. As with more conventional forms of wrecking, the river pirates were not particularly scrupulous in their methodology. If cutting the anchor chains meant that the ship drifted aground on one of the many sandbanks or shoals of the Thames estuary, then so much the better; it simply made it easier prey. If that ship was then wrecked by storms or through collision with another vessel, then that too could prove a blessing: the wreckers would get the timbers, the rivets, the spars and the sails as well. The Thames Estuary was, and is, a fickle passage to navigate. Prone to silting up, littered with old ordnance and exposed to all the North Sea traffic on its way to the Channel, it was not a place for the inexpert or unwary. The pirates and river wreckers took advantage of captains' naiveté and of the likeli-hood of conditions upriver being so crowded that it made escape all but impossible. Much of the time, they had grown so bold that captains could do little but stand back and watch them loot. 'One instance in particular occurred a few years ago,' wrote Colquhoun, 'where an American and a Guernsey ship were plundered . . . by the actual removal both of Anchors and Cables in the view of the Masters of the Vessels, who . . . learn[ed] the fact from the River Pirates themselves; who, as they rowed off, told them that they had got their Anchors and Cables, at the same time wishing them a good morning.'

The pirates were not choosy about the vessels they selected, and in many cases made a speciality of cutting lighters with valuable cargos adrift, following them until the tide carried them to a suitable sandbank, and then wrecking them at leisure.

Naval impressment during the Napoleonic wars had helped to diminish their numbers a little, but Colquhoun seemed confident that they would return in greater force with the outbreak of peace, 'when so many depraved characters will . . . be discharged from the Navy and Army'.

Next were the 'night plunderers' – 'who prefer idleness to labour and indulge in every kind of low extravagance . . . they are in general exceedingly depraved and audacious'. Operating in much the same way as the river pirates, they would bribe their way into collusion with the night watchmen guarding the ships, before robbing their targets and passing the resulting goods on to a network of ready fences. Their methodology had, however, evolved one step further from that of the river pirates; as well as robbing ships at anchor, the night plunderers would occasionally take a crewing job on board one of the more valuable ships. When put in charge of stowing cargo in the hold, they would ensure that the most valuable items were placed closest to the hatches. On a given signal, the plunderer's accomplices would silently board the ship, pick up the marked items and abscond over the side again without being seen. As far as Colquhoun was concerned, the particular villainy in this crime was that many of the thefts were not always discovered until the ship reached its final destination. When the unloaded cargo was checked against the original bills of lading, the discrepancies would become obvious. It was then the captain, not the criminals, who stood to lose both his reputation and his livelihood.

Similarly, the day plunderers, or 'heavy-horsemen', would be contracted to work on the boats as 'lumpers' or loaders, and would supplement their daily income by pilfering as much as they could from the cargo. Most were not much more than petty burglars, who – if Colquhoun is to be believed – spent much of their time wandering the docks dressed as one-man supermarkets. 'Many of them were provided with an under-dress, denominated a Jemmey, with pockets before and behind: also with long narrow bags or pouches, which, when filled, were lashed to their legs and thighs, and concealed under wide trowsers. By these means they were enabled to carry off Sugars, Coffee, Cocoa, Ginger, Pimento, and every other article which could be obtained by pillage, in considerable quantities.'

At the bottom of this unsociable heap were another group of organisms, the human plankton of Thames life. Colquhoun lifted each specimen out with cautious verbal tweezers. There were the mudlarks – 'aquatic itinerants . . . a class of low and miserable beings who are accustomed to Grub in the River at low water for old Ropes, Metals and Coals', and the 'rat catchers' – who would go on board at night ostensibly in order to set traps, but actually to act as informants and accomplices to the night plunderers or the pirates. 'They have even been accustomed to convey the Rats alive from one ship to another,' claimed Colquhoun, 'as a means of receiving payment for catching the same animal three or four times over.' And lastly there were the 'scuffle-hunters' – 'composed of that lowest class of the community who are vulgarly denominated the Tag-Rag and Bobtail . . . considered the Scum of Society . . . they generally come prepared with long aprons, not so much as a convenient habiliment to enable them the better to perform their labour, as to furnish them with the means of suddenly concealing what they pilfer.'

In addition to those who profited directly and actively from river crime, Colquhoun detailed a sizeable group of individuals who benefited passively and indirectly. They included manufacturers of rope and twine who bought raw hemp from the night plunderers, 'female receivers who keep houses of ill-fame', known for seducing the men and then stripping them of their stolen money, and publicans who gave credit to lumpers in exchange for a cut of the stolen cargoes. From a total population of around 37,000 crew members and suppliers working on and around the ships in the Thames, Colquhoun calculated that around 9,600 of those were 'delinquent'. Additionally, there were an extra 10,850 pirates, plunderers, receivers and mudlarks who had no official job or role, but who nevertheless derived their livelihoods entirely from the river.

Unsurprisingly, the few desultory attempts to impose order along the Thames' length had either proved futile or farcical. Night-watchmen posted on boats were often no better than animated scarecrows, since most were so decrepit, infirm and badly paid they could be bribed or overpowered with ease. Mounted watchmen were often responsible for patrolling several miles of unlit shoreline without backup or security. Customs officers were as corruptible as everyone else, and were often bought off with the promise of a well-placed commission. Many had purchased their position, and – when they chose to work at all – could look forward to forty-five holy days and bank holidays a year, plus a working day of no more than three hours.

Pressmen and crimps, feeding the Navy's fathomless appetite for mariners, operated right out at the furthest edges of legality. To fulfil their quotas, most used kidnap, abduction, and the broad-minded interpretation of the phrase 'able-bodied'. Strictly speaking, they were only supposed to take fit young men, preferably with some existing knowledge of the sea. But by the second half of the eighteenth century, the Admiralty's demand for recruits had become so voracious that the press gangs had to employ more imaginative tactics. Instead of seizing men as they left the riverside pubs or brothels, the press men began breaking into houses, raiding the asylums, and overpowering the lawfully employed. Tailors in particular were often taken, since their habit of sitting cross-legged while sewing gave them the same landsick bandy-legged gait as true sailors.

Protests at the press gangs' abuses were frequent – not only from the abducted men, but also from their intended clients. In 1759, one naval captain complained that his latest batch of pressed men included an idiot, a sixty-year-old ex-soldier with a debilitating case of gout, and an assortment of landlubbers who were all either deaf, incontinent, lame, rheumatic or senile. Captains with foresight and time to spare proved cannier, and learned to use impressment's power to their own advantage. In 1800, Lord Nelson was reputed to be searching the Kent coast, 'to procure from among the smugglers in the neighbourhood pilots who were particularly acquainted with the French coast . . .'

Improvement came slowly. In 1797, the West India Company established a pilot police scheme; a security force paid for by the government and initially designed to combat theft and wrecking in the West India Company alone. The force was an unexpected success, Colquhoun claiming that in a single year the losses from West India ships were cut to one fiftieth of their previous level. Certainly, the scheme was successful enough to rouse many of the lumpers and 'lower orders of revenue officers' to a state close to insurrection. Having complained to the shipowners that the new force would put them out of business, they then tried violence. Despite the insurgents' best efforts, however, the system worked. A year later, fifty-one grateful shipowners signed a letter expressing 'our approbation and satisfaction of the Marine Police Institution, as a system which appears to us from actual observation to be of the greatest advantage to the Mercantile Interest as well as the Revenue, both of which have suffered beyond conception by the excessive pillage and plunder which formerly prevailed'.

Three things were ultimately to make a difference to crime on the Thames. Firstly, the publication of Colquhoun's treatise, and the case he made for the establishment of a coherent River Police Force, stirred the government to action, if not to outlay.

Estimating the annual cost of a marine police force at £5,000, the Exchequer offered just under £1,000 of that, while the West India Company committed the rest. In line with many of Colquhoun's recommendations, the force initially consisted of a superintendent, a group of ship surveyors to patrol and inspect the river twenty-four hours a day, police watermen, and a small group of ship constables to supervise the dock gangs. In addition, there was also a surveyor of quays and thirty police quay guards to protect cargoes waiting on shore. That initial investment brought many of the worst excesses under control.

Secondly, the reduction both in the number and the cost of customs tariffs knocked the bottom out of the smuggling trade. By the 1850s, the number of articles eligible for duty had been cut from 1,400 to 30. By raising the penalties and lowering the incentives for crime, Colquhoun and his riverside descendents brought much of the Thames under control for the first time in centuries. And thirdly, the original Thames police worked by using the time-honoured law-enforcement principle of sending a thief to catch a thief. The first recruits to the force were drawn mainly from the ranks of dispossessed naval and merchant sea-men, many of whom were almost as villainous as the criminals they were ostensibly combating. If the shore-going law did not permit them to wound or even kill their targets, then they bent that law until it did. If the law did not allow them to steal the property of criminals, or pay informants, or intimidate witnesses into giving evidence, then that law was insufficient. Even allowing for the River Police's exceptional independence, the force as it then stood was not powerful enough to gain the respect of the criminal classes. The first river recruits therefore made sure they earned their awe by more imaginative means.

Not, of course, that crime on the river stopped outright. Most criminals went underground; some found more ingenious ways to deceive, and some simply slipped below official sight-lines. Fifty years after Colquhoun first described the mudlarks, they reappeared in Henry Mayhew's *London Labour and the London Poor*. Since the turn of the century, their condition and circumstances had, if anything, got worse. Most spent their days picking through the river mud for coal, wood, rope, and old iron, selling them on either to people within their local neighbourhoods or at rag-and-bone shops. At the fall of each successive tide, they would rush out, distribute themselves along the banks and begin scavenging for as long as the light or low-water lasted. Average earnings came to around threepence a day, and Mayhew calculated that by 1850, there were around 550 mudlarks earning a total of about £2,000 a year. 'These poor creatures,' wrote Mayhew,

> are certainly about the most deplorable in their appearance of any I have met with in the course of my inquiries. They may be seen of all ages, from mere childhood to positive decrepitude, crawling among the barges at the various wharfs along the river; it cannot be said that they are clad in rags, for they are scarcely half covered by the tattered indescribable things that serve them for clothing; their bodies are grimed with the foul soil of the river, and their torn garments stiffened up like boards with dirt of every possible description . . . The men and women may be passed and repassed, but they notice no-one; they never speak, but with a stolid look of wretchedness they plash their way through the mire, their bodies bent down while they peer anxiously about, and occasionally stoop to pick up some paltry treasure that falls in their way.

The children, he reported,

> were either the children of the very poor, who, by their own improvidence or some overwhelming calamity, had been reduced to the extremity of distress, or else

they were orphans, and compelled from utter destitution to seek for the means of appeasing their hunger in the mud of the river.

Even now, there are still mudlarks on the Thames, though they are no longer the abject specimens Colquhoun and Mayhew examined. The Society of Thames Mudlarks are permitted to use metal detectors to search the foreshore on licence by the Port of London Authority on the condition that they give up any valuable finds to science or archaeology. From being a desperate community of river-grubbers, mudlarking has become the sport of hobbyists and historians, its transformation proof both of the social changes in the capital since Mayhew's day, and of London's waning interest in the Thames.

In fact, as Bob Jeffries points out when he returns to the museum room, there's only one real use which Londoners still have for the river. He places a file named 'High-Risk Mispers' down on the table. A body has just been recovered from the river, and – as with all other suicides – the River Police are responsible for establishing identity and for dealing with the consequences. The body is the tenth so far this year. In an average year, between 80 and 100 people are known to die each year in the Thames, and 80 per cent of those are suicides. The file contains names and details of all Britain's missing persons: name, age, last known address, identifying characteristics, place where last seen. The body in the river will be checked against the names in the file and on the police database; if it turns out to be one of the lost thousands, then it becomes one more name for the police to cross off their list.

'Jumpers' – the unofficial name for Thames suicides – have always been the River Police's responsibility. Ostensibly, that responsibility is an odd one, since suicides have committed no crime and – if successful – can hardly be brought to court. The police's involvement dates back to an era when suicide was defined by Samuel Johnson as 'self-murder; the horrid crime of destroying one's self', and regarded as a contravention of God's will. Well into the eighteenth century, suicides would be posthumously convicted by the courts; most had their goods confiscated by the state. In some cases, the cadavers would then be 'executed' before having their twice-killed corpses buried under the high road with a stake driven through their chest – presumably as a way of hastening their descent to the fires of Hell. Most suicides were simply declared mad; those who did not succeed were hauled off to prisons or asylums. Astoundingly, it took until 1961 before suicide in Britain was officially decriminalised; even now, coroners will often return either a verdict of accidental death or an open verdict in order to spare surviving family members the stigma associated with suicide.

Given such a history, the River Police's involvement in fishing 'jumpers' out of the river is less surprising. In 1887, Charles Dickens, son of the more famous author, noted in his *Dictionary of the Thames* that, 'An important portion of the duties of the Thames division consists in searching for and dealing with the bodies of suicides, murdered persons and persons accidentally drowned. The dragging process is only carried on for one tide, after which it is considered that the missing body will pretty certainly have been carried out of reach, and it occasionally happens that a corpse will drift into a hole and be covered over before it becomes sufficiently buoyant to rise.' Then as now, the jumpers usually choose either Blackfriars or Waterloo Bridge; between 1817 – when Waterloo Bridge was completed – and 1840, an average of forty people a year hurled themselves from its stone parapets.

Since January 2002, responsibility for dealing with people who either fall or jump into the Thames has been shared by the River Police – or the Marine Support Unit, as it is now known – with the RNLI and HM Coastguard, both of whom recently established stations on the Thames as a result of the

Marchioness Enquiry. The Coastguard is now responsible for co-ordinating all search and rescue on the Thames, a move which has alleviated some of the pressure on the police. In 2002, the RNLI's first full year on the Thames, the lifeboat volunteers were stunned to discover that they were called out 800 times in a single year, and that between 40 per cent and 50 per cent of those call-outs were to deal with those who had jumped or fallen into the river.

But, as Jeffries points out, the numbers of suicides have actually fallen in recent years. 'One of the reasons why the number has dropped, I suspect, is the advent of mobile phones. Previously, people who saw persons acting suspiciously on bridges would have had to find a functioning public phone and then phone the police. Nowadays, people press a button and they're through in seconds.' How do the different organisations work out their duties? Jeffries shrugs. 'It's just a question of who gets there first.' As he notes, 'Those who get into the water don't last for long. Even in summer, that river is dangerous. It's cold, it's fast, there are eddies and currents created by the bulwarks of the bridges . . . The police know from experience that we don't have to search longer than an hour, because no-one who gets into the water would last that long.'

Perhaps reassuringly, it tends not to be the natives who get tired both of London and of life. 'Most of the people who end up in the river originate from outside the capital and so may not actually be Londoners as such. As for their reasons, who knows? I think it's fair to say that many of them are suffering from a variety of mental health problems, and that it's inevitable that the sheer pressure of day to day living on many of them will just be too severe. Why they choose to drown themselves? That's anyone's guess. I am told that once the initial panic subsides and the victim has actually inhaled the water instead of air, then the process is almost peaceful. Unfortunately, I don't know of too many ways that we can easily test the theory.'

Transit to: SIL
Transit date: 6/21/2019,9:30
Transit library: SPLW
Title: The wreckers : a story of
killing seas and plunde
Transit reason: LIBRARY
...em Branch Library

Support Unit's work, however, is
ng Londoners alive than dealing
Jeffries, 'These days, post-9/11,
d with anti-terrorist work.' All
on are now liable to be stopped
the Prevention of Terrorism
lligence that a vessel is due
ip during its stay,' Jeffries
hes will be "satisfactory",
re more than happy for
way, but there are the
n.'

nel also noted, asylum
en be a problem. 'There are
oc ...n report unauthorised passengers who
hav ...emselves aboard ships bound for the Thames,
and ... have been occasions when police have been called
to suspected illegal stowaways. These people have been arrested
and taken to police stations and the relevant authorities alerted.'
But, as Jeffries points out, there are as many holes in the
immigration laws on water as there are on land. 'It's been suggested that the police don't have the facilities to deal with these
people. The usual advice seems to be that the police should
release the suspects and direct them to attend the [immigration]
centre at Lunar House, Croydon. Strangely, many of the
suspects fail to make it to the centre and are often never heard
of again.'

And finally, what about Royal Fish? Does the Marine
Support Unit ever find itself having to deal with dead dolphins
or unexploded whales in the centre of London? Some immature
part of me rather likes the image of helmeted squads of Met
officers pondering the best use for a sperm whale's eyeballs.
Sadly, Bob Jeffries does not oblige. Though he does remember
the dolphin which died upriver a few years ago, 'I have never

heard of any of them being referred to as "Royal". Swans, yes. But fish, no. So I feel I can safely say that the Marine Support Unit does not deal with Royal Fish in any way whatsoever.'

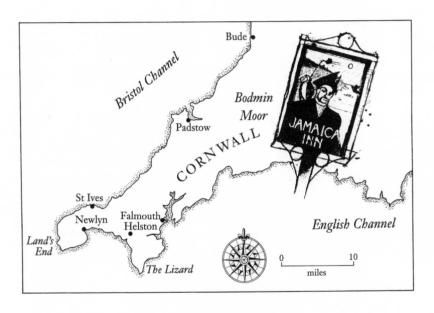

Cornwall

SEVEN

Cornwall

There's a ship on the rocks at Land's End, and by the look of her she's not going anywhere soon. The RMS *Mülheim* lies at the base of a high cliff, her stern aground and her bow pointing a straight course towards the Scilly Isles. By international shipping standards she is a small vessel, 70 metres and 1,840 tonnes unladen, but she slots into the rocky cleft between Land's End and Sennen Cove as if she was made for the space. In line with Cornish tradition, she appears to have arranged her final resting place with some forethought. The cove in which she lies is sheltered, sunny, and – most crucially – provides excellent access for both spectators and salvors. And, on a mild morning in mid-April, there are plenty of witnesses to her indignity.

All along the cliff pathways surrounding the cove stand families with rucksacks and thermoses, making the *Mülheim* into a proper day out. Elderly coach trippers advance with caution over the rocks, holding themselves at a 15-degree angle to the path. Parties of French and Spanish schoolchildren chatter in the bright spring air, most of them looking at the ground, or at each other, or at each other's mobiles, but never out to sea. Couples in their sixties with the air of people who have had plenty of practise with shipwrecks tramp round the headland in mountain boots, pausing once in a while to stop and point. Down on the *Mülheim* herself, men in fluorescent jackets are manoeuvring large claw-handed grabbers slowly in and out of her hold. Each time the grabber goes in, it brings out a handful of what looks like thick black weed and then deposits it somewhere to her seaward side. The *Mülheim* was loaded with 2,000 tonnes of shredded automotive plastic – obsolete dashboard fascias, half-melted car tyres – and every fragment of it has to be removed before both cargo and fuel can become a threat to the local marine environment. The men on the ship and the headland work on, apparently oblivious to the audience they've gathered around them.

There's something inelegant in seeing a big ugly ship caught *in flagrante* with the land, her backside levered up higher than her front and the sun beaming down on her humiliation. Even looking at the underparts of her hull – with its naked steel plates and its unwashed paintwork – feels like glimpsing something intended to remain private. But walking round the cliffside, it becomes evident that it is not going to be easy to restore the *Mülheim*'s dignity. All along her length there are deep black bite marks where the rocks have gnawed away at her hull. The rise and fall of every tide widens the gaps in the steel further, impaling her more firmly on the rocks. Once the salvage teams have retrieved all that they can of her cargo and fuel, she will be left for the Cornish winter to break. When the weather shifts, the sea will pound her up and down on the rocks until her backbone gives way and she begins to fall apart. It probably won't take much more than two or three major storms before she finally dissolves back into her native element. By next summer, there won't be anything here to see except a few scraps of unrecognisable metal.

The story of how the RMS *Mülheim* got here is almost as ignominious as her current position. In March 2003, she was heading from Cork with her car plastics cargo destined for a landfill site in Lübeck, Germany. As she rounded the far west coast of Cornwall on her way toward the Channel, the only person on the bridge was the chief officer. Standing up to check the ship's position, the end of his trouser leg caught in the foot-plate control lever. He stumbled, fell, and blacked out. By the time he regained consciousness, the ship was heading for the rocks. The captain and bosun, alerted by the change in engine noise, arrived too late to prevent the *Mülheim* colliding with Land's End. The chief officer – and his trousers – were later reported to be fine; the ship was not. There have been plenty of other shipwrecks in this area, many of which have been far more catastrophic than the *Mülheim*. But there undoubtedly hasn't been a wreck as silly as this for a very long time.

The tourists, though, see a shipwreck as no more than their due. People swirl around the entrance to the Land's End visitor centre while a small child begins a lengthy and passion-ate dispute with her mother over the use of a see-saw in the 'Wreckreation' adventure play area. Men stand with their hands in their pockets, waiting for their wives to return empty-eyed from 'The Relentless Sea' exhibition. In the toilets, mothers burdened with many bags debate the algebra of family life with their teenage daughters: one trip to the cinema in return for two hours walking round the coast; one trip to the pub plus one trip to the beach plus one unchaperoned night out equals one hour's walk from here to Sennen.

Outside, the seagulls mew with unsatisfied avarice. It is mid-April, and already Cornwall is full – full of day-trippers, families and tourists on coach tours. They are here not just to see the end of England, but to fulfil an old tradition. They want to see what their ancestors probably saw: an authentic wreck. Somehow it seems entirely appropriate that the *Mülheim* should be no more than a short shuffle from a toilet, a car park and the 'Smugglers' Burger Bar'. Land's End has excellent en-suite facilities and a splendid view of the Longships light; surely it should have a shipwreck too? Admittedly, the *Mülheim* falls down on a couple of details: she isn't particularly attractive, she wasn't carrying an interesting cargo, and she can't currently be seen against a Force-12 backdrop; but there's still an un-questioned thrill at the sight of a real live dead ship on the rocks. This is how it should be; this is what people expect.

If Devon does cream and Yorkshire does grit, then Cornwall does shipwrecks. It has always done shipwrecks: that's what it's made for. No other county in Britain can put on a wreck quite like Cornwall can. It is shipping's Ultima Thule, England's legendary resting place, the coast where all the best vessels go to die. Though statistically it is not the county in the UK with the highest number of wrecks per mile of coastline, it is undoubtedly the county with the worst reputation. No other part of Britain comes close to Cornwall's infamy; no other part of Britain would want to try. And if wrecking could ever claim to be a profession, then it was Cornwall which made it so. Though the wreckers of Cornwall were never alone – their work being seconded by a silent band of sympathisers all the way from the Pentland Firth to the Western Rocks – it is un-questionably Cornwall which stands out. Ask anyone, anywhere in the country, what the word 'wrecker' means to them, and the word 'Cornwall' tends to follow shortly after. In this particular universe, the Cornish are kings, dons, godfathers; unquestioned superiors to everyone else in Britain. Those who know about wrecking know that there were whole sections and sub-sections of the local population who were full-time self-employed free-range ship-lifters. They know that the Cornish lured ships onto the rocks, they know they had a whole industry devoted to thieving, and they know they put out false lights. People might have read or seen *Whisky Galore* or have heard of the Goodwin Sands, but what they really know is that the Cornish were at it, harder, fiercer, and longer than anyone else.

To understand why, and how, so many ships have collided with Cornwall, all you need to do is to find a large-scale map or chart of the southern English coast. Though Cornwall is not the largest of Britain's mainland counties, it is the one with the longest area of shoreline. Wherever you are in Cornwall, you are never far from the sea. From the land that proximity is its attraction. The county's mixture of charming beaches and enfolded coves lure the tourists in their tail-backed droves. But from the sea, those coves and cliffs are custom-made repellants, designed to keep the natives in and the foreigners out. Cornwall has it all: a combination of beauty and violence generations of sailors could, and did, die for. Look at a wreck map of the county, and the tiny black crosses cluster like rust around every last inch.

It has been calculated that the past 700 years have brought over 3,500 wrecks to Cornwall and the Scilly Isles; about 13 ships per square mile of coastline. But, like the Scilly Isles twenty-eight miles below it, Cornwall cannot easily be avoided. Shipping heading for America, towards west-coast ports or into the Channel all have to give it the wide berth due to such an infamous landfall. Navigators travelling from any direction can still expect to find every possible configuration of oceanographic unpleasantness, from submerged reefs to unmarked shallows. Despite this, both its coasts have always overlooked a huge variety of domestic and international traffic. The south coast saw East Indiamen heading down the Bay of Biscay, passenger liners on their way to New York, and freight carriers sailing for Dover. The west coast watched over the full fetch of the Atlantic, from small local colliers and trawlers to the traders laden with cargos for Liverpool and Glasgow.

The two seas which border the county – the English Channel and the Atlantic – have entirely different personalities, and thus two competing aims in life. The Channel funnels water through the gap running south-west to north-east between England and France, while the Atlantic rolls all the way from here to America. When the two waters meet they create conflict: shallows, overfalls, unexpected tidal races. Waves and weather conditions coming from the west have had plenty of space –

3,000 miles or more – in which to develop force and momentum, and while the weather on shore can be still to the point of breathlessness, the incoming swells have had a whole ocean to grow in. In Cornwall it is entirely possible to go from a flat calm to uncontrollable pitching within the space of minutes, and it is said that spray from an Atlantic storm can sometimes reach ten miles inland. The weather from the Atlantic comes in like a lion; fast, noisy, dramatic. As Mike Collier, the Maritime and Coastguard Agency's fishing vessel surveyor at Newlyn puts it, the Atlantic gets 'rough, and very rough, and bloody-hell-type rough'. Pounded on their seaward sides, sailors knew that there was not much solace to be sought from the land, since there are few large harbours of refuge along the west coast, and the prevailing wind often converted those which did exist into lee shores. So it is hardly surprising that along this stretch of coastline alone, 2,000 vessels are known to have been lost.

The Channel is more complex. Because of the comparative proximity of land on either side, there is far less space for storms to build up. The Channel, like the North Sea, produces short, steep waves, with deeper troughs and higher peaks than the Atlantic. Weather patterns rise and fall abruptly, with less predictability than on the west. Ships in trouble find themselves racing for the shoreline only to discover what generations of sailors have learned to their cost: the south coast is often deceptive and never safe. While it may be overlooked by a softer coastline than the west, there are more natural hazards and more tricks to fool the eye. From the Lizard Peninsula to Dodman Point, the incoming navigator has to dodge and weave like Homer once did. If in need of a safe harbour, ships coming down from the west would have to turn the corner at Land's End and make it safely into Newlyn or Penzance, running the hazards of the Longships Reef, Mount's Bay or Looe Bar – which appears as a long stretch of sandy beach, but is in fact an underwater cliff. Cornwall's south coast runs for about

100 miles, and over the centuries it has managed to accumulate as many – if not more – wrecks than the fiercer, bleaker west.

But if the county's coastline is repulsive, then its reputation is worse. Part of that notoriety is down to the efforts of one person. Though wrecking was predominantly a male trade, it was a woman who did most to perpetuate it. In 1935, Daphne Du Maurier (born in London but formed in Cornwall) wrote *Jamaica Inn*. The heroine, Mary Yellan, is orphaned young, and goes to live with her uncle Joss and aunt Patience on Bodmin Moor. Their house, and their mode of living, tend towards the gothic; Joss is 'nearly seven feet high' and built to terrify. He does no work, but quite a lot of wuthering. Aunt Patience is feeble and hapless, while Jamaica Inn itself is cold and full of ghosts. For an inn, it is also strangely guest-less, though it does seem to get used as a staging post for midnight couriers delivering large, heavy packages.

One night, a dense fog descends. Uncle Joss – who has by now become almost completely nocturnal – offers Mary a sightseeing trip. When the two of them reach the coast, they find other men have arrived already and are spread out across the cliff tops waiting for something. What Mary thinks at first is a star shining close to the tip of the headland then begins to sway slightly with the motion of the wind. 'The star,' she realises, 'was a false light placed there by her uncle and his companions.' The men and Mary watch and wait, until, 'out of the mist and darkness came another pin-prick of light in answer to the first.' The second light moves closer and Mary is able to see the outline of a ship, creeping through the fog towards the shore. Mary realises that the ship is being drawn towards the false light, believing it to be either a signal of safe harbourage or the navigation light of another ship finding its way more confidently through the dark. The ship plunges towards the coast until, inevitably, it hits the rocks and begins to dissolve. The men, who had remained almost silent while they waited for the ship, 'ran like madmen hither and thither upon the beach, yelling and screaming, demented and inhuman. They waded waist-deep into the breakers, careless of danger, all caution spent; snatching at the bobbing, sodden wreckage borne in on the surging tide ... When the first body was washed ashore, mercifully spent and gone, they clustered around it, diving among the remains with questing, groping hands, picking it clean as a bone; and, when they had stripped it bare, tearing even at the smashed fingers in search of rings.'

As Mary explains to the local vicar – who takes an unhealthy interest in Jamaica Inn's guests – 'They are in it, every one of them, from the coast to the Tamar bank ... they've murdered women and children with their own hands, they've held them under the water; they've killed them with rocks and stones. Those are death wagons that travel with road by night and the goods they carry are not smuggled casks alone, with brandy for some and tobacco for another, but the full cargoes of wrecked ships bought at the price of blood, the trust and the possession of murdered men.' In *Jamaica Inn*, Du Maurier name-checked every single myth about wreckers since the dawn of sailing: the false light, the victims held down to drown, the ripping-off of jewellery, the Faustian bargains struck with the sea. *Jamaica Inn* told the public what wrecking was supposed to be, and who its practitioners were. The rumours which had always swirled around the Cornish were given fictional form and settled for ever in the public imagination.

And yet most Cornishmen will tell you two things: firstly, that what the Cornish mean by a wrecker is subtly but unmistakeably different to what the rest of the country means by a wrecker, and secondly that, despite the overwhelming clouds of smoke, there is no true fire in the belief that any Cornishman ever deliberately caused a wreck. When a Cornishman confesses to wrecking, he assumes that the listener understands that the word does not suggest anything more than mild-mannered beachcombing, or – at worst – the liberation of a few unwanted bits of flotsam. According to the Cornish definition, wrecking is a gentle, vegetarian sport, not the carnivorous industry found elsewhere. As the historian A. K. Hamilton-Jenkin put it in his 1932 book on Cornwall and the Cornish: 'For the latter-day Cornishman, wrecking has come to mean little more than a pastime, representing at the most an occasional opportunity of gaining a few perquisites of a more or less illegitimate kind.' A wrecker in Cornwall is always passive, never active; he is the salvor – or the gatherer – of existing wreckage. He does not cause, or seek to cause, a wreck, and he disassociates himself from those who do. Like the inhabitants of almost every coastal area in Britain, Cornishmen might benefit from the small odd-ments left by a wreck, but they never, ever forced its happening. A true Cornishman is a tender-hearted creature, first to save life and last to profit.

As for the rumours, the Cornish have no idea why they have been so slandered. Though they may have been accused of wrecking by everyone from Scilly to the Shetland Isles, and though they will concede that once in a while they did undertake a spot of conscientious seaside clearance work, most Cornish will tell you that, if it existed at all, wrecking was unquestionably only ever undertaken by Kentish men, or Hebrideans, or boatloads of marauding Scillonians. But definitely not the Cornish. The Cornish never lured ships, they never drowned shipwreck victims, and – most emphatically of all – they never showed false lights. In fact, they probably would not even know what a false light was, and in the extremely unlikely event that they did know, they would pre-sume it a rumour put about by foul-minded outsiders, probably from London. True, there were always a lot of shipwrecks around the coast, and – in the days when Cornwall was almost inaccessible to all but the most fundamentalist customs men – there was undoubtedly a lot of smuggling. When ships did come ashore, the population would often selflessly risk their lives to rescue both crew and cargo. But deliberate wrecking? False lights? No. Never. Anyway, as the Cornish point out, why bother trying to cause a shipwreck when every winter brought ships ashore in their thousands? Why, if they were such savages, did their lifeboat crews go on saving shipwreck victims year after year at such appalling cost to themselves and their families? Why is it only the Cornish who get the notoriety, when – if the old stories are to be believed – half the counties in Britain were out there on the shoreline with carts and lights and axes at the first puff of a storm? Besides, why has no-one ever properly considered the insubstantiality of the false-light story? The legends say that Cornishmen would tie a lantern round a horse's neck or to a cow's horns, and would lead the beasts along the cliff tops so that the motion of the light imitated the swinging of a ship's lantern. But how many people have ever tried tying a hot oil lamp around any part of an animal's anatomy? The reaction – outrage, panic, a strong smell of singed hair – would scarcely suit the stealth of a well-prepared wrecker.

Joe Mills is a local historian living in St Day near Redruth. His voice on the phone sounds middle-aged, but in person he is much older, his face framed by a bright halo of wispy white hair. Though a little deaf, and prone to occasional lapses of short-term memory, one suspects that even now, he doesn't miss much. He served with the Navy on destroyers both during and after the war, though he insists I turn off the Dictaphone before he will talk about it – 'I don't like boasting'. He is also a Cornishman to the bone, and proud of it.

He remembers both his mother and his grandmother telling him: 'We're not English, you know, we're Cornish,' and has spent much of his life studying the differences between the two states. 'We have distinct racial characteristics. The Cornish language was spoken freely well into the eighteenth century, and in the first decades of the nineteenth century it was still prevalent. That characteristic is there. Cornwall has been neglected by the rest of the UK for a very very long time. It has a long history of being comparatively poor. We don't have the big, rich families – not many of them – that you get in the shires. You don't get the sort of farming families that you get in Oxfordshire, Wiltshire, Dorset.'

Inherent to the Cornish sense of identity, he thinks, is the sea and its proximity. 'Cornwall is a narrow promontory, and nowhere in Cornwall are you very far from the sea. At the far end, where we join with Devon, is the widest part, and there you can be forty miles from the sea, I suppose. But down at this end, you're not often as much as ten miles from the sea on one side or another. It makes us very familiar with tides, very familiar with cliffs, very familiar with water. And native Cornish, like native animals of any sort, learn through generations what is dangerous.'

It is not just that sea's length he finds awe-inspiring, but its depth, and what comes up from those deeps. 'We've got an unbridled Atlantic ocean, which meets nothing until it reaches here – the fury of it is unbelievable to people who haven't experienced this sort of shore. It's horrifying. You see the Bishop lighthouse or the Wolf sticking up out of the sea, but you never think of the rocks below it going down and down – it's a mountain, and you're only seeing the mountain top. During my time at sea, I never thought of anything being more than ten feet below what I could see. Like everyone who went to sea for the first time, someone said to me, do you know how far we are from the nearest land, and I would start saying, 350 miles, maybe 400 miles, and they'd say, no, 5 miles. Straight down. Five miles of water – you can't imagine it, can you?'.

For all their familiarity and opportunity, however, Mills categorically refutes the suggestion that the Cornish would ever have taken part in deliberate wrecking, or that the false light story has any validity. 'I don't think they were great wreckers. No, I don't subscribe to any theory that there was deliberate wrecking. I would say never. There is no evidence that [the use of false lights] ever took place here.' As Mills points out, the law always distinguishes between manslaughter and murder, even when the victim is a ship. The Cornish might steal cargo, they might rip a ship to pieces, they might even raid the customs house, but they would not, he says, ever have deliberately drawn a ship towards danger.

There was, however, plenty of passive wrecking. 'The only wrecking done – and they did use the term wrecking – was going out and getting what you could off ships. I remember in my boyhood going off to the coast here and there to see, and also going along the beaches to see what had been washed in. If you heard of a shipwreck – and news does travel fast – it was commonplace to go down to the beach to see what you could get. In my younger days if, for example, a ship went ashore near St Ives carrying packing cases full of paint or something like that, and it came washing in, we'd go down there because paint was worth saving and if you didn't like the colour, you could sell it to somebody else. Also you had people who lived near the coast and who would walk along the beach every day at low tide to pick up the jetsam that was there. Strictly speaking, you're not supposed to keep it, but certainly as far as one's own conscience was concerned, you felt perfectly clear, keeping whatever there was.'

Mills only remembers one occasion when he became involved in what he considers to have been 'serious wrecking'. Round-about 1936, a French or Spanish ship (he is not sure which) shed its deck cargo of wine out at sea, and over the next few days, the barrels floated in along the north Cornish coastline. 'If you were to go to Porthtowan beach and you're looking out to sea, on your left-hand side there's a big rock broken away from the cliff. There's a gap between it as wide as this room is long, and you go through there to the next beach if the tide is out. The rock is called Tobban Rock, and the next beach is called Tobban beach. There's no access to Tobban beach except when the tide is fully out, or you're prepared to climb the cliff above it, which is about 200 foot high there, I suppose.

'I had an Austin 16 Saloon at that time, and I remember taking a couple of buckets and driving it down to the coast. Not down to the beach, but up to the cliff tops, because the barrels which were washed up at Porthtowan had the customs people to guard them, and you couldn't get them. Some of the casks of wine were damaged, some were completely smashed and the sea water had got in, but there were casks – and I'm talking about casks with that sort of diameter' – he stands up and raises his hand to shoulder height, maybe five foot off the ground – 'which were completely unspoilt. So you knocked the bung in, and then you rolled it. And then you would push the thing over so that the wine gushed out, and you held your bucket underneath. And trip after trip! I went up and down those cliffs – I'd love to show you, because you probably wouldn't believe how dangerous and how damn silly it was – but I went up and down with these buckets of wine. I remember I had two buckets of wine I carried up, and when I got to a really perilous part I would put down one bucket, go up with the other, pour it into the churn, and come back for the remaining one.

'The first 10 feet, someone had cut little steps in the cliff, but from then on you were on your own. Perilous – awful, I wouldn't go down there now. And then I poured the wine into a milk churn which was at the back of the car and took it home. It wasn't very good really, but we drank it all the same. The wine was being washed in for two or three weeks, and there were times when customs came over there – they knew it had come in, and they knew we were taking stuff. I remember on one of my trips, coming from the barrels with a bucket if not two buckets of wine, and the customs man met me in that gap. And I thought, "Oh God", and put my buckets down, not that I was in time to hide them. He said, "Anything over there?" I said no. And then he turned and walked away!' Mills laughs. 'In the context of what had been going on for a week or two, you could understand it. He'd been given an impossible task – these damn things washing in all up and down the coast for about twelve or fifteen miles.'

Before I leave, he returns again to the subject of false lights. 'I don't think you'll find much evidence of deliberate wrecking,' he says. 'I'm quite emphatic, and I'm quite convinced, and I'm not trying to protect my forebears – I'm quite convinced that there was no deliberate wrecking of ships.'

The law supports Mills's view, though the evidence does not. A search through the sessions of the local magistrate's courts yields a view of the Cornish as opportunists, but not as murderers. Though there were plenty of convictions for 'plunder and riot', smuggling, theft, and disorderly conduct, there are no known convictions for displaying false lights at any point in Cornish history. In fact, the only evidence points in quite the opposite direction. One of the few verifiable instances of deliberate wrecking in Cornwall occurred in 1680 when the keeper of St Agnes lighthouse was found to have deliberately left the lamp unlit and then to have looted the resulting wrecks. Trinity House subsequently barred any Cornishman from work on the St Agnes light.

In fact the only known case involving a mention of false lights was not in Cornwall at all, but further up the west coast in Wales. According to the *Shrewsbury Chronicle* of 1774, charges were brought by a Captain Chilcote against three 'opulent inhabitants' of Anglesey for 'feloniously plundering, stealing and taking away' several casks of rum and brandy, 'and divers other goods and merchandise'. During a heavy gale in September 1773, Chilcote's ship, the 80-ton *Charming Jenny*, en route from Dublin to Waterford, was said to have been lured by false lights onto the coast of Anglesey and wrecked. The three crew were killed when the vessel struck, though Chilcote and his wife reached the shore on a makeshift raft. 'Nearly exhausted and helpless, they lay for some time, till the savages of the adjacent places, more ravenous than the devouring elements from which they had just escaped, rushed down upon the devoted victims ... Happy to escape with his life, he hastened to the beach, in search of his beloved wife, when, horrid to tell, her half-naked and plundered corpse presented itself to his view – a dismal view!'. When an outraged inhabitant of Anglesey wrote to the paper refuting the claims, Chilcote wrote back claiming that,

> he has never accused any person of the murder of his wife, or of having put out false lights. There is a report in this country that his wife was alive when she was cast on shore, but he cannot say whether it is true or no. He says that she was stripped of her gown, shoes, buckles, cap and handkerchief, and that her pockets were cut off from her sides, wherein were seventy guineas, his watch and other effects. He was not stripped himself, but he says that some time after he was cast on shore, as he lay on the beach exhausted and speechless, but still retaining his senses, he saw a person coming towards him with a knife in his hand, who took his silver buckles out of his shoes; and cut one of his shoes with a knife. That as he lay in this deplorable condition, he saw the greater part of his cargo left on dry ground by the ebbing tide. He says that some time after, a great number of persons with boats, carts, drags and horses surrounded him, and plundered and carried away the whole so cast on shore, within the space of six hours.

One of the accused was acquitted and the other two were sentenced to death by hanging. From that case still lingers the only evidence that anyone in any part of the UK was ever prosecuted for displaying false lights.

And yet the myth of the Cornish as the first and worst of the deliberate wreckers remains persistent. Accounts written by observers – some reliable, some mendacious – make mention of savage practice, and novelists from the sixteenth century to the twenty-first have built on the image of the Cornish as a people just that little bit closer to the fishes than the rest of the country. Daphne Du Maurier was not alone in committing the wreckers to fiction, though she has probably done most to shape Cornwall's image in the public imagination. With *Rebecca* and *Frenchman's Creek*, she established an English version of Southern Gothic which is still recognisable in the way the county sees itself today. Though she told the secret, she was unhappy with its consequences. Returning in the late 1960s to Jamaica Inn, she found that, 'Today everything is changed . . . Motor coaches, cars, a bar, dinner of river-trout, baths for the travel-stained instead of a cream-jug of hot water. As a motorist, I pass by with some embarrassment, feeling myself to blame . . . As the author I am flattered, but as a one-time wanderer dismayed.'

Though *Jamaica Inn* was, and still is, the most famous of the Cornish wreckers tales, other novels told a similar story in equally vehement terms. J. F. Cobbs's *The Watchers on the Longships*, published in 1948, considered the Cornish to be 'a rude, and almost savage, set of people . . . little removed from barbarians'. Other writers went further, suggesting that the Cornish were not only responsible for false lights, but for completely false coastlines. According to the historian Kenneth Langmaid, as soon as local wreckers knew a lucrative ship was on its way towards Cornwall, they would begin constructing a makeshift stage set. The women in the village would be sent out to cut gorse and bracken, and the men would begin filling and trimming the oil lanterns. As night fell, the villagers would take their bundles of gorse and their lights to a hazardous stretch of headland nearby – preferably one which overlooked a convenient submerged reef just offshore. Armed with enough oil to last out the night, the women would station themselves at a point midway down the surrounding cliffs. Extra lights would also be placed at other points along the length of the cliff and near the water's edge. The men would row out a little way from the headland, towing behind them a small flotilla of makeshift rafts. When the target ship was sighted by the lookout, the women would light both gorse and lanterns, and the men would position a lamp on each of the rafts, pushing them out so they floated around the reef. To the approaching ship, the lanterns and the rising smoke on the cliff would look like the lights from a few friendly fishing cottages in a quiet cove, and the bobbing lamps on the rafts like boats at safe anchor. If – as was likely – the captain was by now navigating by dead-reckoning, he would probably not be troubled by the fact that he was four or five miles away from his anticipated destination. Only when his ship struck solid rock and the masts toppled down around him would he realise how completely he had been deceived. Maybe it's only a story. There again, maybe it's not.

There was also confirmation of the local passion for wrecking from more reliable sources. One senior naval officer described the Cornish as a bunch of 'lawless barn-door savages', and a wreck report in 1700 claimed that 'The number of rioters was so great and their threatenings so high, and their proceedings so outrageous that the ordinary ministers of justice durst not attempt to suppress them.' According to the *General Evening Post*, reporting news of a wrecked brigantine driven ashore near Looe in 1751, 'They are so used to night work, so Habituated to Defiance of any Authority and Contempt of the Laws, and generally more or less so inflamed with Spiritous Liquors that they are ever ready to perpetrate any Villainy that their Violent Temper and Love of Lucre shall prompt them to.'

In 1839 the commissioners appointed to look into the possibility of establishing a nationwide constabulary reported that, 'The population on the coast of Cornwall has long been addicted to this species of plunder ... Whilst on other parts of the English coast the persons assemble by hundreds for plunder on the occurrence of a wreck, on the Cornish coast they assemble on such occasions in thousands.' Even in the twentieth century, foreign sailors still talked of the Cornish the way white men talked of 'Hottentots'. 'I have been wrecked in different parts of the globe, even in the Fiji islands,' wrote the Dutch captain of the *Voorspoed*, a general cargo vessel wrecked in Perran Bay in 1901, 'but never among such savages as those of Perranporth.' An old story about a naive young curate posted to a Cornish parish sums up the general view. While out walking, he finds the corpse of a shipwreck victim on the beach. Rushing up the cliff towards the road, he accosts the first man he meets and asks him what he should do with the body. 'Search 'is pockets,' the man replies brusquely, and walks on.

The supposed ferocity of the Cornish was attributable to three things: remoteness, custom, and poverty. Originally, the rights to all wreck belonged to the Crown, which then distributed those rights to local landowners ('lords of the manor') in return for men and loyalty in times of war, or for money in times of peace. The lords thus had claim to anything and everything washed up on their particular section of foreshore. Over time, they found that claim so rewarding that ownership of wreck rights became as disputed as the wrecks themselves. To strengthen their claim, the lords usually enlisted the aid of the most easily bribed local magistrates and as many local troops as they could muster.

In most parts of the country, wreckers usually claimed they

were driven to plunder through destitution, and thus that wrecking should be regarded as a form of fishy Marxism, redistributing wealth and property from rich shipowners to poor labourers. The lords of the manor had no such justification. They were only interested in the redistribution of wealth from the rich to the slightly richer, and were said to requisition anything on their foreshores with an enthusiasm which starving men could not well have matched. To them, a good wreck constituted something between an international interior design consultancy and Ali Baba's cave; half the great houses in Cornwall were said to be furnished with Spanish oak, Flemish tapestries or Portuguese candlesticks. Lengthy disputes arose between shipowners who would demand the return of £10,000 worth of gold ingots or a chest full of jewels washed up on a Cornish beach, and lords, who would reply that the items had been mysteriously lost in transit. The lords also had the power and the resources to make the most of shipwrecks. Instead of one lone wrecker stacking up as much timber as his mule could carry, the lords of the manor scooped up anything and everything that appeared on their sands.

Unsurprisingly, the lords and their tenants loathed each other. The tenants complained that the lords enforced their rights too greedily, and the lords complained that the tenants were no more than axe-wielding murderers. From comparatively early times, the major land-bound industry in Cornwall had been the tin mines. As elsewhere, mining jobs were not lucrative; by the mid-eighteenth century, the average tinner could expect to earn between 16 and 21 shillings per month. In time, therefore, the tinners acquired a savage reputation. Relatively undamaged shipping driven ashore in the area would be stripped so rapidly that the tinners were often down to the ship's timbers by the time the authorities arrived, and it was alleged that the wreckers often consumed so much stolen alcohol that many would simply expire where they lay.

In March 1753, George Borlase, factor to the Onslows of Gulval near Penzance, wrote that:

> The people who make it their business to attend these wrecks are generally Tynners and as soon as they observe a ship on the Coast they first arm themselves with sharp axes and hatchets and leave their tyn works to follow those ships ... they'll cut a large trading vessel to pieces in one tide and cut down everybody that offers to oppose them ... I have seen many a poor man, half dead, cast ashore and crawling out of the reach of the waves fallen upon and in a manner stripp'd naked by those Villains, and if afterwards he has saved his chest or any more cloath's they have been taken from him ... I think whoever shd. forcibly take any goods out of the possession of such shipwreck'd sailor by force shd. suffer as highwaymen [highwaymen were traditionally hanged on a roadside gibbet].

It may well be that Borlase's outrage was genuine and that he was entirely above involvement in such practices himself, though what seems to have irritated him most was not the tinners' violence or amorality, but the fact that they instantly stopped work as soon as they spotted a vessel in distress. Often, the lords' scandalised tones owed more to their outrage at the tinners' success in stripping a wreck than it did to any genuine sense of injustice.

Sir John Killigrew of Arwenack was probably the best known of the lords, and his story exemplifies the combative relationship between landlord and tinner. Historically, the Killigrews had always had a strong family predilection for piracy; in 1583, it was said that a sword-wielding Lady Killigrew had boarded a Spanish ship moored in Falmouth harbour, drowned the crew and requisitioned the cargo. In 1619, Sir John applied to Trinity House for a patent to construct a light on the Lizard peninsula. Trinity House refused, so Killigrew petitioned the Lord High Admiral the Duke of Buckingham instead. He claimed that a light would put a stop to the local practice of showing false lights, and 'I assure your Lordship that most of the houses near the Lizard are built with the ruins of ships.'

Though his petition sounded pious enough, Killigrew was moved less by compassion for distressed mariners than by the prospect of levying dues on all shipping passing the light. Despite Trinity House's protests – and the family precedent – the Duke granted the patent and Killigrew began construction. When half-completed, a group of local tinners attacked the workers and pulled down the half-built light. Killigrew was forced to hire a company of dragoons to keep further incursions at bay, and complained that he had found the whole business, 'far more troublesome than I expected, for the inhabitants near think they suffer by this erection. They affirm I take away God's grace from them. Their English meaning is that now they shall receive no more benefit by shipwreck, for this will prevent it. They have been so long used to reap profit by the calamity of the ruin of shipping that they claim it hereditary, and hourly complain on me. Custom breeds strange ills.' The light became Killigrew's nemesis, since maintaining it in adequate working order cost far more than the sum of any dues he managed to collect. Eventually, Killigrew ran out of money, and the light fell derelict.

In almost all parts of Cornwall the wreckers were also favoured by geography. Now, those who want to get to Cornwall have to join the back of a very long queue. As any seat-sore Bank Holiday tripper knows, getting from London to the south-west still takes as long, if not longer, than it takes to get to Aberdeen – double that on a hot mid-summer weekend in the school holidays. The improvement and expansion of the A30 has speeded access a little, but Cornwall's recent popularity has more or less cancelled out any temporary advantage from better roads. Every last cove and corner of the county is stuffed to the point of discomfort from mid-April onwards. In the past, however, the problem with Cornwall was not its popularity, but the opposite. A mid-nineteenth century journey to Penzance from London by mail coach would have taken at least three days, which was seventy-two hours too long to effectively protect any wreck which came ashore. No-one came to Cornwall, so no-one saw. Though the county had its usual quota of magistrates, coastguards and preventive men, Cornwall's distance from London – the very thing which now renders it so popular – proved to be the wreckers' most effective weapon.

Besides, even when the law could have got there in time, there was no guarantee they would have found their targets. Cornwall seems to have been custom built for secrecy. The county is filled with tiny lanes enclosed by high hedgerows so thick with age and overgrowth they seem as much part of the natural landscape as the cliff tops, steep village streets down which nothing wider than a bicycle can pass with comfort, unexpected coves appearing and disappearing behind another few miles of switchback road, twisting river mouths and thickly wooded hillsides, glimpses of water vanishing behind ambiguous headlands, similar-sounding place names, and always that dreamlike sense of having passed this way a little time before. It is that confusion, the sense of having stumbled across a half-discovered land, which forms so much of Cornwall's attraction. You could stay in the same place every summer for twenty years and still get lost every time. The fishing village at the bottom of a near-vertical hillside with its bath-sized cove, its perfect pub and its peeling red phone box might be there one weekend but have vanished by the next; the patch of beach on which you built a fire and cooked an impromptu meal might seem vivid in memory but no longer exists in fact. Walk along the same stretch of headland and somehow the path leads you off to a different place on each revisitation. Sail up one of the inlets and stare round you as the sun goes down; whatever you see will be gone by the time you return. Landmarks get nearer or further, headlands appear or repeat; expected signs refuse to materialise. Cornwall is England's mirage, parts of it always vanishing before your eyes. From land and sea, it is a cartographer's nightmare and a wrecker's dream – a place that could not possibly have been better designed for concealment.

In the past, those visitors who did make it safely into the county – either by land or by sea – had often been sent there by the Church. Most protested vehemently against the wreckers. In a lengthy report by the Reverend G. C. Smith in his mid-nineteenth century letters to a friend (later published as *The Wreckers, or A Tour of Benevolence from St Michael's Mount to the Lizard Point*), he wrote that:

> Natural depravity and the custom of centuries have inspired the inhabitants of the coast with a rapacity for plundering those wrecks ... the name of 'Wrecker', therefore, applies to vast numbers, who inhabit the various parishes along the coast; and unfortunately such has been the frequency of wrecks every winter, that the people look as naturally for them at that season, as the sharks for the devotees who perish in the waters of the Ganges. Men, women, and children usually join in this work; and if the vessel contains a cargo of wine or spirits, it is not uncommon for five or six persons to drink so much as to perish on the beach, or in the adjacent lanes ... When the news of a wreck flies round the coast, thousands of people are instantly collected near the fatal spot; pick-axes, hatchets, crowbars, and ropes, are their usual implements for breaking up and carrying off whatever they can. The moment the vessel touches the shore she is considered fair plunder, and men, women, and children are working on her to break her

up, night and day. The precipices they descend, the
rocks they climb, and the billows they buffet, to seize
the floating fragments, are the most frightful and
alarming I ever beheld; the hardships they endure
(especially the women) in the winter, to save all they
can, are almost incredible. Should a vessel laden with
wine or spirits approach the shore, she brings certain
death and ruin, to many with her. The rage and
fighting, to stave in the casks and bear away the spoil, in
kettles and all manner of vessels, is brutal and shocking.
To drunkenness and fighting, succeed fatigue, sleep,
cold, wet, suffocation, death and – what? An eternity!
Last winter we had some dreadful scenes of this
description. A few in this neighbourhood, it seems,
having a little more light than others, scrupled to visit
a wreck that came on shore last winter, on a Lord's
day, lest it should be breaking the Sabbath; but they
gathered all their implements into a public house, and
waited until the clock struck twelve – at midnight,
therefore, they rushed forth, all checks of conscience
being removed. Imagine, to yourself, my dear Sir, 500
little children in a parish, brought up every winter in
this way, and encouraged both by precept and example
to pursue this horrid system.

But even Smith drew back from accusing the wreckers of
murder:

The Wreckers seldom or ever reap profit by these
nefarious labours, for they are found at the end of the
year nearly the same as the beginning. It appears, for
the credit of the country, that these are confined to a
few western parishes, and that even there no deeds
of personal inhumanity towards the unhappy sufferers
have been performed in modern times, even by the

plunderers themselves ... Inheriting from their ancestors an opinion that they have a right to such spoils
as the sea may place within their reach, many among
the enlightened inhabitants secure whatever they can
seize, without any remorse; and conclude without any
hesitation, that nothing but injustice, supported by
police, and sanctioned by law, can wrench it from
their hands.

On closer inspection, however, anomalies begin to appear.
G. C. Smith's account can be found almost word-for-word
in a variety of different sources. Which is fine, except that in
one or two of the accounts, small details become large ones,
plain anecdotes grow ornaments, and the wreckers turn inno-
cent or guilty according either to the date of writing or to
the intended readership. Sabine Baring-Gould, parson, squire,
folk historian and composer, was the first writer to consolidate
an image of his flock as a bunch of godless murderers swinging false lights on cliff tops. And the Reverend Hawker of
Morwenstow, whose account of wrecking near Bude makes
Dickens's description of the death of Little Nell look even-
handed, has been soundly discredited by several recent writers.
Hawker was born in 1803 and became vicar of Morwenstow
on the west coast of Cornwall in 1834, during which time he
became famous for his eccentricities and his overactive imagination. Even his son-in-law and first biographer, Charles Byles,
conceded that Hawker, 'never let facts, or the absence of them,
stand in the way of his imagination'.

In part, the outrage of vicars such as Hawker was undoubtedly genuine, not least since it usually fell to them to organise
(and, in many instances, to pay for) some form of Christian
burial for unclaimed shipwreck victims. Until the early nineteenth century, corpses were either left to rot where they lay or
buried in shallow graves along the cliff tops or in rough ground

close by. Old local habits proved hard to shift. In common with many coastal communities, the Cornish believed that those who saved a drowning man would be repaid with their own death. The distaste for touching the deceased remained so profound that an act was passed in 1808 offering a 5-shilling bounty to anyone reporting a corpse, while penalising them £5 for failing to do so. The act only made a partial impression. Hawker claimed that he supplemented this with a further five shillings of his own, though even with financial incentives it cannot have been a pleasant task to go in search of 'gobbets' on the beach – the lumps of flesh and bone which was often all that remained of a crew after the sea and the wreckers had done their worst – or to have answered the midnight knocks on the door to find someone bringing news of a hand, a foot, or a severed head ashore.

Hawker may have often altered or inflated his own role in events, but what was unquestionably true was that between 1824 and 1874, eighty-one vessels were recorded as having been wrecked around the coast near Bude, and that as the local vicar, Hawker would have been forced to deal with them. During his time in Morwenstow, he claimed to have personally buried over forty victims. In 1868, after yet another wreck, Hawker wrote: 'I do indeed pray that I may be spared as much as possible the misery and indeed danger of proximity to the dead when far advanced in decay . . . If it were not for the fact that burial of the dead is one of the seven acts of mercy that God will surely requite, my heart would fail me.'

Though there is little doubt that the majority of Cornish vicars fulfilled their calling with honesty and fortitude, there is equal evidence that some went spectacularly native. The ancient smuggling rule that a couple of casks would be laid aside for the local man of God extended to wrecking as well. When the authorities began a search for the missing cargo of the *Lady Lucy*, wrecked off Porthleven in 1939, they discovered four hogsheads of brandy hidden in the cellar of the local parson. Any vicar who had been posted to a parish in which every single inhabitant had been brought up since birth with the firm conviction that plundering ships was not only a duty, but a God- and law-given right, would very likely find it more their life's worth to object. In truth, some Cornish vicars probably were in league with the wreckers, some did all they could to oppose them, and some merely turned a blind eye. There is an old anecdote of a man bursting into church with news of a wreck on the rocks nearby. The parson hears the man out, turns back to his congregation and orders them to remain seated. But instead of continuing with the service, he flings off his surplice, and announces, 'Now we can all start fair!' before bolting for the door and the path to the beach. The story, inevitably, always concerns a Cornish church, and a Cornish parson. Another early account on similar lines claimed that:

> If a wreck happened to occur in Cornwall while Divine Service was being held, notice of it was given out from the pulpit by the parson. It is said of the wreckers, I know not with what truth, that the strongest among them would swim out through the breakers and drown the exhausted survivors by thrusting them under water as the poor wretches struggled, with failing strength, to reach the shore. There were even pious fanatics who went so far as to admonish the people that it was sinful to succour a vessel in distress upon the Sabbath; that it was, in fact, sinful to save life. On the other hand, refusal to do so was a proof of true religiousness since it showed that they realised it was God's will that the ship should sink and the crew perish.

As the 1839 Commission on establishing a national constabulary heard, both the Cornish wreckers and their most zealous imitators in other parts of the country had been able to create a perfect circle of violence. Because they always appeared in such numbers, because they came armed and because they would stop at nothing – not even extreme personal risk – to attack a wounded ship, it was almost impossible to stop them. Besides, there was also confusion over the different official roles and duties. Lloyd's agents were expected to save and account for both ships and cargo, but had no power to protect vessels from plunder. The coastguard was regarded with suspicion and considered to be acting without legal authority, and those guards who did appear on the seething beaches usually felt themselves to be undermanned and overwhelmed. Customs officers were expected to protect property but were rarely given the means to do so, while the police force had no true force at all. It was hardly surprising that the only method left open to the various different officials was to call in the army – a device of last resort which took time and did little to instil confidence among either victims or shipowners.

Occasionally, not even the presence of soldiers was enough to suppress the looting. In 1817, when the brig *Resolution*, carrying a cargo of wine and oranges, was wrecked at Porthleven, a full-scale orgy was in progress within an hour. The local customs officer, realising that he was overwhelmed, galloped off in search of reinforcements and returned with a party from the Inniskilling Dragoons. The wreckers simply drove the soldiers from the beach and continued drinking well into the next day. It was not until twenty-four hours later, and the arrival of further military reinforcements, that the rioting was brought under control.

Even when the coastguard or the army did reach the coast quickly and saved some items from the predators, they could not always guarantee that their salvings would remain safe. Another particular Cornish speciality was the storming of customs houses and the removal of items put there for storage and disbursement. From the wreckers' point of view, they were doing no more than reclaiming what was rightfully theirs, but the threat of continuing violence even after cargoes had been locked up provided yet another deterrent to prevention.

But despite all this evidence – the victims, the lords, the shipowners, the sea-captains, the vicars, the officials – the locals remain adamant that there is no such thing as a real Cornish wrecker. In bookshops and libraries, in museums and harbours, in bars, shops, hotels and tourist traps, the answer is always the same: the Cornish never deliberately wrecked ships, and they never used false lights. In most places, the fact that I'm asking these questions at all is taken as further proof – if proof were needed – of bad faith. 'There was no wrecking here,' says the manageress of a bookshop in Falmouth. 'That was all just stories made up.' So how come so many of those stories were 'made up' by the Cornish themselves? 'They weren't,' she says. 'They were made up by Outsiders.' Outsiders like Du Maurier, Hamilton-Jenkin and Borlase? I browse for a while among the shelves and then buy two books off her, one called *Cornish Wreckers*, the other *Cornish Shipwrecks*.

Falmouth high street is bright and busy, with shops selling knick-knacks to the passing trade: Cornish rock, Cornish pasties, Cornish boats, Cornish pictures, Cornish key fobs and tea towels. Over the years, Cornwall has become very adept at flogging its past. Just down the road, the new Cornwall Maritime Museum is nearing completion. Land's End has a real wreck and The Relentless Sea. Charlestown has an entire museum devoted to shipwreck and rescue, offering pirates, smugglers and an appropriately salty version of the county's criminal past. And Jamaica Inn is still open and still recycling its old myths. Almost every shop in the county is filled with images of bearded, peg-legged sea dogs clutching swords or pasties on everything from beer mats to key rings. Over the years, it would seem that the Cornish has figured out how to have things both ways, selling images of themselves as swash-

buckling plunderers to the tourists, whilst simultaneously deny-
ing that anything actually took place.

And so, having exhausted more conventional methods of
research – libraries, salvage websites, statistics, legal reports,
local histories – all that remains is to try a less conventional
method. In mid-April, the port of Newlyn is already sluggish
with tourists loitering down the narrow side streets. Cars move
slowly along the coastal road between Mousehole and
Penzance; families stop to gaze up at the fishermen's cottages,
looking for something – anything – to buy. At some time in the
past, Newlyn and Penzance were two separate towns, but the
years have coupled them together. Like Edinburgh and Leith,
the larger and the smaller now co-exist, one working, the other
idle. Penzance is more grown-up and developed, rich with
tourists and visiting yachts. Newlyn also gets the tourists, but
has managed – just – to cling on to its day-job. Remove the
tourists, and it would be a quiet place: small, solid, sure of itself,
built to stare straight towards the worst of the Atlantic weather.
It looks like the sort of place that hasn't changed much since
the wreckers were rampant – if, of course, there ever were any
wreckers.

It therefore comes as something of a shock to realise that
this port, with its couple of acres of sheltered water and its
modest practicality, is now England's largest fishing port. In
other words, England's fishing fleet has shrivelled so completely
that this place, with its nineteen or so trawlers, is now as good
as things get. This morning, there are seven or eight fishing
trawlers lined up against the quay, some warming quietly in
the spring sun, some inflamed by a cold fountain of blue sparks.
Two or three men are moving around their decks, taking a
welding torch to the winches and the rusted fish hatches. The
boats are not large – maybe 80-foot long – and each of them has
evidently sailed through many years of Atlantic gales. On most,
the paintwork is rusty, the fenders have split, the decks are

rutted and the wheelhouse glass is opaque with age. There is no glamour here, no dazzling white multi-million pound super-trawlers, no proof of much more than the most basic levels of equipment and comfort. Instead, there's just a bunch of old boats doing the same job as they've done for the past thirty years. The only evidence of success – or even of modest pros-perity – are up on the masts, almost out of view. The radar equipment and satellite aerials on most of the boats are new, and look it: big, expensive equipment designed not only to alert the rest of the maritime world to the vessels' existence, but to hunt down every last fish they can from here to Newfoundland.

In a small office overlooking the quay, Mike Collier sits surrounded by the evidence of wreck. He is the Maritime and Coastguard Agency's local fishing vessel surveyor, a post which requires him to enforce the regulations on ship safety and to deal with casualties if and when they happen. On the wall are a number of photographs, one of the *Cita*, one of a large ugly vessel heeled over in shallow water with most of her hull exposed, and two of private yachts high and dry on the rocks. Collier himself is friendly and amiable, fielding calls throughout our conversation and obviously at home in his chosen occu-pation. Looking out at the trawlers moored outside, I wonder how many vessels he is responsible for. 'Gosh,' he says, thinking carefully. 'The boats vary in size – we've got some of 35 metres right down to five metres. And there must be about sixty boats which come into the bigger category – the over 15 metre category. Below 15 metres, we've probably got something like a hundred, I suppose, in total. It's quite a big fleet. The only problem is, it's quite an ageing fleet. They'll invest in equip-ment and they'll keep the boats up to scratch, but there hasn't been much investment in new tonnage down here – it's stayed fairly static. We've got one new boat in the port and a couple that are nearly new, but that's all. It isn't because they can't afford to, it's because people don't want to change their boats –

they're quite happy, they're familiar with the boat that they've got. If you've got a boat which is paid for, it doesn't owe you anything, and all it's costing you is the maintenance, then I can see the point of not investing. Because to buy a new boat is going to cost you probably – I don't know, let's be conservative and say £500,000 to buy a good new fishing boat. You might get something a bit cheaper than that, but that's the usual price.'

Since all fishermen are expected to be expert sailors, any problems which arise are less due to human error than to mechanical failure. 'Anything that's mechanical or floats on the sea is liable to be beset at any time by problems. You can have your car serviced regularly and still the finger of fate will come out of the cloud one day, and say, "You, you bastard, snap" . . . the water pump breaks, but you just coast to the side of the road and get on to the AA or Britannia, and they'll come and get you, but if you're 150 miles south-west of here and it's blowing howling hooligan and the water pump packs up, you've got a problem.' Which, presumably, is exacerbated by all the risks in fishing off a dangerous coast. Collier considers. 'It is, but fishing is done by people who know that it's dangerous and there-fore react totally differently than if . . . Fishing is a controlled danger, it's an accepted danger, it's not just a perceived danger for people standing on the shore.'

Many of the shipping casualties caused by human error are due to watchmen falling asleep. Sailing of any kind can be both physically and mentally exhausting, and it is unsurprising that those left on lookout during the night often succumb. As Collier points out, the pressures are even greater for fishermen. 'It happens – it's one of these things that can happen in the best regulated vessels. Human beings get tired at night; the automatic reaction in the hours of darkness is sleep, and they're working very hard.' He points to the picture of the yacht. 'That one was sleep-induced . . . Poor bloke – that was his worldly possessions, all gone. And all through tiredness – if he'd stayed out in the Atlantic, he'd have been alright.' Then, of course, there is the *Cita*, another infamous loss caused simply by some Polish sailor's need for a nap. Collier was involved in the salvage operation, and remembers the *Cita* with affection.

Had he come across instances of wrecking before then? 'Not directly, not causing vessels to be wrecked. It's a hearsay thing. But I am quite confident that it did happen, because certain areas, like this one, tended to be much more insular than they are now. People tended to stick more in their own little communities, and because of the poverty, any shipwreck would produce vast wealth for a small community, vast wealth. I mean, it would provide more than enough timber to keep them going for all their needs, for housing and repairs and stuff like that, and the cordage and the rope and the sails – just the basic ship itself would bring a tremendous amount of riches. I'm sure that it must have happened at some stage. Whether it happened to any great extent, well, that's another matter. I'm quite sure that it probably did happen, I'm sure it's not just folklore.'

The Maritime and Coastguard Agency evidently believes that wrecking occurred, though I suppose that even the knowledge-able and pragmatic Collier could be dismissed as yet another Outsider. I say goodbye to Collier and walk across the road. On the door of a nearby pub, there is a notice: 'Don't Bomb Iraq, Bomb Brussels Instead.' Inside, folded away from the midday heat, are a group of men in jeans and lumberjack shirts. The television is on and the sunshine through the windows flings beams of orange and gold light to the floor. The men gathered round the bar have evidently been there for some time and will be there for some time to come. As I walk in, they are clustered around a tall man standing slightly to the left of the bar, reminding him – in stereo and at length – that he recently failed to answer one of the preliminary questions on *Who Wants to Be A Millionaire* correctly, a question apparently so simple that only donkeys and foreigners could possibly have got it wrong.

Their target smiles back, neither shamed nor riled by the insults.

I wait by the door, watching the half-full pints glowing in the shadows and the layers of gauzy fag smoke drifting sideways through the draught. Finally, the man on the barstool turns. 'Yes?' he says. Does anyone know any wreckers round here, I say. 'What?' he says. A wrecker, I say. Wreckers. 'Wreckers?' he says. 'What sort of wrecker?' He looks hostile, all goodwill gone. False lights, I say. People who plundered ships. People who once lured ships onto rocks. *Whisky Galore*, *Jamaica Inn*, the *Cita*, that sort of thing. I now have the undivided attention of all the men in the bar, and only the TV is still laughing. People, I say hastily, who could theoretically have lured ships onto rocks. The men gaze at me – my bag, my Dictaphone, my librarian's smile – for a long time. No-one says anything. It's for a book, I say, looking at the floor. The silence continues long enough for the traffic noises outside to become audible and to overhear the conversation between two dog walkers out on the street. Perhaps, I think, as I listen to the receding footsteps, I could run away and get a proper job, a job in an office involving spreadsheets and meetings and half an hour set aside every day for kicking the photocopier. Not a job which involves walking into fishermen's pubs and asking complete strangers if they or their forebears ever took part in the kind of illegal maritime activities which gave Cornishmen a bad name, and if they would furthermore be prepared to discuss those illegal activities on the record, thus potentially opening themselves up to criminal prosecution several decades after the actual event.

'Mike Pearce,' says the man on the stool. 'Mike might talk, if you ask the right questions.' For a moment I just stand there, so startled not to have been either lynched or drowned that I cannot move. 'He's in The Dolphin every lunchtime. You'll catch him there.' I smile gratefully and walk back into the sunshine. Sure enough, across the road in the shadows of another bar is Mike Pearce: late middle-age, rough white hair, the rolling walk of a landsick man. When I explain my mission he chuckles. 'Give me a moment,' he says, 'and buy me a drink.' I get him a pint, and leave him to gather his thoughts. After a few minutes, he beckons me back over to the bar, breathing heavily into the Dictaphone. Like Joe Mills, he wants first of all to emphasise the difference in definitions. 'Put it this way, the word wrecker covers a lot of things. It's such a bad theory – I mean, if you pick up a lump of wood, you're wrecking, if you went aboard a ship, you were wrecking. A lot of people would call it looting, but it were wrecking, same again. I reckon half the houses in Scilly, and even over here in Newlyn, I reckon half the timber in those houses came from out of the wrecks. Only some of these' – he gestures southwards, down towards Mousehole and Newlyn's seafront houses – 'is paid for, I reckon.'

Pearce has lived in Cornwall for well over twenty years, though he was born and brought up in the Scilly Isles. Does he know if his own family were wreckers? 'I suspect so, put it that way. My grandfather was a very respected man in Scilly, and he used to have a pilot gig of his own. He came from St Martin's, but what he got up to I don't know.' Are the Cornish different to the Scillonians in their attitude to wrecking? 'Yes, they are. They are. Altogether. I think they're more . . . they're more . . .', he pauses. 'There wasn't really much in it – they'd both do anything for a bit of wrecking. Where we [the Scillonians] would cheer for the merchant men that was on these ships, they would come to make sure they were first at the wrecking. All from the Lizard side and that, it was what they could find first, and then they'd look after the crew. But in the old sailing days, they used to fear the Scillies, because they had a ferocious name. They had a worse name than round the Lizard and that way there.'

But it was the Cornish who became notorious, I say, not the

islanders. 'Yes, yes, I know, they do have a bad reputation. But the thing was, everybody knew the Scillies, and that was the first port of call you hit, so you used to get more wrecks there than what you did over here. Certain ships like the TW *Lawson*, the biggest sailing ship ever made, she sank there. The men over there risked their lives – and some of them lost their lives – rescuing the crew off her. We had a different look at life over there, we did, to what they did in Cornwall. Our advantage comes from the sea, and we relied on wrecks, because we were all fishermen and things like that. We'd say, look out for the crew first, but in Cornwall, half the people weren't even seamen – they were farmers. They were used to doing the wrecking, but they didn't have the same thought about the men at sea as proper seamen does. They'd say, "to hell with the crew, we'll have the cargo first".'

So what would happen when they got news of a wreck? 'If you could get aboard of her, you would get aboard of her – it was as easy as that. First thing would always be to make sure the crew were safe, and then grab what you could. Don't matter if there's police and customs sitting on every rock – there'd be a way to get aboard her somehow. After that, it's fair game. And if the weather was too bad and she was breaking up, you'd put your boat so as to pick up all the jetsam and flotsam out of the water then, and then wait ashore when the wind was the right way – we knew exactly which tide she was in. So you used to follow the flotsam around, you know. But it's surprising what used to get washed ashore. We used to like finding them big bales of crepe rubber. Crepe, you know, like what teddy boys used to wear on their shoes. There was quite a lot of them used to wash up, and they were worth quite a bit – a tenner a bale. That was quite a lot of money for them days.'

Which were the best ships? 'Oh, general cargo, yes, definitely, definitely. You'd find out what it was, you know, and if it was general cargo, you used to smile and if it carried coal you used to . . .' He scowls theatrically. 'The only thing any good then was things like what was in the galley: bottles, fags – nothing else was much good. You couldn't dive on her for scrap or nothing like that, because we didn't have no diving suits.' And would they expect to fight the customs for possession? 'In them days, if you picked up a matchstick, you had to give it to the Customs, and they've got to prove who has the ownership of it. And if they can't prove who owns it, then you get it. Oh, the Customs were very strict on these things – anything you salvaged had to be declared to 'em by law.' It sounds, I say, almost as if you treated it as a kind of game. 'Oh, yes, yes, with who could get away with it. You'd have one man distracting them, someone else as lookout, someone going out at midnight, going out in a gale of wind, getting aboard of her, things like that. They'd think "Oh, it's lashing down with rain, nobody'll be there tonight", and we'd already been there!.'

What was the best thing he ever got from a wreck? He takes a long thoughtful sip from his pint. 'The first banana I ever seen came off a wreck. That was off a tank landing craft that went ashore in Scilly. We went aboard of her, and wondered what these things were hanging up, and they were bananas.' He stops, then starts again. 'There was another one. I can't think of her at the moment, but she went on the Scilly rocks. Italian job. The *Isobel*? Mussolini struck a medal for all the local people who saved her crew off her. I've still got my grandfather's medal at home, signed by Mussolini. She went down, but she had everything from grand pianos to cattle aboard of her. There were men on Bryher seen burying grand pianos. I remember a grand piano in our house, in our front room. My father used to play it quite a lot.' And no-one ever had any suspicions about how it had got there? 'Well, everybody knew, didn't they? On a small island, you can't keep nothing quiet. Everybody knew.'

Where did people usually hide things? 'The pond. The field. Or in caves. On the seafront, under rocks. If you know a place, you'll always find somewhere. With the pianos, they waited six months till everything had cooled off, then they dug 'em up and . . .', he shrugs, 'we had pits already dug on the farms. As soon as we got ashore, we buried it. All ready, it was. Covered it over, and that was it – nobody ever found it. It was in the field – under barn floors was easy to find. We daren't hide anything near the houses, so we put it in the pond.'

He remembers other wrecks, other storms, whole households of wreckage. 'I got a radar set off one, I got a lifeboat off one. Oh yes. When I left Scilly, I loaded up all my furniture and I came across in that lifeboat. I had everything in it – television sets, everything, even household coal I had. I remember a good wreck in the 1950s. There was quite a controversy about her because certain people took a lot of the captain's personal gear and things like that. They had the Lloyd's detectives trying to trace the stuff. Her cargo weren't no good, but she had good pickings on her from up the crew side of it. We were aboard of her that night [she was wrecked] but the lifeboat couldn't go to sea. They knew roughly who it was because they knew there was only one boat good enough to get out there, and she was missing from her moorings in St Mary's. And then the lifeboat went out, and they had to stand off. Next morning, it was still very bad, mountains of sea going in, and the lifeboat thought they'd try and get out there again. And when they got out, there was nothing left. We'd been aboard of her that night.' What did you get off her? 'Oh, quite a lot of things. Well, I had a lot of things: boots, radar, bearings, compass, chronometer, all the stuff from the wheelhouse. But somebody nicked the captain's best silken hat and all that lot, and he didn't like that.'

He sits reminiscing for a while longer, stopping and starting, breathing into the tape recorder. So if a general cargo ship went ashore now, what does he think would happen? 'Well, you'd have the fishery protection boats there, you'd have the Customs cutters there, but there are so many of them these days with the drug smuggling and that, I reckon they would just completely put a circle around it. They'd have helicopters, all these things there. It would make it harder.' So does he think wrecking has finally died out? He shakes his head, vehement. 'It's never died out. Never has died out. You don't get so much of it now because of all these modern navigational aids and global navigation and all that, but it's still there.'

He's probably right. The *Cita* provided plenty of modern proof that the spirit of wrecking remains alive and well. And – though Mike Pearce is keen to draw a distinction between the methods of the islanders and the mainlanders – it probably would not have been the kind of difference that a shipwreck victim would have noticed. Besides, in many areas, people risked their own lives to make sure that crew and passengers on shipwrecks reached the shore safely. In the majority of cases, it was probably fair to assume that the wreckers were neither so callous nor so interested in the survivors that they would risk either injury or murder. They would save or assist shipwreck victims and consider their subsequent plunder as due repayment-in-kind. So why then do most Cornish people become so indignant when accused of wrecking? Perhaps because they know that while the county may still profit from selling skulduggery back to the tourists, it has also been affected by the ineradicable suspicion that anyone landing at its ports cannot always be guaranteed a helpful welcome.

Walking back across the harbour after saying goodbye to Mike Pearce, it occurs to me that, technically speaking, even he isn't properly Cornish. He might have been a wrecker, and he might have lived here for over twenty years, but still . . . Later on, in one of the local libraries, I chat to one of the archivists about the research I've been doing. She shakes her head. 'You won't find anything like that here,' she says. 'Maybe in the eighteenth century, but even then it was nothing like as bad as people from Outside said it was.' And so we're back where we started. What the English might say is their own misguided business. But the Cornish will sell you one thing and tell you another; they'll sell you the image of the false light, and tell you till the end of time that there is no such thing as a Cornish wrecker.

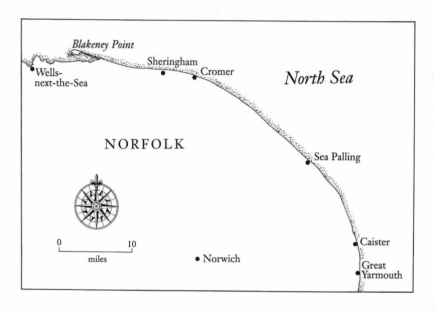

The East Coast

EIGHT

East Coast

Some people ornament their gardens with gnomes. Some people like sculpture, or gazebos, or patio sets. Richard Davies has boats. Two of them, upended, their prows setting a straight course for the sun and their sterns sailing along six feet under. The boats are painted black and red and are the first thing anyone who comes to the house will see. They stand proudly above the surrounding hedges and trees, sailing away to their ethereal destinations. These two additions to the local horticulture are Davies's way of telling the world (or at least a small Norfolk section of it) what he is and what he stands for.

The sea is everywhere here, lapping at the doorsteps, watermarking the walls. Davies and his family have been part of that sea for as long as anyone round here can remember. He is the ex-coxswain of the Cromer lifeboat, and one of a long line of Davies to make a living from fish. He's a thick-set, gingery man, blunt-spoken and solid as a tank. He recently retired from the RNLI and now devotes much of his time to running the family fishmongers in Cromer, though he has kept the look of the sea about him: electric blue eyes and the appearance of someone so at ease out of doors that he seems outsized inside. Meet him in the street and you might guess at his profession, but what you would not get is the fact that he and his family have between them been awarded three gold, five silver and nineteen bronze medals by the RNLI.

During the twentieth century, lifeboat medals were awarded sparingly and only for exceptional valour; a gold RNLI medal is now considered the equivalent of the military VC. At home in East Runton, Richard has so many framed copperplate commendations for his work that they stretch halfway up the stairs. And the two boats moored in his garden: proof both of his erstwhile profession and his continuing interest in wreck.

The pattern of Davies's life was set as soon as he was born; he would be a fisherman, and he would be on the lifeboat crew. Was his father a fisherman? 'Yes, and his father, and his father ... There's seven generations of fishermen in our family.' And you wanted to be, as well? 'No bloody way, no,' he says vehemently. 'But there was no question; I had to be, and that was that.' Why? 'Because my father said so. I said to him, "I want to be a farmer, I'd rather work on a farm." He said, "You're going out." Then I said, "I want to go in the Navy." He said, "You're going in the bloody Navy – the Cromer Navy!" And that was it.'

Having learned his trade in the fishing boats, Richard was then recruited to the lifeboats. When did he first volunteer? He shakes his head. 'It weren't like that. You didn't volunteer, you were just put into it. There weren't no choice, there weren't no choice at all. I know it's supposed to be a volunteer service, but that's not how it was here – if your father was a fisherman, you were expected to be in the local lifeboat crew, because he'd been in it, and his father, and his father before him. And before they worked the lifeboats, they were wreckers.'

He stops. For a couple of seconds, he looks at me, a level gaze with an edge of defiance. He knows what he is saying. Back in the age of Nelson, when his great-great-great grandfather was still alive and before the lifeboat services had been established, the Davies family were wreckers, just the same as all the other fishermen in Cromer. 'Have you heard of the hovellers?' Yes, I say; there were hovellers down in Kent, servicing the ships on the Downs. 'Well, up here, the old boats used to be called hovellers, and the crew were called hovellaires.' And hovelling was one step up from wrecking? 'Yes. They was pirates, if you like. They had these fast, shallow boats, and there'd be a race between the different families – they always went for the prize, they were racing each other to get out to the wreck first, racing each other. The first boat got the best pickings, and the last boat would bring the bodies out. The first got the free-for-all, and the last got the mean pickings. A wrecker didn't go after human beings. They left them. They was just dead weight. And that was how the RNLI started, no matter what the official history says. They was wreckers first.'

If the Stroma men made wrecking an art form and Cornwall made it a trade, then on the east coast it finally became an industry. Wrecking on the east had a professionalism which set it apart from the amateur efforts of ship-lifters in other parts of the country. Here, wrecking was business as well as pleasure, a semi-legal occupation protected by law and practiced in daylight. In the work of the beach companies, the hovellaires and – later – the tug men, wrecking developed a respectability and status which was absent elsewhere. The combined efforts of so many different sub-species were ultimately responsible not only for developing much of the modern-day salvage and diving industries but for openly acknowledging what the rest of Britain could only hint at. Whereas wreckers elsewhere did everything they possibly could to avoid detection, the local solution to the problem of dealing with cheap vessels carrying valueless cargoes was to walk straight into the nearest court of law and ask for a slice of both. The ancestors of today's professional salvors were wreckers born and bred, and the RNLI owes its current impeccable reputation to those ambiguous beginnings. Because, as Davies and his compatriots point out, all anyone could do round here was to make the best of a very bad sea.

There's nothing subtle about the east coast. To the west there are mountains and cliffs, rocks and unexpected islands; to the south there are quicksands, white cliffs, and smuggler's coves. On the north there are 12-knot tidal races and a plunging coastline. But the east coast is more pragmatic. There's always a sense of incompleteness on the east, a sense that whoever designed this place got called away at the crucial moment. All the essential elements are here, but the adornments which soften or lift a place are missing. Though there are cliffs and beaches, they aren't particularly spectacular. The North Sea can't be bothered with the complicated geological novelties of Britain's Atlantic front. It doesn't do whirlpools or white cliffs; most of the time it doesn't even do a decent safe harbour. Instead, the east coast does the three slabbed lines: earth, sea, sky, each element stacked in rigid accordance with the rule of thirds. And that's it: just a bald arrangement of greys and browns painted just the same way from Margate to Thurso. Sometimes the combination of cliffs and water achieves a brutal kind of grandeur, and sometimes – on a sunny day – it almost looks majestic. The east coast can certainly put on a fine storm or a pleasing beach walk. But there is never anywhere here which makes you want to run away to sea. Gaze out from a headland on the east coast, and all you end up wondering is what's for tea. The west coast speaks of dreams. The east coast just whispers 'piss off'.

But it is not water which dictates the east coast's character. It is the wind. Though Britain is a narrow land, there are still supposed to be distinct east-coast attributes: strength, caution, parsimony, and an unforgiving spirit, as if the wind has sidled through the cracks in people's characters and tightened them against the world. Every mariner who ever sailed these seas dreads that wind's unpredictability and its violent switches of temper. The North Sea is a small, steep sea, bounded by the Continent on one side and Britain on the other. When the wind and weather rise on the west, the resulting waves have 4,000 miles of open ocean to roll, a distance which gives them both momentum and regularity. The North Sea gets the same combination in a more restricted space, so each wave will be steeper, each squall more abrupt, and each wind a little chillier.

There are other weather conditions particular to the east coast. There are the haars, those cold other-worldly mists rolling inland from the coast and rendering everything – people, cars, trees, buildings – as no more than lonely arrangements in grey. A haar also changes the definition of sound so that normal city noises become ghostly silhouettes of their usual reality. But the haars also have their opposites. The spectral quietude of the sea fogs is offset by something which happens much more rarely, but which undoubtedly lives up to its local name. In Norfolk and Essex, where the coastline is low and the point where land meets water remains debateable, certain configurations of wind and tide can force a surge called a rage. Once every fifty or sixty years, a high spring tide in flood combines with a heavy swell and a wind pushing away from the coastline. The wind holds the tide back, but if that wind turns, all the pent-up power of the water is unleashed against the land. Instead of moving steadily from north to south and round through the English Channel, the sea behaves instead like a tidal bore, swinging round and rushing inland.

The last major rage was in 1953, when large parts of north Norfolk were entirely overwhelmed by water. In many low-lying areas, the sea simply swatted the sea defences aside, raced over the breakwaters and invaded the living rooms of half of Norfolk's coastal towns. In total, 32,000 people had to be evacuated, and over 300 lives were lost. Richard Davies remembers the last rage well. 'I was eight or nine, and I remember my father getting me out of bed and taking me up onto the cliff to watch the storm. And he said, "I hope you never see this again in your lifetime." That was bad. It blotted out the pier, the promenade, lifted the lifeboat out of the boathouse, took half the land with it . . .'

The rages are a reminder – if any were needed – that this corner of the country is not stable. The west's reefs and rocks may be hazardous, but at least the majority of those hazards do not shift or alter. On the east and south coasts, things are not so concrete. This is a land which picks itself up and walks, perpetually in retreat from an old enemy. What is coast and beach today was a hill or valley yesterday. In the nineteenth century, long-lived residents reported that ships sailed in places where crops had once been grown. England's fat haunch is losing weight by the year: south-east England is currently sinking relative to the sea level at the rate of a foot a century, while the coastline itself recedes steadily inland.

The process of loss is caused in part by East Anglia's position. As the sea rounds the north coast of Britain and funnels down towards the Channel, it picks up speed and momentum. Caught between island and continent, and driven onwards by the wind, it strikes East Anglia's protruding coastline with huge force. Since that coastline is geologically unstable, the land cannot resist. The cliffs are built up from layer upon layer of clay, chalk and sandstone, all with differing densities and all with differing capacities to resist the sea. Each accumulated winter's worth of gales undercuts the cliffs a little further, while rainwater sidles between the expanding cracks and pushes yet more of the county over the edge. Over the centuries, the North Sea has managed to eliminate around eleven separate towns along this stretch of coastline. The most famous is Eccles. Originally a village of 2,000 acres, it ended up with its church tower stuck like a rock stack in the middle of the advancing beach.

Travelling round East Anglia in 1722, Daniel Defoe was

struck by the process of erosion. Orford, he noted, 'was once a good town, but is decayed, and as it stands on the land-side of the river, the sea daily throws up more land to it, and falls off itself from it, as if it was resolved to disown the place, and that it should be a sea port no longer'. And Dunwich 'is manifestly decayed by the invasion of the waters ... [it] is, as it were, eaten up by the sea; and the still encroaching ocean seems to threaten it with a fatal immersion in a few years more.' The Haisborough Sands, now eight miles out to sea, were once part of the mainland. Bromholm Priory was eleven miles inland in the twelfth century; now it is half a mile from the coast. In just under four decades, between 1915 and 1953, Caister was supposed to have lost 200 foot of beach. The local response to the sea's encroachments has been to keep adapting. In many areas sea defences have been built and have held, but in some parts of the county the population has had – almost literally – to pick up its buildings and run. At Sidestrand, when the old church was threatened with immersion in 1880, it was moved stone by stone a mile or so inland.

The changeable coastline is part of the reason that the east coast has so few safe harbours. Here, what you see is what you get. And what you get are variations on the basic theme: high cliffs, a deep sea bed, long fingers of corrugated rock poking out from the coast, a sandy beach with rocks below. Offshore, ships had to pick their way past several notorious sandbanks: the Dudgeon, the Gunfleet, the Kentish Knock, the Haisborough. Captains negotiating their way southwards would be faced with a gamble: to give the coast a wide berth – avoiding the major hazards, but also increasing the danger if bad weather overtook them – or to sidle along close to the coastline and hope they would have time to bolt for the closest land. Ships caught somewhere in the 150-odd miles of ocean between the Humber and Harwich had no choice but to run before the wind or to risk calamity. Though in many places breakwaters and sea defences

were constructed, a high sea often made it impossible for boats
to nip back safely between the harbour walls. Even in relatively
placid conditions, vessels could also find themselves trapped on
a lee shore and drifting towards the submerged rocks. Ships
heading down from Thurso would find themselves plummeting
towards Morayshire's coastline, while boats from Scotland and
the north east would collide with Norfolk's unforgiving flank.

The skippers of vessels in these waters knew what was going
to happen, and they knew that – very likely – there was nothing
they could do about it. The consequences of that danger can be
understood just by glancing at a map of the distribution of the
RNLI's lifeboat stations around the British coast. The south
and south-west coasts are well covered, but there are also areas
where fewer stations have been established: nothing between
Portree and Lochinver, only one along the north coast, surpris-
ingly few around Oban. The east coast has about ten lifeboats to
every inch: Dunbar, St Abbs, Eyemouth, Berwick-upon-Tweed,
Seahouses – at times it seems almost as if there must be a boat
for every inhabitant.

That disproportion is also played out in the statistics. As
previously explained, it is not Cornwall or the Pentland Firth
which have the dubious honour of the highest number of shipwrecks per mile of coast. It is Durham, a tiny county with a tiny
sliver of coastline, with 43.8 losses per mile. Further south,
Norfolk has 25.6 and Suffolk 25, both of which make south
Cornwall's total of twenty wrecks per mile seem almost modest.
Further north, over 1,200 casualties have been identified in
the stretch of coastline between Duncansby Head and Stone-
haven. Much of that total is explained by the type of traffic
using the North Sea. Generally, the Atlantic got the glamour
and the North Sea got the work. Shipping around the west
or south was rich and varied, but on the east, there was coal.
Just coal. Coal from Newcastle and to Newcastle, coal from
northern ports to southern ones, and – later – coal to fuel the

colliers themselves. Occasionally, for variety, there would be fishing boats, passenger steamers, or freighters carrying goods to the Continent. That comparative uniformity of traffic, and the fact that the majority of vessels were making short journeys close to the shoreline, does much to explain the atrocious casualty rate.

All of which makes the history of wrecking in the area something of a curiosity. It was one thing for the Cornish to plunder an East Indiaman stuffed with desirable merchandise, but it was quite another for someone in Norfolk or Lincolnshire to wreck a collier owned or crewed by someone as poor as the wreckers themselves. Though they might get some temporary warmth from the stolen coal, the boat would not be worth much. It would have no special equipment and no costly navigational equipment – nothing but the basic boat-building materials they could have found on their own doorsteps. Worse, since that collier or fishing vessel might belong to a port only a few miles away from the wreckers' own territory, there was the very real possibility that looters were merely robbing their own kind.

Nevertheless, wrecking remained as animated here on the east coast as it was in other quarters of the country. When Daniel Defoe reached East Anglia he claimed to be 'surprised to see, in all the way from Winterton, that the farmers and country people had scarce a barn or a shed, or a stable; nay, not the pales of their yards and gardens, not a hogstye, not a necessary-house but what was built of old planks, beams, wales and timbers etc the wrecks of ships, and ruins of mariners' and merchants' fortunes'. More than a century later, the situation had not altered much. In February 1837, the 160-ton *Raby Castle* was wrecked and driven on to the beach at Cley while on its way from London to Stockton with a valuable general cargo. Both crew and passengers were rescued, but as the *Norwich Mercury* later reported, a free-for-all ensued:

Immediately after she broke up, the beach was strewn with Spirits, Wine, oranges, nuts, toys, Hampers, boxes etc. The scene beggared description. The most outrageous and beastly conduct was exhibited. There, might be observed a group breaching a spirit cask and letting it run into their oilskins, hats, shoes etc. There, another stood filling their pockets and handkerchiefs. Further on, another party secreting a cask etc, until a more favourable opportunity presented itself of disposing of it, and all this in the face of day and in a civilised country. Plunder, wholesale plunder appeared to be the order of the day in spite of contingents of coastguard men. Many who were charged to watch the property became themselves intoxicated. Many were conveyed from the beach, literally dead drunk, and it is with disgust that we add that many women were in the same state.

So effective were the wreckers that only £800 worth of goods were recovered from a cargo originally valued at £5,000. As J. M. Bate, the commanding coastguard officer for the area subsequently reported, his men had an additional problem in persuading the wreckers to stop looting. 'In many cases, the [Coastguard] have difficulties to contend with, it appearing to be a generally conceived opinion that they act without authority, and are doing so from interested motives.' If the wreckers regarded the Coastguard as mere criminals in uniform, in other words, then it was not surprising that robbery went unchecked.

One hundred miles further north, the *Haddingtonshire Courier* was roused to popeyed horror by the events of October 1864. During a heavy storm, a 'neat and well-built' French schooner named the *Louise* was driven onto the reefs near Scoughall on the North Berwickshire coastline on a Saturday night. As with the SS *Politician* on Barra, the *Louise* was carrying a cargo of hard liquor, though in this case the drink in question was not whisky, but brandy – 110 tons of it, half in casks and half in bottles. By the time the crew and skipper had been rescued, the brandy had begun to float ashore. 'Truth compels us to state,' continued the *Courier*, 'that, in connection with the stranded cargo, the conduct of many of the country people who had been attracted to the spot was in the highest degree reprehensible. We are willing to believe that it was not till after the last man was landed from the vessel that they began to help themselves to the brandy; but, once they commenced, they were not slow in availing themselves of the opportunity to make themselves for once at least in their lives acquainted with the taste of genuine cognac. One cask after another, which had been washed out of the bottom of the wreck and partially stove in, was surrounded by groups of country people – young lads and boys being among the number – and the contents drank of so freely and recklessly that scores of them sank down beside the barrels in a state of helpless intoxication ... The scene witnessed on Sunday afternoon on the wreck-strewn beach at Scoughall was utterly disgraceful to the character of the people who took part in it, and would seem to indicate that where strong drink can be surreptitiously obtained, neither the honesty of some of our Scottish peasantry nor their respect for the sacredness of the Sabbath are proof against their desire to get it.'

Sabbath or no Sabbath, the 'Scottish peasants' were obviously not that quick off the mark; out of 2,000 casks of brandy, 1,000 were ultimately preserved by the coastguard intact. In a subsequent letter to the *Courier*, the local customs official, Mr Brodie, attempted to restore a little of his countrymen's dignity. 'All that were found intoxicated – and their numbers were greatly exaggerated – were Irish or farm labourers from a distance, and strangers to me,' he wrote. 'It is a pity that the disgraceful conduct of a very few should detract from the meritorious conduct of the many.' However his version of events is contradicted by one local woman born after the event who was told that 'everyone drank brandy, and it is said even the pigs were drunk. The inhabitants hid brandy on the links and then drank so much that when they again became sober, they could not remember its whereabouts.'

If the *Raby Castle* and the *Louise* illustrated the conventional side of east coast wrecking, then there were other elements which were not so familiar. The most striking variation was in the evolution of the Norfolk beach companies. Beachmen were a singular breed, combining the roles of salvor, hoveller, pilot, fisherman, lifeboatman and wrecker all in one semi-official package. In the century or so between 1780 and 1870, a series of companies were established along the length of the north Norfolk coastline, each with its own boats, look-out posts and equipment, and each with between twenty and thirty members. Like the hovellers of the Kent coast, the beach companies evolved as a response both to the need for guiding and pro-visioning the ships passing their stretch of coastline, and in order to take advantage of the almost limitless opportunities for salvage. Unlike the hovellers – or, indeed, wreckers in any other part of the country – they were regulated, ordered, paid, and organised all the way from the coxswain at the top to the company cat at the bottom.

In their own way, many of the beachmen were also legal experts as well. Since they spent much of their time in court, two or three company men would become fluent in the high grammar of maritime salvage law. In most respects, their boats – the Norfolk yawls – were oversized versions of the Pentland Firth yoles: large, clinker-built, undecked vessels with a single lug sail and enough space for about twenty oarsmen. The yawls were speedy and capacious, with a wide beam, a shallow draught, and a moveable keel which could be hauled on board as soon as the boat touched the beach.

The first law of all beach companies was that only those who touched the boat were eligible for a portion of the salvage. The rule included the crew and those who helped launch the boat, but not the lookouts or absent crew members. When a vessel at sea in trouble was spotted, lookouts (either posted along the cliff tops or in specially built huts on stilts) would alert the waiting men. A crew of around twenty-five would rush down to the beach and launch the boat into the water, rowing like fury towards the wreck. In most areas along the north Norfolk coastline, there would usually be two or more company yawls competing against each other, so the trip from shore to ship (most likely undertaken during a gale, and in filthy sea conditions) would also be a race, since the first boat alongside the wreck would also be the one which got the best loot. Assuming the vessel had not yet capsized or broken up, they would then begin haggling with the captain, trying to convince him that he and his ship were in mortal danger and that his only chance of saving her was to engage the beachmen. Rookie captains, fearful and responsive, were easily convinced, but experienced ones – especially those who knew the coastline and its companies well – were not. As in Kent, many captains regarded the beachmen as no better than organised extortionists, and were fully aware that as soon as they agreed to take a tow line, they would be sacrificing a sizeable portion of their vessel's value. In cases where the captain was only a hired hand appointed by a distant shipowner, this was less of a problem. But when the captain was also owner and skipper of his own vessel, or when he feared for his future position, the disputes could be long and acrimonious. In practice, this could lead to the curious sight of a captain debating the finer points of salvage policy with a boatload of beachmen amid the shrieks and cracks of a Force-10 gale. Occasionally, the beachmen hurried the argument along a little. When faced with a particularly intransigent skipper, anchor chains might mysteriously break or otherwise sound hulls spring leaks. In the beachmen's view, they hadn't risked livelihood and limb in order to exchange an hour's worth of legal pleasantries.

Once agreement – however reluctant – was reached, the beachmen would instantly begin salvaging both ship and cargo. In the early years of the companies, the beachmen's first priority was to save property, not life. A crowd of wailing women and children clinging to the foredeck of a sinking freighter might look affecting, but it would not help put food on their tables. According to Richard Davies, any survivors 'had to pay. And if they didn't have the money, the beachmen let 'em stay. If you took your ring off and gave it to them, then you might get in the boat. People would say nowadays, "Oh, no, but they'd get the survivors off first." Well, that's a load of squit. Those men were hungry, they had families to feed. You can't feed families on dead bodies and you can't feed them on live bodies unless those bodies are going to pay you. But if you could salvage things, then you could sell them.'

Davies looks at me again, that same slight defiance; judge them if you dare. Those passengers who were beyond saving were also ignored. Bodies were, literally and metaphorically, dead weight. 'It was a hard life round here; most people was just trying to survive. If you was starving, and you can get money out of ship's cargo, you aren't going to bother saving anyone, are you? If you was filling your boat up with prize, think how much space and weight a body would take up. You wouldn't want a dead body if you could have something valuable instead, would you? It's like Lockerbie, isn't it? If you get piles of money falling out of the sky, you're not going to leave it lying in a field. It's just human nature.'

Besides, it would rarely be the best of the beachmen who dealt with survivors anyway. Assuming three or four different company yawls had all raced out to the wreck, the first boat would take the best of the cargo and equipment and the following crews would get whatever was left, including – in many cases – all that could be stripped from the corpses of the dead. 'When they was wrecking, they'd take clothes off the bodies as well,' says Davies. 'If he's dead, he ain't going to want them no more, is he? So you looked at it, specially if he had a nice-cut jacket on, and you didn't have nothing, you had rags. And then you'd go out on a Sunday and stick your chest out. Everybody would know exactly where it came from, but they don't ask questions, do they? Ask no questions, tell no lies. And if there was dresses or shoes, they'd have them for the wives. Socks, boots, jewellery, everything. Oh, yes. In the First World War, how many British soldiers do you think wore German boots? My grandfather, he fought in the war. There were a couple of dead Germans close by him, and he could see they had decent boots – his army boots were worn out. He got the first one off the body, put it on, perfect fit. He took the other one off, and it still had the German's leg in it. Gave him a fright, but he still kept those boots.'

If the vessel could be refloated, it would then be towed to a safe harbour. If it could not, then the beachmen would offload as much of the cargo as possible onto their own boats and return to shore. Once back on dry land, the real work began. Having itemised their various gains, and, if possible, patched up and refloated the vessel, the beachmen would then present their case for a salvage award to the local Admiralty court. As direct descendents of the old vice-admiral system, the courts were responsible for the settlement of disputes between shipowners, salvors and Lloyd's agents over salvage. The courts were supposed to be impartial – as courts generally are – but the majority of judges regarded the beachmen at best as a necessary evil and at worst as a kind of maritime Cosa Nostra, lying, extorting and, if necessary, killing their way to a living. Thus most Admiralty court disputes followed a familiar pattern: captains and shipowners would argue that both cargo and vessel were worth nothing and the beachmen had rendered either minimal assistance or none at all, after which the beachmen would argue that the vessel was worth a small fortune and that they had been single-handedly responsible for saving every last plank. The judge was responsible for finding some cheerless middle ground between the two positions, and for setting a percentage of the total value as a salvage award. Finally, either the shipowner or the shipowner's insurance company would – with bad grace and loud complaint – pay the beach company. Returning home, the beachmen would then share out the payment in lots to all those who had touched the boat before she launched.

Though the early history of the beach companies was relatively lawless, its later development intersected with the establishment of the lifeboats. Once the lifeboats became involved, the incentive to kill or abandon survivors of shipwreck diminished. The first beach companies were founded in the 1780s; a quarter of a century later, the first lifeboat was stationed at Cromer. In 1823, the Norfolk Association for Saving the Lives of Shipwrecked Mariners was established (initially acting as an entirely separate entity to the RNLI), and provided an additional six lifeboats plus six mortar lines at points around the coast. With the evolution of the early lifeboats (and their eventual amalgamation into the nationwide service) the beachmen began concentrating solely on salvage.

But as salvage flourished, so the companies dwindled. By the late nineteenth century, salvage had become a daylight occupation with the dignity of obligation and the endorsement of law, a profession which no longer settled its differences on a dark beach with a crowbar, but on paper in court. To be a good salvor required skill, foresight and nerve, a shrewd understanding of oceanography and fluency in several languages. Though born out of criminality and regarded with suspicion, it gradually gained both an acknowledged role and a veneer of respectability. As one nineteenth-century law historian put it, salvage 'offers a premium by way of honorary reward, for prompt and ready assistance to human sufferings; for a bold and fearless intrepidity; and for that affecting chivalry, which forgets itself in an anxiety to save property, as well as life'. Then, as now, its aim – as defined by the International Salvage Union – is that 'the salvor should be encouraged by the prospect of an appropriate salvage award to intervene in any casualty situation to salve the ship, property, and, in particular, to save life and prevent pollution'. In practice, most shipowners afford the salvage industry the kind of grudging respect that the general public gives to morticians or rat catchers; they know they're there, they know they're necessary, but they don't ever want to have to make use of them. At the same time, it is also true that salvage retains something of its old reputation for rapacity, and stories still persist about clusters of vulturine tugs in pursuit of a kill.

Syd Weatherill, Ben Dean and John Porteus are all amateur salvors who have spent their working lives probing the reefs and bays of England's north-east coast. Based in Whitby, they set up a salvage company concentrating on the recovery of non-ferrous metals (gold, silver, brass, copper, lead) from wrecks in the area. They exemplify the adaptability and resourcefulness of the east coasters, and their ability to turn even the most unpromising cargoes into hard brass. Most wrecking in the area, Dean thinks, was mundane. 'When ships came ashore here, it was mainly people going down and salvaging some of the coal for their own fires, or wood to make sheds. It wasn't really expensive cargoes until the wars, when ships were carrying more expensive things. But still, it was mostly small stuff.' Syd Weatherill interjects. 'It would be coal. People could use coal, and if you could get a few bags of it, that was just great. They're still picking up coal further north, from the tips. I have a relation up near Newcastle and she said her family used to go to the beach and collect what we call brash, small fine coal, and wrap it in newspaper, and it would be fine, wouldn't it? It was something for nothing for the poorer people.'

The relative uniformity of traffic on the east meant that salvors usually knew what they would be dealing with. 'Round here, most ships would be carrying coal or iron, or they'd be bulk carriers carrying a single cargo,' says Dean. 'If you wanted a diverse cargo, it would all be in containers. A lot of foreshore recovery work, or salvage, in the old days during our lifetime, was timber, deck cargo. At one time, North Yorkshire and Durham were big coal-mining areas, all using pit props which came from countries which had lots of little trees to make pit props from, like Scandinavia. Props were pine, and at all the major ports – Whitby, Hartlepool – there used to be stacks and stacks and stacks of them waiting to go to the mines. They had to be dried out because they were lighter when dry, and when they lost their weight they could be handled easily down the pits. But while they were standing in stacks, of course they were very handy for people who fancied a bit of firewood. Then they went on to steel girdering, and that particular trade stopped.'

As Dean points out, part of the reason why the salvage industry became so strong along the east coast was the time and effort required to deal with metal-hulled vessels. 'Steel ships, they're not so easy to loot. They don't break apart. You go with a horse and cart, and go aboard a steel ship that's come ashore, and you've got 40 foot of straight steel to deal with. It's not so easy, and the authorities can control it better. The old wooden ships were the ones which were good for wrecking because they had a shallower draught, they'd drive well inshore on the beaches and rocky areas, break up and the cargo would be just littered about.'

A wooden ship could be wrecked and picked clean within hours, but 'when a ship came ashore in this area, we all knew, and there was a certain amount of excitement. We call them rockers round here, a rocker was a ship come ashore on the rocks. And then there would be a little bit of a race to try and do some salvage, to try and get a line on board, to help take a kedge anchor off, or something like that. That was really where the money lay, in trying to be part of the salvage crew.'

In the past the main salvors around Whitby would have been fishermen. 'You hear these apocryphal tales, when a ship comes ashore and somebody gets to know about it, the seamen running down to their boats, carrying their sea boots over their shoulders so they're not disturbing anybody, all of them going down in this rush, because it was the first to get a line on who had the chance for some salvage.' Dean adds, 'The removal in a gentlemanly manner of other people's equipment and possessions is universal, and everlasting. Where the sea meets the land, there'll always be a place for the entrepreneur, the risk-taker, the person who's going to be able to survive in a basically hostile situation. The fishermen and the smugglers and the wreckers: they're a breed, a certain type of resourceful person. You can use the coast – you can catch fish or you can collect bits washed ashore, or climb the cliffs and get eggs to feed the family, but all of those things are extremely risky. And wherever the sea meets the land, the risk factor is there all the time. It's quite unforgiving. If you get the wrong side of the tide, that's it. So it breeds the type of person who is aware of their environment, lives with their environment, and their environment has shaped their lives.'

Part of which, I say, relies on the perception that the sea washes things clean of ownership. 'Yes,' says Dean, 'but everything is still owned by somebody. The vast majority of people, particularly people who aren't on the coast, think it doesn't belong to anybody. But everything in the sea belongs to someone.'

John Porteous points out that if a cargo of coal came ashore now, few people would bother gathering it. 'It's all electricity now, and the coal comes from Australia,' adds Dean. Weatherill nods. 'A lot of the stuff that comes on the shore now, even good timber, a lot of it would just be left. Nowadays, if people want timber, they're not using it for fires like they used to, so a lot of it just gets wasted. You look at the timbered roofs in old houses in Whitby, and they're totally salvaged. Specially the ones that haven't been too much renovated, and you find ships' timbers in the beams. I think this community itself has changed vastly over the years. Once upon a time in Whitby and Staithes and Robin Hood's Bay, the community was local. Everybody knew the person next door, and the sons and daughters were living in a very tight community. And people in those days were quite poor, and the beach was the place to find odd bits of this, that and the other. There's odd ones that still comb the beaches for things, but they're very few and far between. They don't need to nowadays. If a small trawler came ashore now, nobody would really be interested, would they? It's got no non-ferrous metal on board like the old ones, it's just a heap of scrap really. And nobody's interested in the metal because it would cost them too much to do anything with. So unless it had a cargo on board which was of any value, everybody just forgets about it, don't they. That tramp down at Salford – that came ashore, and it was just left.'

'It's down to what makes the working communities on the coast tick,' says Dean. 'When we started diving in the 1950s, we'd all been on the beach since lads. And then we got involved in scuba diving. I would think, though it's a gross over-simplification, that's where the beachcombers went. It's a strange thing, but beachcombing moved out. We moved out and went down, and we found things. And the strange thing about divers and particularly salvage divers is that once they've seen something on the bottom that they think they can get at, you will shift anything to get it. It's just the fact of doing it. We've raised old fishing boats, and when you first see them on the bottom, you've got to get it. And you make a small profit by selling them back to the insurers. We've taken fishing boats apart on the bottom of the ocean, so we could sell their engines and their machinery and suchlike. The last stuff we brought up, about five years ago, was a great big lump of lead. When we first started, we would have thought, that's smashing, that'll pay for the fuel for this job . . . But nobody wants it. Not worth the value of carrying it, even. When we were wrecking, we were mainly looking for the non-ferrous metal to salvage. But a lot of the younger divers are not wanting to do that. They want to see a wreck in order to tick it off in their book – it's like bird-watching. So the vast majority are sports divers. But for us, it was different. We were more like the old beachcombers rather than what the modern divers are like.'

Back down in Norfolk, Richard Davies made his living by more conventional means. He might have been a reluctant recruit to the fishing grounds, but there is no question that he was a skilful one. 'I picked it up as I went along. I watched my father, and I learned like that. The whole Davies family were known for being good fishermen.' And what does he consider makes a good fisherman? 'A good fisherman is someone who can put food on the table at the end of the week. Never mind knowing the sea or the area or the fish, that's all that counts in the end. I've had old people in the town coming up to me and saying, "If it wasn't for your grandfather, we'd have missed a lot of suppers." Their sons were killed in the [First World] War, and there'd be no-one to be the breadwinner, and if it wasn't for my grandfather hanging a bag of something on the door – a couple of crabs, a bit of cod, whatever he had that week – on the door, they'd have gone hungry. He'd get stuff off the local poacher to give to people when he didn't have any fish.'

The local fishing industry is now depleted, but it is not yet dead. Richard's son John has taken up his father's trade, though Richard hopes for better prospects for his grandson. 'There are about twenty-five fishermen in Cromer now. There's mainly crabs, whelks, cod – not so much of the cod now as there used to be, but we're good, we look after the stocks. In the 1950s there was maybe sixty full-time fishermen. At one stage it went down to about fifteen – after the war there was a whole generation missing, killed. I had two uncles drowned in 1953 at the time of the Coronation – I can remember all the flags out, the celebrations, coming home and being told they'd drowned.'

The Davies family was also helped by the beginnings of mass tourism. 'In the summer, my family would be doing the beach thing – they had bathing huts down on the beach. It was big business at one time. They had seven or eight people hiring out the bathing huts and the bathing costumes. In those days you wouldn't buy a swimsuit, you'd hire them – those big things, with the stripes, great big things, like a music-hall comedy turn. They'd look stupid now. They'd do the bathing machines as well, hiring those out. My father had both sides of the beach – my father would walk four miles every day before school to pick up the carthorses from one of the local farmers, take them down to the beach, and they'd be towing the bathing machines up and down the beach all day. The women would go into the water in the bathing machines, everything hidden except their heads – like swimming in a tent.'

Like many families in Cromer, before the tourist industry began to develop, the Davies' made extra money through hovelling or membership of one of the local beach companies. When does he think the beachmen lose their murderous edge? 'Oh well, you're going back a long, long time – early 1800s, I should think. Late 1700s maybe. It evolved into the lifeboats. But they were wrecking all the way through. They wreck now.' The RNLI? The British charity that today has an almost 100 per cent public approval rating, a £100 million annual turnover and a record of saving over 136,000 lives? Is he really serious?

'There would be wreckers in the lifeboat, yes, of course. They were all wreckers.'

Davies pauses again. It is evident he knows what he's talking about. 'If they were called out to a wreck, and they'd got all the crew off safely and they knew the boat was going to sink, what's to stop them pulling the clocks off the wall, taking the barometer and the compass and the prize? The crew would go aboard with a sack, a screwdriver, a knife, and get what they could. They'd go in the wheelhouse and had a little look around with a screwdriver or something. They'd have the compass off the gimbal if they could get it, they'd have a clock – anything out of the wheelhouse, they'd have anything what was going. The bell ... You'd know the boat was going to go down soon, and you'd look around the bridge, and you'd think, "I'll have that." It would just go to waste otherwise, wouldn't it?' Well, yes, but . . .

'The first priority is get your people off, and if the ship was breaking up, the next priority is to get off what you can.' He laughs; a huge, contented sound. And did the RNLI know about it? 'Of course they knew about it. We weren't pinching from a thing what was still alive, if you get me. If that ship was breaking up, then no-one was going to get it. Now the wreckers nowadays are going there in rubber suits and diving down and wrecking. But we wrecked it before it was underwater.' So the lifeboat volunteers regarded wrecking as payback for the risks they took? 'That's right, yeah. As long as there was no-one hurt over it. You'd save the crew and if you went back the next day to just check over, and she'd gone to pieces, well, you'd just help her out a bit, wouldn't you? The lifeboat crew would be there at a wreck first, and if they got some perks off it, well ... They were doing it for free, and they didn't get much out of it, did they? But you didn't do it for money. You know, if you could save a life, that's it.'

On the other hand, there are alternative methods. Why, for

instance, did the lifeboatmen not just claim salvage? In cases where the ship can be refloated and towed, the RNLI does still (reluctantly) permit claims by lifeboat crews. 'Oh, yes, they could claim salvage, but it was much easier just to wreck,' says Davies. 'If you were going to do the salvage, you had to have a good solicitor, you needed a Lloyd's Open Form, you'd need to prove your claim, and you'd be up in front of the courts no question. And the RNLI don't like them doing it, the RNLI wash their hands of it. You have to pay the RNLI for the fuel, and if you damage the lifeboat, you got to pay for that.'

Any prize was doled out in just the same way as the beach-men had doled things out many generations before. 'The way it went, the coxswain would share the prize out when they got back home, otherwise the mechanic and the shore crew wouldn't have got anything. It made it fair that way. It was the coxswain's job to dole it out fairly – they'd have a raffle some-times. The hovel would all go in the far part of the lifeboat, and they'd come home and have a share out. They'd put it in lots, so say there was twenty people, and you had twenty lots, and you'd put the lots all in a different place, and then you'd turn the fellow round so he'd be facing all the crew, and someone would shout, "Whose is this?" And he'd say "That's so-and-so's." You'd go all along the line – "Whose is this?" "That's so-and-so's." "Whose is this?" "Give that to my brother".'

So, I ask, looking around the room – the brass lantern, the engraved mirrors, the polished candlesticks – have you ever done any wrecking? 'Me?' He looks up, wide-eyed. 'Never done any wrecking in my life.' His wife Julie – a tall, quiet-spoken woman who now manages the family fishmongers – walks into the room. 'Yes you have,' she says drily, 'you've wrecked my life.' Davies roars with laughter. 'Just after we were married I came back home with some contraband,' he says after she leaves the room. 'My wife looked at it, and she looked at me, and she cried. She said, "Is this the kind of man I've married?".' What kind of contraband was it? 'Fags, drink. I brought them over from the Continent, and brought them up here stuffed down inside my boots.' So what was the best wreck you've been out to? 'The wreck itself is good. Any wreck. There's been some odd things – Henry Blogg [the UK's most decorated lifeboatman, and a distant relation of the Davies family] had a St Bernard dog once. I've found a canary – my mother kept it for years – and the cage as well.' He points to a couple of things standing in the grate of the fireplace. 'These are all off wrecks. I've got a ship's lantern there, that was the stern lantern off one, that was. I got that the next day. That old tabernacle there, that come out of another one. My mother's got a clock, I can't remember what ship that come off.'

As in other parts of the country, a wreck in Norfolk was an event, an impromptu local festival. 'During the war, there was a ship that went on the sandbank full of oranges. There was no fruit in the country, and there was that many oranges coming ashore, people was waiting for a full box and the lifeboat was steaming through an orange sea. The sea was all orange, just coloured orange. There was everyone down there. All the women from the country were coming down, biking down with the kids and filling their sacks full of oranges. They hadn't had no fruit. They started off with anyone who had a van or a vehicle would fill it up with oranges, go up to Norwich market, and start flogging them oranges, because there hadn't been no oranges during the war, had there? And then there was vanloads going everywhere – London ... All black market, just orange upon orange.

'Then there was a general cargo vessel wrecked on some rocks off Cromer, what we call a shoal. It was carrying everything – whisky, tools, dolls, bikes – everything. Being wartime, they had to get everything off. All the fishermen were down there, on the beach. When the tide went out, they could get in the holds, and they started emptying stuff. The lifeboat crew were all down there as well. Everyone had a new bike, my daughter got a new doll, and I got the whisky. Because of the way the ship had settled, there was water slopping in and out of the hold, and some of it had got into the whisky. If you got a clear bottle then it was still alright, but if it was cloudy, the sea-water had got in and you had to throw it down the toilet. That film *Whisky Galore* – that was everywhere. My mother had three or four bottles in the cistern.'

And what would you do if a ship went ashore today? 'If a timber ship sank today, you'd still have to have all the wood. Half Cromer would be along the beach with barrows. When it happened in the past, my father and my grandfather would be out there so fast … They'd get the wood and they'd make chicken sheds and pig styes out of it and then they'd sell them round the town. The rest of the wood they'd sell to the local builders. The builders knew where it came from, alright. But my father would stop them getting to the beach.' How? Davies inclines his head. 'Oh, he'd ask them nicely, of course,' he says sarcastically. 'They controlled both sides of the beach. They could stop anyone else getting down there. My grandfather always knew where the ship had sunk, they knew what the tide was doing – the builders didn't, and it was usually a long time before the coastguard turned up.' Julie comes in again, holding a load of fresh ironing and wanting to know about Davies's plans for the evening. They talk for a while and I loiter by the kitchen door, looking up at the line of framed RNLI commendations and the paintings of old lifeboats rowing through vast grey valleys of ocean.

A few minutes later I am on the coast road to Sheringham. There on the main street is the local RNLI shop, bright and professional, and filled to the rafters with the kind of things you never knew you needed: pads to kneel on while weeding the garden, faux fur cushions, clogs, biscuit barrels, lifeboat microfleeces, torches, bird-feeders, sweatshirts, aprons, and the inevitable little model boats. The shops have come a long way since the days when all you could find was a lifeboat tie pin, though at present the shop's only customer is a fat pigeon with good manners and an eye on the till. This is the familiar side of the RNLI, the spruce red-white-and-blue Institution commanding the boundless goodwill of the British people. Unlike many large UK charities – Oxfam, Greenpeace, Save the Children – it is not affected by a perception that it is a political or campaigning institution. It exists simply 'to save lives at sea', and leaves the majority of the campaigning work to the Maritime and Coastguard Agency.

Standing here in the shop surrounded by tea towels and garden truckles seems a very long way from Davies's tales of bare-knuckle wreckers. Given the minuscule numbers of prosecutions for wrecking, it would be hard to verify his account, though it undoubtedly makes sense. But he has done no more than to openly state what Matt Lethbridge on the Scilly Isles had hinted at, what David Stogdon in Caithness had guessed, and what I have also been told off the record in several other parts of the country. I also suspect that it is no coincidence that the most highly decorated lifeboatmen are also those who turn out to know most about the RNLI's shadowy early history. Firstly, the majority come from the old local families who have lived in one area for generations, and who – like Davies – know every last puddle in the place. Modern RNLI volunteers are far more likely to be incomers – dentists and doctors and teachers – who have moved from the city and who want to contribute to their adopted communities. And secondly, the older lifeboatmen's individual histories speak for themselves; they have nothing to prove.

The RNLI and every other international lifeboat service has for many years considered it an article of faith that to save a life will prove its own reward both in this world and the next, and that no price should ever be put on that service. In fact, like many of the British institutions or services most closely associated with humanitarianism – the lighthouses, the fire brigade, the ambulance service – the lifeboats were originally established not through some sudden collective impulse of compassion, but because it was found to be cheaper to save lives than to waste them. Besides, why should the RNLI have to maintain an image of spotless heroism when their crews were drawn from the same communities as those who built their houses and furnished their parlours with wreck? After all, if you were standing in the wheelhouse of a sinking ship surrounded by a couple of thousand pounds' worth of electronic equipment or a case of best malt whisky, if you knew the crew and passengers were safe, and if you knew that from now on it was a straight contest between you and the phytoplankton, what would you do? If you'd just risked your life to save the lives of others, then who really has the right to quibble about the disappearance of a clock or a brass compass? I think I prefer my heroes to remain human. And to have boats floating through their flowerbeds.

EPILOGUE

'No photographs,' says Ajay without turning his head. 'Apologies. Photographs is not permitted at Alang.' There is a silence. I should have known. The Indian government has never been keen on photography at its official installations, and whipping off a dozen or so films of an internationally infamous ship-breaking yard in a country apparently intent on war with Pakistan seems, on reflection, to have been a little over-optimistic. Outside the car windows, two warthogs bristle at us from the summit of a rubbish heap. Is there any chance of obtaining temporary photographic permits? Another silence, during which both Ajay and Mr Patel try to look as if they do not understand the question. 'We go at Alang,' Ajay says, sounding his horn irritably at a passing cyclist. 'You will see.'

At this time of year, downtown Bhavnagar is a cheerful place. Every few yards, a boy sits by the side of the road, winding an endless line of pink string onto a hexagonal metal frame. Beside the wheels are wooden stalls selling paper kites in bright sugar-spun colours, while passers-by stand and wait to have their choice of kite attached to a length of the string. Out in the street, Ajay has to dodge to avoid the people practising their flying technique in the middle of the road – men in office clothes, schoolchildren, even a couple of policemen. Mr Patel points to the small paper squares dipping through the sky. 'January every people do kites in Gujarat. Today is people practise for festival.' I look up. Each of the telegraph wires along the road has a line of torn paper bundles hanging down like multi-coloured fruit bats. A soldier runs across the road in front of us, holding his pink string high above his head, indifferent to the traffic. Ajay opens the car door, spits out a mouthful of betel juice in the soldier's direction, closes the door and drives on.

Beyond the edges of Bhavnagar, the kite-fliers are replaced by opulent fields of onions and mango trees. Parties of schoolchildren walk along the side of the road, all the girls in dark glossy pigtails and blue uniform *salwar kameez*, all the boys in shorts. We pass temples, mountains, canyons in the tarmac. Though it is January, it is a hot afternoon. When I open the window, clammy lungfuls of air rush in, flavoured with salt and exhaust fumes. The journey begins to take on a pleasant monotony; emerald fields, stalls, an occasional abrupt thumping as the car's suspension protests at another pothole. Having recovered from the earlier awkwardness, Ajay has moved on to the safer conversational ground of the caste system. 'I am Brahmin,' he says. 'Bhatt is name for Brahmins only. Brahmins are high caste. Priests and religious peoples only.' He slaps Mr Patel softly on one knee. 'Mr Patel is Rajput. Not so high as Brahmin.' Mr Patel smiles.

Ajay is the younger of the two, and they are professional equals, but it is always Ajay who touches Mr Patel in that affectionate sexless Indian way – his arm across the gear stick, the faint click of a gold ring against the back of the passenger headrest. Both of them were born and raised in Bhavnagar. Ajay trained as a civil engineer, spent a while in Bombay and then returned to Gujarat when Alang was set up in 1983, having realised that marine engineering along the Gulf of Cambay was likely to be more lucrative than writing reports on road surfacing aggregates. 'High margins,' he says simply, when I ask what brought him back here. 'Good business, high margin. Here is good work, life, opportunity. At Bhavnagar and Alang I am meet peoples from all countries, have good businesses, be close at Mumbai.'

284

Ajay takes a couple of calls on his mobile, arguing rapidly and snapping the phone closed with a dismissive flick. Mr Patel stares out of the car windows at the roadside stalls selling tepid Pepsi and the dull blue sky. Once in a while, we pass a truck laden with ropes or stacked with long metal canisters moving slowly down the road. Men crouch on top of the trucks, nesting in the coils of the ropes and watching the countryside pass by.

Twenty kilometres out of Bhavnagar, the scene changes abruptly. Under the shade of a large wooden shed, ten or fifteen lifeboats lie beached in the middle of a field. The sun has faded their paintwork from emergency red to romantic pink, and a thin brown dust covers their gunwhales. A line of lifebelts has been strung from the eaves of the shed above a pile of fire hoses coiled one on top of the other. 'Scrap,' says Ajay, nodding towards the sheds. 'Scrap shipbreak plot.' The fields of crops and the roadside shrines vanish, replaced by row upon row of small allotments on both sides of the road. A little further on, Ajay stops the car and we get out to wander among the stalls, observed but unchallenged.

Here in the middle of the hot green fields is everything it takes to make a ship except the sea. Vast engine parts turned verdigris with exposure, satellite masts, lifebelts, porthole glass, rolls of lino flooring, stacks of sheet metal, security doors, lists of health and safety rules in Greek and Russian, coffee machines, industrial mixers, a whole empty audience of armchairs, crockery, fridges, anchor chains, ropes, cupboards, filing cabinets, port and starboard lights, an angled pile of files in Serbian, Italian, Turkish, Dutch and Japanese, radar operating instructions, Admiralty lists of lights, a first-aid box, mirrors, tables, sheets of glass with their edges shining sea-green in the sun, doors, windows, plates, salt and pepper shakers, empty gas cylinders, pots, jam jars, runcible spoons, samovars, colanders, a stack of bright stools, fire exit signs, muster instructions, industrial cake mixers, ancient computers, a Russian station bill, curtain materials arranged by colour, a plan of a long-dead ship's layout in French, a small icon of the Virgin Mary, a picture-postcard painting of an imaginary rural scene with the legend 'They Conquer Who Belive [sic] They Can' written above it . . .

A lopsided 'LIGHT OFF' notice bangs softly against a pillar and a stack of dirty mattresses sags in the dust. One plot is selling reading matter: salvage guides in Russian, manuals for long-obsolete electrical parts, bowed paperback copies of Wilbur Smith or Jackie Collins. Another table has a pile of *Admiralty Instructions to Mariners* dating back to the 1950s. The only thing missing among all this reading matter is the library of porn traditionally considered necessary to keep most ships afloat. Here and there someone crouches beside a large pair of scales, weighing scraps of steel or polishing an unidentifiable lump of metal. Some of the allotments show a very Indian gift for presentation: a line of upended sinks being used to weigh down a shed roof, a skein of ladles and spoons tinkling like wind chimes in the breeze, a stack of colanders with flowers growing through their holes, someone using red and green port and starboard lights as illuminations round a small private shrine to the Hindu god Ganesh. A woman in a dark sari sorts through old materials, holding a remnant of an orange curtain up to the light, haggling idly with the stallholder.

Perhaps all these things would seem a bit less incongruous if we didn't feel so far from the ocean. But there's nothing to suggest that the Gulf of Cambay is only a couple of kilometres further on – no sea-smell, no wind, no cooling of the midday heat. Nothing except these dry green fields and the miles of sea-marked items. After half an hour or so, Ajay motions for us to get back into the car, and we drive on. Finally, a notice appears by the side of the road: 'Welcome to Alang. Safety is our motto.' More plots, more lifebelts, more dispossessed possessions. And then, finally, poking out of the tops of the scrub and the pylons, is the bridge of a ship, a white square block with narrow portholes and tear stains of rust running down its sides. Floating above the landscape, it could just as well be the outrider to some large city suburb. Seen from the road, it gives the sense of having stumbled across a large seventies office block drowned in the middle of a country field. A little further beyond, the remains of a radar mast sticks out through the branches of a tree. Then a cluster of huts, their corrugated iron roofs strapped down with an assortment of ship's rope ladders. At the entrance to the yard, Ajay fiddles with the gears, says something in Gujarati to Mr Patel and stops the car. Two uniformed officials look in and shake their heads at us. Ajay gets out. There is an argument, and then – more calmly – a discussion. Money changes hands. We drive on.

Here, finally, is a beach and a sea. Earlier that morning, far above Alang in the plane from Mumbai to Bhavnagar, distance leant an oily enchantment to the Gulf of Cambay. The sea appeared pale and flat in the sun, and down beyond the white squares of the salt flats, a line of ships stuck out at right angles to the coastline. Out in the bay, four or five tankers lay at anchor, waiting to clear Customs before they too would be run up the beach to their graves. Once back down on the ground, things seem darker. The ground is dark, the sand is dark, the air is dark, the sea is dark. All along the seaward side of the road, sections of derelict ship loom over the walls to the ship-breaking plots. Bony cranes and winches poke up into the air, groping for unseen pieces of steel.

There is the sound of hammering, sawing, the scream of metal against metal. The sea and the land seem so immense and the implications reach so far beyond an ordinary horizon that it is difficult to take in anything except small-scale details – two dogs attacking a younger, smaller dog by the roadside, a line of washing hung outside a tiny grey-black hut, a rope and a fire extinguisher hanging on the sawn-open wall of a 40,000 container vessel. From deep inside a ship's bow section comes a sudden bright fantail of sparks. Some of the ships are freshly beached and almost completely intact, others are now no more than a cross-section of bridge and a sliver of hull. Sliced open, the empty store rooms and cabins gape in the daylight. Not everything has been removed from the cabins before the demolition work began, and many of the cabins still have life-jackets hanging on pegs or charts on the wall. It feels somehow intrusive looking at these tiny human-scale items hanging in such a huge inhuman space, as if someone had taken a guillotine to an apartment block and left its innards hanging out for the world to see.

Until very recently, Alang was the world's largest ship-breaking yard. It dismantles ships from 4,000–52,000 tons, and can cope with everything from passenger ferries to fish factories to aircraft carriers. It was established in 1983 with three plots and now runs to over 200, having spread all the way up the coast and absorbed the neighbouring beach of Sosiya. The beach itself is owned by the government (in the guise of the Gujarat Maritime Board), who collect customs and export dues from shipowners bringing ships to Alang, issue permits for breaking and licence the plot owners.

When Alang was set up, demand and margins were high. Owners with redundant ships to sell would advertise through a broker such as Lloyd's of London, and ship breakers, having assessed the potential value of the scrap, would put in a bid. If successful, the owner would then be expected to deliver the ship to Alang, pay the customs dues, and hand it over to the breaker. The breaker would then hire a team of cutters and winchers on short-term contracts (no-one, not even the most skilled cutter, is engaged for longer than a month), winch the ship up the beach and begin taking it apart. It is an arrangement which has worked well for the past twenty years, partly because Alang once held a near-monopoly on the world's unwanted shipping, and partly because the geography of Gujarat's coast is so uniquely well-suited to the task. The beaches on the west of the Gulf of Cambay have an exceptionally shallow gradient, and are subject to exceptionally high and low tides. Ordinary daily tides rise and fall by 20 feet, fortnightly spring tides by between 30 and 35 feet. The tides and the gradient make it possible to run very large ships up the beach, stabilise them, remove all ballast and take them apart by hand. Each section from bow to faraway stern is sawn off piece by piece, winched away and cut into manageable sections. As the ship vanishes, the workers haul the remainder further up the beach until nothing but the rudder remains.

As with all things, there is a scale of desirability. The majority of ships here are no more than about twenty or thirty years old – oil tankers generally live fast and die young – so the scrap plots of Alang are filled with the industrial design flaws of the sixties, seventies and eighties. According to Ajay, a 'good ship' is one in which there has been minimum weight loss (no ship should lose more than 5 per cent of its unbalasted weight through natural wear and tear, though some vessels can lose up to 15 per cent) and minimum corrosion. The steel should be in reasonable condition (oil tankers are particularly coveted, since oil preserves the weight and condition of steel in a way that seawater does not), and the original workmanship should have been of high quality. Ideally, the vessel should contain plenty of well-preserved raw material – non-ferrous metals, brass, copper cabling – which fetches a comparatively high price and is easy to melt down for re-use. And if possible, the ship should have originated in either Europe or America, since US and EU vessels are liable to arrive at Alang in better condition than Russian, Korean or Polish ships. Passenger vessels are time-consuming and difficult to break because they have so many fiddly internal divisions. Once in a while, Alang does get naval ships and aircraft carriers, but most countries are increasingly jumpy about security, and the Americans have now stopped sending any military vessels to be broken abroad.

Unfortunately, Alang's international image hangs not on its tonnages or its tidal statistics, but on its reputation as the world's most glamorous environmental scandal. In 1989, the photographer Sebastião Salgado shot a series of famous images of Alang – lines of ragged workers hauling ships up the beach, broken oil-tankers leaching poisons into the sea, dying cargo-carriers picked apart by (so the implication went) dying workers. The photographs were published across the globe, and Greenpeace followed in their wake, agitating for international reforms to ship-breaking procedures. As an environmental campaign, Alang had it all. It was filthy, Third-World, photogenic and – as Greenpeace argued – both economically exploitative and politically corrupt. Soon afterwards, the charity scored a notable publicity coup by protesting over Shell's intended sinking of the Brent Spar oil platform. During the subsequent enquiry, the International Labour Organisation published the findings of the Basel Convention on the safe dismantling of ships, noting that, 'Ship breaking compl[ies] with the principles of sustainability. Unfortunately, the procedures adopted in extracting and regenerating do not.' For a while, it seemed as if Alang's number was up. Strangely enough, nothing happened. The world admired Salgado's photographs, paid desultory lip service to the dishonour of Asian ship-breaking practices and continued sending their arthritic supertankers off to the Gulf of Cambay just as they always had.

In part, that international indifference was based on bland economic logic. At present, the truth is that if ships don't get broken at places like Alang, then they don't get broken at all. As Greenpeace found out, the alternative to sending ships to India or Bangladesh or Pakistan is to scupper them at sea, thereby releasing all their toxins onto the ocean floor and creating what would, in effect, be several thousand Brent Spars a year. While ships continued to be broken at Alang, the environmental damage was at least limited to a 12-kilometre stretch of Gujarati coastline where it could be adequately monitored. No-one claimed that Alang was anything to be proud of, only that the alternative was worse. Furthermore, as things stood, only Asia and the third world could make the arithmetic of ship-breaking work. In the mid-1990s, America – galvanised by scandals of its own – introduced safe practices to its local breaking yards. Very shortly afterwards, it then discovered that the cost of safely scrapping a ship far exceeded any possible rewards from that scrap. Even in India, the high margins which had so attracted Ajay back in the late 1990s had dwindled away to almost imperceptible levels. A decade ago, the price of scrap steel was $200 per ton; now it is $70 to $100, if they're lucky. Besides, other yards, capable of breaking much larger ships were being set up, in competition with Alang. The numbers of breakers bidding for the best wrecks had doubled, trebled, and then quadrupled. Today, the majority of ship breakers at Alang can expect to make a profit of no more than 10 per cent to 20 per cent on the value of their steel, and to pay American-style wages with American-style safety rules would cancel that fraction out completely.

Nor is it Alang's fault that everything here is just a bit more naked than it is elsewhere; the malpractices so flagrant and the damaged physics so evident. What irritates the West about Alang – and, for that matter, the rest of India – is that it has no capacity for guile and no interest in disguise. It is simply not possible to hide eight miles of dead and rotting shipping visible from sea, air and land. It is not possible to hide the damage, or the exploitation, or the danger. Or the double standards, given that half the flags of the signatories to the Basel Convention are still flying from the masts along the beach. Perhaps in Europe and America things would be better hidden – the beach more remote, the security more effective. But sophistry costs money, and Alang isn't paying.

Ajay acknowledges the contradictions. 'Accidents happen,' he says. 'Alang is never being totally safe. Now is better, not perfect.' He was on site last year, he says, standing at the entrance to one of the breaker's plots when a worker cut into the hold of a cargo ship and the sparks from his torch ignited the toxic gases remaining inside. Ajay remembers the rush of the explosion, and the fire. 'Two hundred, three hundred people killed,' he says calmly, watching the road. 'Many peoples.' In theory, shipowners are legally responsible for ensuring that all toxic materials are removed from the ship before it passes through Customs. If they do not, the ship will not be permitted to beach. But corruption inevitably ensures that plenty of unsafe ships do pass through Customs, do get beached, and do kill or maim their dismantlers. In addition, the fuel the cutters use is Low Pressure Gas – the same cheap poor-quality stuff used for barbecues and storage heaters. Acetylene gas would be safer, but it would also be more expensive.

When Greenpeace returned to the site in 2001 they discovered that many of Alang's 30,000 workers had learned to accept the devil they knew. 'Greenpeace come at Alang,' reports Ajay, 'and they met two workers. They say, we could make sure Alang is stopped. Is this what you wish? Workers say, if Alang close, we have no money, we die. At least this way we are living for half a century.'

In truth, as Ajay tacitly acknowledges, there are probably only a few more years left for Alang. The new ship-breaking yard in Bangladesh was only started up five years ago, but already it is having an impact on Alang's trade. Between 1998–99, Alang broke 361 ships with a total tonnage of 3,037,882 tons; by 2003–4, that figure had been reduced to 294 ships and 1,986,121 tons. For all its age and fame, Alang is still unable to deal with the really immense ships – the 60–80,000 tonners –

and workers in Bangladesh are now working underwater in conditions even worse than Alang.

In Ajay's manner – part pride, part defensiveness – it is possible to read a much broader local ambivalence. Alang has been condemned by the outside world as a source of shame, and yet it is the major employer in this area: ship-breaking in India generally is calculated to support over half a million workers either directly or indirectly. Ajay and the ship-breakers fear what I or anyone else is going to see and write about Alang, but at the same time the local hotel cites it as a sightseeing attraction and one of the prime sources of local pride. Both Ajay and Mr Patel are heavily involved in the shipyard: Mr Patel is one of the site contractors, repairing and dismantling electrical equipment. Ajay's role is more complex. He has his own ship-breaking plot, but he also acts as an unofficial spokesman and as a broker between different interests. Though Ajay is keen to advertise Alang's reputation as the oldest, largest and best of the Asian yards, and declares that 'Alang never stops,' he admits in more reflective moments that a 10 per cent profit margin is no margin at all, and – in his own attempts at diversification through the website and publicity – that he himself can see the day when he too will move on.

Ajay stops the car by one of the larger plots, gets out and motions for us to follow. Stepping out of the air-conditioned cool of the car, the smell hits us like a physical force. That smell tells us all we could possibly want to know about this place. Whatever it's made up of – oil, rubber, burning plastics, dioxins, petrol, stuff no-one wants to think about – it's a bad, thick, messed-up smell. There is no breeze to disperse it, so the smell and the darkness just hang immobile in the midday heat. A thick grey smirr of pollution hangs over the bay, as tangible as the ships themselves. As we walk towards the entrance of the plot, one of the staff moves towards us, motioning to Ajay to get back in the car and go. After a brief argument we are allowed to stay for an uncomfortable five minutes, peering down a narrow field of vision at a ship, a field of steel plates, a hut at which workers were queuing for fresh LPG canisters, the oil-black sea, and the concrete base of a new staff office spiked with reinforcing rods made – appositely enough – from recycled Alang steel. Ajay points to the yellow safety helmets the cutters are wearing. 'Safety,' he says as we watch a man in flip-flops and a filthy dhoti slicing into a 15-foot section of hull, 'very important at Alang.' The sparks from the man's torch cascade over the steel, and the little white light of the flame creeps closer to the edge. We watch, mesmerised. After a couple of minutes, Ajay turns and hustles us back to the car. We drive off at speed, back through the entrance gates and up the road to Bhavnagar.

The next day, I ask if it is possible to go back again. Two hours of strained diplomatic manoeuvring follows. 'I am sorry,' I say, meaning it. 'I know it is difficult,' Ajay looks away. 'Later,' he says, 'later maybe.' Then, hopefully, 'You are wanting see other things? Mountains, sadhus, temple, tiger, luxury beach resort, shopping?' 'No,' I say. 'Alang. Only Alang.' Ajay fidgets with his mobile. 'Yes,' he says. It is a flexible 'yes', containing several different meanings, one of which is 'no'. 'You go hotel now.' I go back to the hotel and start washing my hair, not hopeful of my chances. But in the late afternoon, he is there, standing by his car. This time, it is dusk by the time we arrive. Perhaps this is the best time to see it – the lights of the welding torches firing brightly against the silhouettes of the tankers, the winches and cranes fingering the horizon, the black ectoplasmic line of pollution hanging above the bay in exactly the same place as it had been the day before. A small fire burns at the side of one plot, a tiny flame outlined by the darkness of the surrounding sand.

We stand at the end and look back down the way we have come. Around us are smaller plots where the ships being broken are puny things by Alang standards – 4,000-ton customs vessels and 3,000-ton fishing trawlers. Beyond them is the skeletal remains of a 20,000-ton cargo carrier which had arrived intact three months previously and is now no more than bones. Parts of the hull are poking up out of the water and a latticework of winch ropes strain to keep what remains of the hull upright.

It is now, staring at all this infernal beauty, that I start to wonder about ships and their souls. Did these ships have a lifespan, and if so, is this where they died? Certainly the majority of vessels here are pretty decrepit. Most are the emphysemic old folk of the shipping world, leaky and brittle-boned. The majority of them were never designed to live beyond thirty and have probably been kept alive this long as much through wish-fulfilment and judicious bribery as through adequate maintenance. Looking at the dirty skeletons lined out all the way down the beach it is difficult to feel any particular affection for them; Alang hardly qualifies as a yard full of Fighting Temeraires. But still, when these ships were driven up the sand by their captains and their lights went off for the last time, did anything else depart in that final decisive instant?

Lloyd's of London's recent announcement that they would no longer be referring to ships as 'she', but 'it' implies that a fishing trawler or supertanker is no more capable of possessing a character than a road or an airbus. But most skippers would disagree. Captains once went down with their ships, a tradition built as much on the unbounded loyalty the vessels themselves commanded as the practical difficulties of doing otherwise. More than any other form of transport, ships are floating homes, places where people live and work for months at a time. And if it is possible to attribute a personality to a house – bleak, cosy, welcoming, cold – then it should not seem surprising that people also anthropomorphise the vessels which hold so many lives between their unreliable rivets. Floating in the middle of a featureless sea, crews had no choice but to make a friend or an enemy of the ship which carried them. Though apparently unmourned, each vessel which ends up on the beach at Alang still has a history, a youth, a set of individual whims. I turn to Ajay. Does he ever get emotional about his work? A sharp, unguarded laugh. 'No!' Never? He shrugs. 'Ships like all other thing. They live, they die, some part is for used again. Alang is like vulture, for taking away of bones. It is cycle of life, same with all other thing.' He pauses. 'It is exciting.'

After a while, we get back into the car and turn away from the beach. Driving back that night, the haze is so thick that each car's headlights form a perfect cone of light as they come towards us. Most of the journey back to Bhavnagar passes in silence. I stare out of the windows at the passing scrap plots. Every few yards someone has strung together a set of green and red navigation lights around a shrine to Ganesh or Shiva or Kali. Figures move in the darkness, fixing meals or sitting in the discarded armchairs watching the truckloads of LPG canisters thunder past. Men stoop by the shrines, rearranging the sprays of flowers or adjusting a starboard light, while above them a thousand abandoned cutlery sets tinkle in the breeze. It is hard not to wonder who exactly will one day drive down this road and discover in themselves a sudden unsatisfied need for an incomplete set of forty-seven mismatched muster instructions for a 1976 Estonian-registered bulk carrier or four rolls of damaged orange lino. The only item which is not much in evidence here is steel. Steel – from the hulls and innards of the ships themselves – is the point of this place, but steel, in general, has no need to sit and rot in the sun. Most of it is taken direct to re-rolling mills and turned into the concrete reinforcing rods used in construction. Between 60 and 80 per cent of it will stay in Gujarat, since most reprocessed steel is too low in quality to be sold for export. So, in effect, the ships of Alang will be transformed into the infrastructure of India itself.

Perhaps Ajay is right. Looking at the little shrines with their landlocked navigation lights now being used for more heavenly reasons, Alang makes better sense. Those broken ships on the beach may or may not have souls. But if India is the recycling capital of the world, then Alang is where it finds its darkest incarnation.

It may seem an odd way to end, in a wrecking yard without any wreckers. But in its own stark form, Alang represents part of what has happened to ships and to the people who live off them. Back in the days of wooden sailing vessels, any ship which hit the coast would not be expected to remain intact for long. Whether or not it was seized and stripped by wreckers, the hull itself would be unlikely to survive a winter on the rocks. But as ships got larger and steel began to replace timber, ships began to last. And last, and last. Steel doesn't rot, it just lies there on the ocean floor providing prefabricated housing for the algae. No-one, not even the most dedicated wrecker or salvor, was ever going to be able to find a use for 30,000 tons of rusting hull. Shipowners had a choice; they could either sell their obsolete vessel to a scrapyard like Alang, or they could hope that the sea did the same job for less money. And so, alongside the development of huge international ship-breaking yards, there was also the development of another, less ostentatious form of demolition; the deliberate wreck.

When the Shipwreck Committee was appointed in 1836 to 'inquire into the increased Number of Shipwrecks, with a view to ascertain whether such improvements might not be made in the Construction, Equipment and Navigation of Merchant Vessels, as would greatly diminish the annual Loss of Life and Property at Sea', the committee members discovered that captains were often as likely to be responsible for the destruction of their ships as sandbanks or hovellaires. Their report exposed an industry riven with mendacity and turpitude. As they concluded, there was a clear chain of corruption reaching all the way from the Houses of Parliament to the dockside tavern. Shipowners took shortcuts because legislation allowed them to do so, and crews had become so accustomed to working in overcrowded and dangerous conditions that most did not expect to survive more than ten years at sea.

In the preamble to its report, the committee established ten principal causes of shipwreck. Firstly, ships were often poorly designed and defectively constructed – a tendency which was, if anything, actively encouraged by the system of ship classification which designated all new ships as inherently stronger than all old ships, however lame and shabby they might be. In the committee's view, the system induced 'shipowners to build their ships in the cheapest manner, and with the least degree of strength that was sufficient to sustain their vessels through the shortest period named'. Since it was evidently useless spending good money on a bad ship, and since the strength of foreign competition had already peeled profit margins to the bone, owners would rarely bother to maintain their ships in a seaworthy state.

Overloading, fraud and inadequate supervision only worsened the situation. Shipowners, knowing that they could claim on the insurance and that the cost of the premiums could be passed on to the cargo owners, would scarcely bother ensuring that their ships were seaworthy. Many of the emigrant coffin ships of the nineteenth century were barely capable of making it out of their home port, let alone across the Atlantic. Shipowners bought semi-derelict hulks, extorted a small fortune out of each passenger, and sat back in the confident expectation that the deliberate drowning of 300 half-starved Irish peasants was unlikely to trouble the British authorities.

Besides, if the ships themselves weren't at fault, then the crew probably were. As the committee discovered, 'the frequent incompetence of masters and officers appears to be admitted on all hands . . . some are appointed to command merchant vessels at periods of such extreme youth (one instance is given of a boy of 14, all of whose apprentices were older than himself), and others so wholly destitute of maritime experience (another instance being given of a porter from a shipowner's warehouse who was made a captain of one of his ships) that vessels . . . have been wrecked on coasts from which they believed themselves to have been hundreds of miles distant at the time.'

A bad situation was, in the committee's view, worsened by the lack of adequate harbours of refuge on many areas of Britain's coast, and by the fatal inaccuracy of most navigational charts. When ships did run aground they found that 'there is on many points of the coast a want of that moral principle which should inculcate a just regard for the rights of such [shipwrecked] property. It is rather looked upon as a chance gift, which each has a right to scramble for as he can, notwithstanding the laws which have been passed from the earliest period, to prevent or punish such depredations . . . The plunder of shipwrecked property on the coast has been carried on to an enormous extent.' More terrible still was the fate of the victims. The committee reported on two or three cases in which 'the crews of several ships in each year having been reduced to the necessity of existing on the remains of their comrades'.

But perhaps worst of all, in the committee's view, was the menace of rum. 'Drunkenness,' they stated, 'either in the masters, officers, or men, is a frequent cause of ships being wrecked . . . the practice of taking large quantities of ardent spirits as part of the stores of ships, whether in the Navy or in the Merchant Service, and the habitual use of such spirits, even when diluted with water, and in what is ordinarily considered the moderate quantity served to each man at sea, is itself a very frequent cause of the loss of ships and crews.' As an example of the benefits of nautical temperance, the committee pointed westwards, 'there being at present more than 1,000 sail of

American vessels traversing all the seas of the world, in every climate, without the use of spirits by their officers or crews, and being, in consequence of this change, in so much greater a state of efficiency and safety than other vessels not adopting this regulation.' By the early nineteenth century, the daily grog ration was as much of a tradition within both the Merchant and Royal Navies as sodomy and insubordination. Until 1824, the daily ration for one adult rating in the Royal Navy was a pint of rum diluted with a quart of water, and for officers, an undiluted pint.

In August 1836 the committee reported its findings. Among their recommendations were the immediate establishment of a board (the Mercantile Marine Board) to regulate and police the merchant service, the enforcement of a universal maritime code, and the establishment of proper courts of enquiry to look into individual shipwreck cases. They also wanted the system of ship classification tidied up, design and construction regulated, proper consideration given to the various life-saving devices shown to the committee, and a system of schooling for both officers and ratings 'in which some attention should be paid to their habits of cleanliness, order and sobriety, and the preservation of their moral characters, all of which are at present unhappily neglected'. Prospective candidates for the service would now also be expected to pass examinations in 'seamanship, navigation, and nautical astronomy', and to wear a recognisable uniform. Ambitiously, they suggested that Britain begin negotiations with most of the other major maritime powers to ensure that shipwreck victims were properly treated, and 'in order to supersede, if possible, the present barbarous practice of plundering the ships and men thrown by misfortune on dangerous shores'. They also recommended that the daily grog ration be discontinued immediately, and a 'more nutritious and wholesome' beverage such as coffee, cocoa, chocolate or tea be provided as a substitute.

The committee's findings did not meet with universal approval. Many shipowners felt that the report was no more than the ramblings of parliamentarians drunk on statutory meddling, and argued that to put even a tenth of the committee's recommendations into effect would cost Britain her place in world commerce. As they saw it, there were and would always be risks involved in sea travel, and a dangerous coastline was just one of those God-given things.

In 1843, following the loss of 240 British ships and 500 lives within the space of three years, the committee reconvened. During the intervening years, laws had been passed restricting deck cargoes in ships plying between Britain and America, but casualty numbers remained too high and the committee found it necessary to spread the terms of their inquiry more widely. This time, the committee examined not just external wreck preventives – lighthouses, floating breakwaters, lifeboats, coast-guards, rockets and mortars – but internal ones as well. Health provision was improved, attention was paid to the supply of on-board anti-scorbutics, and issues concerning employment, wages, training and the system of shipboard punishment were addressed. For the first time, they also recommended the fitting of 'watertight divisions in steam-vessels'. But it would take a further seventy-one years and the loss of 1,500 lives in the Titanic disaster of 1912 before the fitting of bulkheads became compulsory.

Changes in maritime drinking habits were also slow to take effect, since – despite the committee's best efforts – neither the Royal or Merchant Navy showed the slightest inclination to swap alcohol for hot cocoa. Over the course of the nineteenth century the grog rations were gradually reduced, or gin substituted for rum, but it was not until 1970 that alcohol was finally banned by the Royal Navy.

Despite both shipwreck enquiries and the subsequent advances in legislation, the changes made almost no difference to the casualty statistics. Throughout the nineteenth century, the figures kept creeping upwards: in 1851, 692 registered vessels were wrecked on the British coastline with 900 lives lost; by 1880, 1,303 vessels were wrecked and 2,100 lives lost, and by 1909 – by which time the average tonnage and passenger capacity of each vessel had increased, meaning an exponentially greater loss of life when ships did founder – 733 vessels were wrecked and 4,738 lives lost. Although on-board conditions improved steadily throughout the twentieth century, two world wars also took an appalling toll on British shipping, and though the Royal Navy did its best to provide escorts for merchant vessels, they had neither the resources nor the equipment available to fully defend the convoys against the depredations of German wolf packs and dreadnoughts. Between June 1940 and June 1941 alone, three and a half million tons of British merchant shipping was sunk in the North Atlantic.

Late twentieth century improvements to charts, navigational aids and buoyage have, however, reduced the numbers of shipwrecks. Ostensibly, the sea is now a safer place. Technology has been responsible for much of that change. The bridges of many modern ships now look more like games arcades than wheelhouses, and captains are now more likely to need a masters degree in IT than a feel for the sea. But increasing dependence on electronic equipment carries its own risks. Computers fail or crash, and when they do so captains have to fall back on more old-fashioned skills. If those skills atrophy through lack of use, then there is a genuine risk that the sea will once again start taking its old rake-off. Besides, improvements in technology are rarely matched by improvements in human physiology. Half the wrecks mentioned in this book were caused by someone falling asleep or misreading the charts, a form of fallibility that no amount of legislation will ever eliminate.

There are other difficulties as well. Advances in technology have inevitably led to advances in misuse of that technology.

Over the past ten years, the Global Positioning System has become almost ubiquitous in the maritime world. GPS works by adapting the old-fashioned navigational technique of triangulation to modern technological methods. Instead of a sailor taking two compass sights off the nearby coastline and thus managing to fix his position, the GPS system triangulates from the land to a number of satellites and back again, giving the mariner a reading of his position accurate to within a few feet. Theoretically, it is possible to 'spoof' the satellite signal – to send out a false signal with a higher power than the real one, so that the receiver (and therefore the sailor) will read only the stronger of the two signals. By forcing the on-board GPS receiver to listen to the false signal, any would-be wrecker could ensure that the sailor mistakes his position, thereby making him, and his valuable cargo, uncomfortably vulnerable to grounding or collision. The principle is almost exactly the same as that of putting out false lights: beguiling those on board a ship into believing that they are where they are not. Another alternative would be to jam the signal by broadcasting white noise over the same frequency, thus making it impossible for the receiver to read the satellite correctly. As James Taylor, chief executive of the Northern Lighthouse Board puts it: 'The technology which allows ships which drive on satellite navigation autopilot for most of their lives is also the technology which allows someone else to drive it ashore, or onto a reef, and wreck it.'

Other forms of modern wrecking, including scuttling, *Mary Celeste*s, and ships which mysteriously disappear overnight, are all encouraged by the complexities of the modern shipping industry. The *Prestige*, an oil tanker which broke up near the coast of Spain in 2002, is a case in point. Originally named the *Gladys*, she was a single-hulled ship and over twenty years old. She was also built in Japan, flying a Bahamian flag, owned by the subsidiary of a Greek company based in Liberia which had bought her cargo of oil on the stock market in the Baltic states, had been chartered by an offshoot of a combined Russian-Swiss company based in Switzerland, was captained by a Romanian but crewed by Filipinos and was insured in London but licenced to operate by the United States. Disentangling who exactly is responsible for her is complicated enough; making those people pay for the damage she caused is near impossible. As the Galicians have found with the *Prestige*, and the Scillonians found with the *Cita*, every ship is now a floating disunity of nations. For anyone interested in wrecking ships – or in global terrorism – the twenty-first century has proved the perfect moment. The technology to save lives may have improved, but the technology to 'lose' both vessels and cargoes has improved at just the same rate.

For as long as there have been ships, there have been wrecks, and for as long as there have been wrecks, there have been wreckers. There always have been and there always will be. Not just because both the sea and technology still make it possible, but because wrecking always did satisfy some very fundamental side of human nature.

After a while, the front rooms of wreckers, salvors, divers, fishermen, lifeboat volunteers and coastguards all acquire a uniformity of appearance. Alongside the disproportionate numbers of cats occupying the best chairs, most have a surplus of maritime knick-knacks: paintings, books, odd bits of brass-work, glass buoys, tea cups, plates stamped with some dead ship's insignia. Some of this loot – whether legally or illegally gained – is unquestionably both beautiful and desirable. The elegant brass lantern by the fireplace, the old ship's bell and the captain's silver napkin ring all have a shining role to play in their new land-bound lives.

But what is also striking is how many of these objects appear completely valueless: piles of obsolete low-denomination coins, blunt table knives, broken crockery, brass portholes so covered in algae that the glass is now opaque. To someone who knows none of its history, it just looks like junk-shop clutter. It is junk-shop clutter. But to the person who found it – dragged it from the sea bed, plucked it from a wheelhouse, grabbed it in the last few instants before the ship went down – it has a value unconnected to money. The sea once stole it, and now they've stolen it back. In the Scilly Isles, there's a shop that sells bits and pieces from various wrecks including the naval flagship, *Association*. Displayed on one of the tables is a broken spoon-handle, a bent and rusty fork, a chipped tea cup, a comb – things that even the most desultory car-boot flogger would be ashamed of. The spoon handle was priced at £25, and the rusty fork at £32. To the shop owner – and, presumably, to many of his customers – all these useless things had been elevated by their connection with the *Association* into a different place. They had come from a wreck and been washed by history, and those facts alone justified their price.

Most wreckers will emphasise the usefulness of a good shipwreck: the raw materials, the timber, the fuel oil. But in practice, it is not always the useful things that they most prize, it is the souvenir and the pointless ornament. They do not show visitors the mahogany cross beam over the lintel or the three extra tractor tyres, they show them the clock and the captain's jacket. For the truth is that wrecking was never just about need, it was also about want. As Richard Davies in Norfolk puts it: 'The wreck itself is good. Any wreck.' In other words, wrecking is theft, and stealing things is fun.

The sheer pleasure in theft might have been one reason why the wreckers wrecked, but there were also more subtle forces at work. If it is partly Britain's physical circumstances which brought the wrecks, then it is also our island psyche that made the best of them. Infamously, we are a nation of shopkeepers and bargain-hunters; secretive, materialistic and enterprising. We prefer a broad moral fudge to narrow fanaticism, we dislike outside interference, and we have never been averse to taking a little bit extra on the side. Perfect qualities, one could say, for the trainee wrecker. Add poverty, necessity, and superstition to the equation, and it is hardly surprising that wrecking throve as it did.

There is also some irony in the fact that the most notorious wreckers were often the bravest sailors. In all cases and all places, the finest prizes went to those who risked their own lives to save both the survivors of shipwreck and their property. From Crooked Jack in the Pentland Firth with his peg leg and his fearsome seamanship, to William Stanton floating half-drowned above the Goodwin Sands, to Richard Davies and his never-ending commendations, the story is the same. Those men were there on deck rescuing survivors and stealing the captain's hat not just because they were thieves, but because there wasn't a soul on this earth who had the skill to follow them. For many wreckers – both past and present – the prospect of loot remained an opportunistic afterthought to be considered only once the crew had been rescued and the ship correctly salved. And though it is comparatively easy to rush to judgement against the foxholes full of grand pianos and single malt whisky, it's always worth wondering if that isn't a very small price to pay for the life of a survivor in conditions even the coastguard wouldn't venture out in.

Like fly-fishermen, every sailor has his own cache of tall tales: the longest storm, the deepest depression, the greatest escape. But, as those who use the sea for a living know (and as the wreck statistics confirm) it is not always the most difficult conditions which prove the most treacherous. When the glass is falling and the gale is at its height, both the skipper and his crew will remain on deck, braced for disaster. It isn't that difficult to consider calamity when caught in the eye of a roaring Force 12. It is, however, much more difficult to think of things going wrong on a calm day, in a still sea, on a functioning boat – which, of course, is when many casualties do happen. Collisions and groundings occur when the sailor takes their eye off the horizon and their mind off the compass bearing. Out in the middle of the ocean on a fine day in good company, it's hard for any navigator not to relax and forget the miles of buried wreck below his sunlit decks. In the same way, it's just as hard for the same sailor not to feel when he approaches shore after many days at sea that he has finally sighted safety again. Whatever that sailor knows is waiting for him on land – comfort, debt, argument, a well-stocked bar – he does at least have the security of knowing that here, at last, he can relax into a solid element.

Sometimes, though, it isn't out at sea among the reefs and rising sands where the greatest hazards lie. Sometimes there are things just beyond the warm harbour's glow just as alarming as those at sea. Sometimes the old rumours turn out to be true. And sometimes even the darkest night at sea can be better than the false lights of home.

BIBLIOGRAPHY

General

BOOKS

Bernstead, C. R., *Shallow Waters* (Robert Hale, London, 1957)

Bull, J. W., *An Introduction to Safety at Sea* (Brown, Son & Ferguson, Glasgow, 1981)

Cotton, Sir Evan, *The East India Company's Maritime Service* (Batchworth Press, London, 1949)

Davidson, James, *Scots and the Sea* (Mainstream Publishing, Edinburgh, 2003)

Dunn, Douglas, *Scotland – An Anthology* (Fontana, London, 1991)

Forsberg, Gerald, *Salvage from the Sea* (Routledge Kegan Paul, London, 1977)

Golden, Frank and Tipton, Michael, *Essentials of Sea Survival* (Human Kinetics, Illinois, 2002)

Hamilton-Paterson, James, *Seven-Tenths* (Hutchinson, London, 1992)

Hope, Ronald, *A New History of British Shipping* (John Murray, London, 1990)

Langton-Jones, Cdr R., *Silent Sentinels* (Frederick Miller, London, 1944)

Larn, Richard and Larn, Bridget, *Shipwreck Index of the British Isles, Vols 1–5* (Lloyd's Register, London, 1995–2000)

Lockhart, J. G., *The Life of Sir Walter Scott, Bart.* (A & C Black, London, 1893)

MacAlindin, Bob, *No Port in a Storm* (Wittles Publishing, Caithness, 1998)

Rule, John G., *Wrecking and Coastal Plunder*, Essay in *Albion's Fatal Tree – Crime and Society in Eighteenth-Century England* (Pantheon Books, New York, 1975)

Smith, Gavin D., *The Scottish Smuggler* (Birlinn, Edinburgh, 2003)

Stevenson, Robert Louis, *Records of a Family of Engineers* (Wm Heinemann Ltd, Tusitala Edition, 1924)

Warner, Oliver, *The Lifeboat Service* (Cassell, London, 1974)

ARTICLES AND REPORTS

Langewiesche, Wm, 'Anarchy at Sea', *Atlantic Monthly* (September 2003)

Lloyds Register, Casualty Returns (Lloyds Register, London, 1890 to the present day)

Lloyds Register, Wreck Books (Lloyds Register, London, 1892–1940)

Roberts, Dr Stephen, 'Seafaring – Britain's Most Dangerous Occupation', *Lancet* (August 2002)

'Select Committee Report on Shipwreck', 1836

1. *False Lights*

BOOKS

Aitken, Henry, *Salvage Awards in England and Scotland Contrasted*, Juridical Review, Vol. XIII (Wm Green & Sons, Edinburgh, 1901)

Court of Session Papers, 416, 169 (Murray & Cochrane, Edinburgh, 1800, 1780–83)

Morrison, Wm Maxwell, *The Decisions of the Court of Session*, Vol. XXXVII – Wreck (Bell & Bradfute, Edinburgh, 1907)

Newson, Harry, *The Law of Salvage, Towage, and Pilotage* (Wm Clowes and Sons Ltd, London, 1886)

Stair Memorial Encyclopaedia, The Laws of Scotland, Vol. 21 (Law Society of Scotland, Butterworths, Edinburgh, 1994)

Steel, David W and Rose, Francis, *British Shipping Laws, Kennedy's Law of Salvage* (Stevens & Sons, London, 1985)

STATUTES

Aviation and Maritime Security Act 1990 (Current Law Statutes, London, 1990)

Malicious Damage Act 1861, Section 47

Merchant Shipping Act 1894 (57 & 58 Vict)

Merchant Shipping Act 1846

Merchant Shipping Act 1894 (57 & 58 Vict)

Merchant Shipping Act 1995 (Part IX – Salvage and Wreck)

Protection of Wrecks Act 1973

Statute of Westminster 1 (3 Edw 1)

Statute de Praerogitava Regis (17 Edw 2, c11): Act 12, Anne c18; Act 26 Geo 2 c19; Act 7 & 8, Geo IV, c30, s11

ARTICLES AND REPORTS

Gohre, Sanja, 'From Shipyard to Graveyard', *ILO Magazine* (December 2000)

Griffiths, Ben, *Wrecking – A Legal Perspective* (Independent legal research, London, September 2003)

Langewiesche, William, 'The Shipbreakers', *Atlantic Monthly* (August 2000)

WEBSITES

www.encyclopaedia.org – see entry on 'Wreck'

www.mcagency.org/row/law

www.admiraltylawguide.com/documents/oleron

2. *Goodwin Sands*

BOOKS

Carter, George Goldsmith, *The Goodwin Sands* (Constable & Co., London 1953)

Chamberlain, David, *The Goodwin Sands Man of War, 1703–2003* (David Chamberlain, Kent, 2002)

Eden, Revd Robert, *An Address to the Depredators and Wreckers on the Sea Coast* (J. G. F. and J. Rivington, Leigh, 1840)

Gattie, George Byng, *Memorials of the Goodwin Sands* (London, W. H. Allen, 1890)

Lane, Anthony, *Shipwrecks of Kent* (Tempus Publishing, Stroud, 1999)

Larn, Richard and Larn, Bridget, *Shipwrecks of the Goodwin Sands* (Meresborough Books, Kent, 1995)

Major, Alan, *The Kentish Lights* (S. B. Publications, Seaford, 2000)

Stanton, William, *The Journal of a Deal Pilot* (Simpkin Marshall Ltd, London, 1929)

ARTICLES AND REPORTS

Lloyds Salvage Association, 'Report on the Subject of Wreck and Salvage on the Coast of Kent' (A. Williams, London, 1867)

3. Pentland Firth

BOOKS

Baird, R. N., *Shipwrecks of the North of Scotland* (Birlinn Publishing, Edinburgh, 2003)

Ferguson, D. M., *Shipwrecks of Orkney, Shetland and the Pentland Firth* (David & Charles, Devon, 1988)

Gibson, W. M., *Old Orkney Sea Yarns Vol. 2* (Kirkwall Press, Kirkwall, 1986)

Houston, Anne (ed.), *Lest We Forget, The Parish of Canisbay* (Congregational Board of Canisbay Parish Church, Caithness, 1996)

Lockhart, J. G., *Life of Sir Walter Scott* (A & C Black, London, 1893)

Miller, James, *A Wild and Open Sea* (Orkney Press, Kirkwall, 1994)

Townsey, Kate (ed.), *Orkney and the Sea, An Oral History* (Orkney Heritage, Kirkwall, 2002)

Tulloch, Peter, *A Window on North Ronaldsay* (Kirkwall Press, Kirkwall, 1995)

Wood, Lawson, *The Bull and the Barriers* (Tempus Publishing, Stroud, 2000)

Young, Donald (ed.), *Stroma* (North of Scotland Newspapers, Wick, 1992)

ARTICLES AND REPORTS

Aitken, Margaret, *The Island of Stroma* (Northern Printers, Thurso, undated)

Brown, John R., 'The Wreck of the Johanna Thorden' (*Orcadian*, 24 September, 1 October and 8 October 1931; 29 August and 12 September 1935)

——'The Wreck of the Svecia' (*Orcadian*, 20 November 1980)

Ferguson, David, 'Orkney Crime in the Latter Part of the 17th Century', *Orkney View* (Kirkwall, May 1997)

Fraser, John, *Three Years of Shipwreck* (Proceedings of the Orkney Antiquarian Society, Vol. XIV, 1936–37)

Manson, Sutherland, 'Some Wartime Memories of Stroma', *Orkney View* (Kirkwall, June 1990)

——'No Rest for the Navigator', *Orkney View* (Kirkwall, Sept 1999)

Pottinger, Morris, 'Stroma', *Orkney View* (Kirkwall, Feb/Mar 1993)

'Report of the Deputy Receiver of Wreck', South Ronaldsay District, 27 August, 1931

Towrie, Sigurd, 'The Wreck of the Johanna Thorden' (*Orcadian*, 13 January 2000)

WEBSITES

www.caithness.org/history/articles/sailingdirections.htm
www.caithness.org/history/historyofcaithness/chapter1
www.caithness.org/history/articles/wrecksofpentlandfirth.htm

4. Scilly Isles

BOOKS

Austin, Keith, *The Victorian Titanic, The Loss of the SS Schiller in 1875* (Halsgrove, Tiverton, 2001)

Beattie, John, *Lifeboats to the Rescue* (David & Charles, Vermont, 1980)

Boyle, Martin, *Bishop Rock* (B & T Publications, Southampton, 1997)

Chaplins, W. R., *The Story of St Agnes Lighthouse in the Scilly Isles* (Unpublished manuscript in possession of Trinity House, no date)

Cowan, Rex, *A Century of Images – Photographs of the Gibson Family* (Andre Deutsch Ltd, London 1997)

Larn, Richard and McBride, David, *The Cita – Scilly's Own 'Whisky Galore' Wreck* (Shipwreck and Marine, Cornwall, 1997)

Larn, Richard, *Shipwrecks of the Isles of Scilly* (Troutbeck Press, Cornwall, 1999)

Lethbridge, Richard, *Behind the Eyebrows* (Arden Craig Publications, Plymouth, 1999)

McBride, Peter and Larn, Richard, *Admiral Shovell's Treasure* (Troutbeck Press, Cornwall, 1999)

Stammers, M. K., *Ships' Figureheads* (Shire Publications Ltd, Buckinghamshire, 1983)

WEBSITES

www.lloydslist.com/lloydscasualty.com (16 October 1997)
www.divernet.com/wrecks/cita997

5. West Coast

BOOKS

Campbell, J. L. (ed.), *The Book of Barra* (Acair, Stornoway, 1998)
Hutchinson, Roger, *Polly – The True Story Behind Whisky Galore* (Mainstream, Edinburgh, 1990)
Johnson, Samuel and Boswell, James, *A Journey to the Western Isles of Scotland* (Yale University Press, Avon, 1993)
Lawrence, Martin, *The Yachtsman's Pilot to the Western Isles* (Imray, Laurie, Norie & Wilson Ltd, Huntingdon, 1996)
——*The Yachtsman's Pilot to Skye and Northwest Scotland* (Imray, Laurie, Norie & Wilson Ltd, Huntingdon, 1997)
——*The Yachtsman's Pilot to the Isle of Mull and Adjacent Coasts* (Imray, Laurie, Norie & Wilson Ltd, Huntingdon, 1999)
Linklater, Andro, *Compton Mackenzie* (Chatto & Windus, London, 1987)
Mackenzie, Compton, *Whisky Galore* (Penguin, London, 1947)
Maclean, Alasdair, *Night Falls on Ardnamurchan* (Birlinn, Edinburgh, 2001)
Martin, Martin, *A Description of the Western Islands of Scotland* (Birlinn Ltd, Edinburgh, 1999)
Michael, Chris, *The Wrecks of Liverpool Bay* (Liverpool Marine Press, Merseyside, 1994)
Smith, Noel, *Almost An Island – The Story of Wallasey* (Self-published, Wallasey, 1998)
Stevenson, Alan, *Account of the Skerryvore Lighthouse* (A & C Black, Edinburgh, 1848)

ARTICLES AND REPORTS

Dunn, Bill, 'Gulf of Corrievreckan Swim', *The Canoe Camper*, No. 171, Ardfern (Winter 1981–2)
Farrer, T. H., 'Wrecking in the Hebrides – Report to Board of Trade' (PRO, Edinburgh, 1867)

'First Report of the Commission Appointed to Inquire as to the Best Means of Establishing an Efficient Constabulary Force in the Counties of England and Wales' (Charles Knight, London, 1839)

Place, Geoffrey W., 'The Fate of the Charming Jenny', *Mariner's Mirror*, Society for Nautical Research, Vol. 76 (1990, No. 2)

Rodgers, N. A. M., 'Legends About Wreckers', *Mariner's Mirror*, Society for Nautical Research, Vol. 71 (1985, No. 2)

Scott, Sigurd, Private letter to the author, January 2003

6. Royal Fish – London

BOOKS

Colquhoun, Patrick, *A Treatise on the Commerce and Police of the River Thames* (Patterson Smith, New Jersey, 1969, reprinted from the London 1800 edition)

Jeffries, Bob, *A River Thames Guide, Woolwich to Battersea* (private publication, undated)

Martin, Frank, *Rogues' River* (Ian Henry Publications, Essex, 1983)

Mayhew, Henry, *London Labour and the London Poor* (Penguin Classics, London, 1985, reprinted from 1865 edition)

Minois, Georges, *The History of Suicide – Voluntary Death in Western Culture* (Johns Hopkins University Press, Baltimore, 1999)

ARTICLES AND REPORTS

Marriott, John, 'Sweep Them off the Streets', *History Today* (August 2000)

Redman, Nicholas, 'Whalebones in Orkney', *Orkney View*, Kirkwall (January 1995)

Sabin, Richard, Bendrey, Robin, and Riddler, Ian, '12th Century
    Porpoise Remains from Dover and Canterbury', *The
    Archaeological Journal, Royal Archaeological Journal*, Vol. 156
    (1999)

WEBSITES

www.historyonline.chadwyck.co.uk/pfto
www.nhm.ack.uk/zoology/stranding/history.html
www.beachcombers.org

7. *Cornwall*

BOOKS

Brendon, Piers, *Hawker of Morwenstow, Portrait of a Victorian
    Eccentric* (Jonathan Cape, London, 1975)
Baring-Gould, Sabine, *Cornish Characters and Strange Events*
    (Bodley Head, London, undated)
Cobb, James F., *The Watchers on the Longships* (Wells Gardner,
    Darton & Co. Ltd, Surrey, 1948)
Carter, Clive, *Cornish Shipwrecks – The North Coast* (Pan Books,
    London, 1978)
Du Maurier, Daphne, *Jamaica Inn* (Arrow Books, London, 1992)
——*Vanishing Cornwall* (Penguin, London, 1967)
Hague, D. and Christie, R., *Lighthouses – their Architecture, History
    and Archaeology* (Gomer Press, Wales, 1975)
Hamilton-Jenkin, A. K., *Cornwall and its People* (Augustus M
    Kelley, New York, 1970)
Langmaid, Kenneth, *The Sea, Thine Enemy* (Jarrolds, London,
    1966)
Larn, Richard, and Carter, Christie, *Cornish Shipwrecks – Vols 1, 2
    and 3* (David & Charles, Newton Abbot, 1971)

Mudd, David, *The Cruel Cornish Sea* (Bossiney Books, Bodmin, 1981)

Noall, Cyril, *Cornish Lights and Shipwrecks* (D. Bradford Barton Ltd, Truro, 1968)

Parker, Derek, *The West Country and the Sea* (Longman Group, London, 1980)

Smith, Revd G. C., *The Wreckers; or A Tour of Benevolence from St Michael's Mount to the Lizard Point* (J. Hill, London, undated)

Vivian, John, *Tales of the Cornish Wreckers* (Tor Mark Press, Penryn, 1989)

Waugh, Mary, *Smuggling in Devon and Cornwall 1700–1850* (Countryside Books, Cornwall, 1999)

ARTICLES AND REPORTS

Place, Geoffrey W., 'The Fate of the Charming Jenny', *Mariner's Mirror*, Society for Nautical Research, Vol. 76 (1990, No. 2)

WEBSITES

www.historyonline.chadwyck.co.uk/pfto (22 September 1818)

8. East Coast

BOOKS

Benham, Hervey, *The Salvagers* (Essex County Newspapers Ltd, Colchester, 1980)

Cameron, Ian, *Riders on the Storm – The Story of the RNLI* (Weidenfeld & Nicholson, London, 2002)

Ferguson, David M., *Shipwrecks of North-East Scotland 1444–1990* (Mercat Press, Edinburgh, 1991)

Higgins, David, *The Beachmen* (Terence Dalton Ltd, Lavenham, 1987)

Hooton, Jonathan, *The Glaven Ports* (Blakeney History Group, Norfolk, undated)

Jarvis, Stan, *East Anglia Shipwrecks* (Countryside Books, Newbury, 2003)

Leach, Nicholas, *Never Turn Back – An Illustrated History of Caister Lifeboats* (Tempus Publishing, Stroud, 2001)

Malster, Robert, *Saved from the Sea* (Terence Dalton Ltd, Lavenham, 1974)

Weston, Chris and Weston, Sarah, *Claimed by the Sea* (Wood Green Publications, Norwich, 1994)

Young, Ron, *Shipwrecks of the North-East Coast, Vols 1 and 2* (Tempus Publishing, Stroud, 2001)

ARTICLES AND REPORTS

Rabagliati, Lucy, *Wrecks on the Coast Near Scoughall* (RLS Club Yearbook, Edinburgh, 1995)

INDEX

Abbey Gardens (Tresco) 112–13, 114
Ajay 283–5, 286–7, 289, 292, 293, 294, 296
Alang 286–97
alcohol
  banned by Royal Navy (1970) 301
  and *Politician* grounding 154–7, 159–60
  seen as cause of loss of ships by Shipwreck Committee 299–300
Alderney Race 144
Alexander 51–4
ambergris 184–5
Anglesey 227–9
Argyll, Duke of 172
Association 16, 124–5, 126, 305
asylum seekers 56, 211
Atlantic Ocean 3, 218, 219
Atlantis 39

Bangladesh
  ship-breaking yard 292, 293
Baring-Gould, Sabine 238
Barra 23, 157–9, 162, 164
Basel Convention 290, 291
Bate, J.M. 264
beach companies/beachmen 266–70, 276–7
beachcombing 176–7, 179–81
Bermuda 163
Bhavnagar 283–4
Bishop (rock) 57, 123
Blogg, Henry 279
bodies
  shipwrecked attitudes towards 137–8, 238–9
body temperature 1–2
Borlase, George 233, 242
Boswell, James 152

Bow Street Runners 197
Bray, Julian xxii
Bremner, William 83, 84, 85, 88
Bromholm Priory 261
Brown, Bruce 71
Burnie, William 164
Byles, Charles 238

Caister 261
Caithness 97, 98
Canadians xviii
Cape Wrath 150
Capek, Karel 151
Caribbean wrecks xviii
Carter, George 34
cetaceans 184–5, 186–7 *see also* whales
Channel 218, 219
  difficulties in navigating and hazards 56–9
Channel swimmers 56–7
Charming Jenny 227–8
Cheshire wreckers 166–71
Chilcote, Captain 227–8
Cita 103–10, 118–19, 129–30, 246, 252, 304
Coastguard, HM 209–10, 235
Cobbs, J.F.
  The Watchers on the Longships 229
Coke, Lord 9–10
Coll 178
Collier, Mike 108, 219, 244–6
Colquhoun, Patrick 192–3
  'The Commerce and Police of the River Thames' 198–9, 200–1, 202–3, 204, 205
Commission of Inquiry (1839) 21, 166, 168, 231, 240–1
Conrad, Joseph
  Heart of Darkness 197

Lethegus Rocks 126
lifeboats/lifeboatmen
  on east coast 270
  and salvage 136, 278
  Scilly Isles 134–40
  as wreckers 136, 257, 276–7, 282
  see also RNLI
lifesaving xxiii–xxiv, xxv–xxvi
lighthouse keepers 175–6
lighthouses xxv–xxvi, 119
  during Second World War 173–4, 175
  protest at construction of xvii, 233–4
  St Agnes 227
  Skerryvore 172–3
Liverpool 166–8, 170
Lloyd's agents 171, 241
Lloyd's of London 295
Lloyd's Register of Shipping xxvi, 6, 7
Lloyd's Salvage Association
  Report (1867) 41, 44, 45–6, 48–9, 50
Loe Bar 219
London Labour and the London *Poor* (Mayhew) 198, 207–8
Longships 110, 138–9, 219
lords of the manor 231–2
Louise 264–6

McColl, Charles 159–60
MacCulloch, John 157
Mackenzie, Compton
  Whiskey Galore 153–4, 160
Maclean, Alasdair 176–7
Maclean, Angus 164–5
Macleod, John 155–6
Malicious Damage Act (1861) 15–16
'man or beast' ruling 11, 20
Marine Support Unit (was River Police) 209–10, 211
Maritime and Coastguard Agency 16, 18, 55, 244, 246, 281
Martin, Martin 152
Mayhew, Henry
  London Labour and the London Poor 198, 207–8
Men of Mey 144
Mercantile Marine Board 300

Merchant Shipping Act (1894) 16, 81
Mills, Joe 223–7
Minnehaha 119–20
Mount's Bay 219
Mowatt, Willie 77–8, 80–2, 82–3, 88, 89, 90, 100–1
mudlarks 203, 206–8
Muir, Tom 95–6, 97, 98, 99
Mülheim, RMS 214–17
Mussolini, Benito 250

Natural History Museum and whales 186, 187–8, 190, 193
Nelson, Lord 205
Nevada 2 178–9
Newlyn 243–5
Norfolk 7, 259
  beachmen/companies 266–70
  number of wrecks 262
  yawls 266
Norfolk Association for Saving the Lives of Shipwrecked Mariners 270
North Ronaldsay 96
North Sea 3, 258, 259, 260, 262
Northern Lighthouse Board xvi, 173
Northumberland 33

Ogle Castle 32
Orkney 71, 75, 76–7, 80, 81–2, 91, 97, 99, 100, 184
Orwell, George 142–4, 147
overboard, falling 2–4

Patel, Mr 283, 284, 285, 293
Peacock, Bob 28–9, 32, 33, 36–7, 38, 39
Pearce, Mike 247–52
Pennsylvania 78–86, 89, 91
Penrose, Rod 190
Pentland Firth xvi, 62–101
  currents and tides 70–1, 71–2
  hazards and dangers of 73, 74
  and *Johanna Thorden* tragedy 93–6
  and *Lena* wreck 96–7
  map 61
  navigation of 72
  number of wrecks 75

SILVER FALLS LIBRARY
410 South Water St.
Silverton, OR 97381
(503) 873-5173

910